Between
Totalitarianism
and Postmodernity

Between Totalitarianism and Postmodernity

A Thesis Eleven Reader

Edited by
Peter Beilharz, Gillian Robinson, and John Rundell

THE MIT PRESS
Cambridge, Massachusetts
London, England

The contents of this book were first published in *Thesis Eleven* (ISSN 0725-5136), a publication of The MIT Press.

The following selections are copyright © *Thesis Eleven*:

Peter Murphy, "Socialism and Democracy," *Thesis Eleven* 26 (1990); Johann Arnason, "The Theory of Modernity and the Problematic of Democracy," *Thesis Eleven* 26 (1990); Peter Beilharz, "The Life and Times of Social Democracy," *Thesis Eleven* 26 (1990); Julian Triado, "Corporatism, Democracy, and Modernity," *Thesis Eleven* 9 (1984); Ferenc Fehér, "The Left After Communism," *Thesis Eleven* 27 (1990); Alain Touraine, "Is Sociology Still the Study of Society?" *Thesis Eleven* 23 (1989); Andrew Arato and Jean Cohen, "Civil Society and Social Theory," *Thesis Eleven* 21 (1988); Agnes Heller, "Are We Living in a World of Emotional Impoverishment?" *Thesis Eleven* 22 (1988); Cornelius Castoriadis, "Individual, Society, Rationality, History," *Thesis Eleven* 25 (1990).

The following selections are copyright © the Massachusetts Institute of Technology:

Edgar Morin, "The Anti-totalitarian Revolution," *Thesis Eleven* 30 (1991); Gunnar Skirbekk, "The World Reconsidered: A Brief Aggiornamento for Leftist Intellectuals," *Thesis Eleven* 30 (1991); Zygmunt Bauman, "A Sociological Theory of Postmodernity," *Thesis Eleven* 29 (1991); Axel Honneth, "Pluralization and Recognition: On the Self-Misunderstanding of Postmodern Social Theorists," *Thesis Eleven* 31 (1992).

Selection and introductions, copyright © 1992 by The Massachusetts Institute of Technology.

ISBN 0262-52179-2

Second printing, 1993

Library of Congress Cataloging-in-Publication Data

Between totalitarianism and postmodernity : a Thesis eleven reader /
    edited by Peter Beilharz, Gillian Robinson, and John Rundell.
        p.   cm.
    Includes 13 articles previously published in *Thesis eleven*.
    Includes bibliographic references.
    ISBN 0-262-52179-2
    1. Social history–1970- 2. Totalitarianism. 3. Democracy. 4. Post-communism.
5. Postmodernism. I. Beilharz, Peter. II. Robinson, Gillian. III. Rundell, John F. IV. Thesis eleven.
HN17.5.B434   1992
303.4–dc20   92-28663
                                                                                                          CIP

CONTENTS

*Between Totalitarianism
and Postmodernity*

Notes on Contributors

Andrew Arato is Professor of Sociology at the Graduate Faculty, New School for Social Research, New York. He is co-author of *The Young Lukacs* (with Paul Breines) (1979) and more recently *Civil Society and Political Theory* (with Jean Cohen) (1992). He is also co-editor of *The Essential Frankfurt School Reader* (with Eika Gebhardt) (1978) and *Gorbachev: The Debate* (with Ferenc Fehér) (1989).

Johann Arnason is Reader in Sociology at La Trobe University, Victoria, Australia. His publications include *Von Marcuse zu Marx* (1971); *Zwischen Natur und Gisellschaft* (1976); and *Praxis und Interpretation* (1988). He has also written extensively on Japan as well as Eastern Europe.

Zygmunt Bauman is Emeritus Professor of Sociology at Leeds University, England. He has written extensively on the debate between modernity and postmodernity. His most recent publications include *Modernity and The Holocaust* (1989); *Modernity and Ambivalence* (1991); and *Intimations of Postmodernity* (1991).

Peter Beilharz teaches social theory at La Trobe University, Melbourne. A co-founder of *Thesis Eleven*, he is author of *Trotskyism and the Transition to Socialism* (1987), *Labour's Utopias* (1992), editor of *Social Theory* (1992), and co-author of *Arguing About The Welfare State* (1992).

Cornelius Castoriadis founded *Socialism au Barbarie* (1945–1965). He is now a practising psychoanalyst and Director of Studies at the Ecole des Hautes Etudes, Paris. His main writings in English are *Crossroads in the Labyrinth* (1984); *The Imaginary Institute of Society* (1987); *Politial and Social Writings* (1988); and *Philosophy, Politics, Autonomy* (1991).

Jean Cohen teaches in the Department of Political Science, Columbia University, New York. She has published extensively on political and critical theory. Her books include *Class and Civil Society: The Limits of Marxian Critical Theory* (1982) and *Civil Society and Political Theory* (with Andrew Arato) (1992).

Ferenc Fehér is Professor of Literary Studies at the New School for Social Research, New York. He has written extensively on political theory, with a particular emphasis on the Soviet Union and Eastern Europe, as well as aesthetics and literary criticism. He is author of *The Frozen Revolution* (1987); and the editor of *Reconstructing Aesthetics* (1986).

Agnes Heller is Hannah Arendt Professor of Philosophy at the New School for Social Research, New York. Among her many works are *Beyond Justice* (1987); *General Ethics* (1988); *A Philosophy of Morals* (1990); and *Modernity's Pendulum* (with Ferenc Fehér) (1992).

Axel Honneth is Professor of Philosophy at the University of Konstanz. His publications include *Social Action and Human Nature* (with Hans Joas) (1988);

Critique of Power (1991); *Die zerrissene Welt des Sozialen: Sozialphilosophische Aufzatze* (1990).

Edgar Morin, although retired, is associated with the Ecole des Hautes en Sciences Sociales. Among his many publications are *L'esprit du Temps: Essai sur la culture de masse* (1962–1975).

Peter Murphy lectures in politics at Ballarat University College, Victoria, Australia. He is a political philosopher, and an editor of *Thesis Eleven*. Some recent essays of his are included in the forthcoming anthology *Essays for Agnes Heller*.

Gillian Robinson is completing her dissertation on the work of Hannah Arendt. She is an editor of *Thesis Eleven* and teaches social theory at Monash University and La Trobe University, Victoria, Australia. She has also published in *Thesis Eleven*.

John Rundell is a lecturer in the Department of Anthropology and Sociology, Monash University, Victoria, Australia. He is an editor of *Thesis Eleven*. His publications include *Origins of Modernity: The Origins of Modern Social Theory From Kant to Hegel to Marx* (1987).

Alain Touraine is Professor of Sociology at the Ecole des Hautes Etudes en Sciencs Sociales. He is best known for his work on social movements. Among his publications are *The Self Production of Society* (1977); *The Return of the Actor* (1987); *Solidarity* (1983).

Julian Triado is a founding editor of *Thesis Eleven*. He lives and works in Melbourne, Australia, where he maintains his lively interest in social and political theory. He is now a member of the Editorial Advisory Board of *Thesis Eleven*.

Gunnar Skirbekk is a philosopher at The University of Bergen, Norway. He is the editor of *Praxeology* (1983); *Die pragmatische Werde* (1987); and *Essays in Pragmatic Philosophy 11* (forthcoming).

Part One:
Two Faces of
Modernity

INTRODUCTION: BETWEEN BOLSHEVISM AND DEMOCRACY

Peter Beilharz

Who would have imagined, five years ago, a world in which there would be one Germany, and no Soviet Union at all? For those who grew up with them, the two Germanies, constructed in different ways by Nazism and Social Democracy, and the Soviet empire which was the long-term result of the October Revolution through two world wars were simple facts. For those who lived with them, these facts lost any finer sense of contingency. Contingency seemed to have hardened into fate, as though the world could never really change again. Now, into the 1990s, the Berlin wall down, the various republics hoping to flourish, the euphoria is all but gone. The television images portray more misery and poverty than could before have been imagined in the queues which hit the streets of Moscow. The news analysis in the press and on radio present a renewed sense that even within the reunited Germany there are still two nations.

On the face of it, social democracy and communism seem both to be definitively exhausted. Except that elsewhere, the spectre of Keynes and the New Deal are revived as radicals and conservatives alike argue again that economic regulation is, in fact, a form of moral regulation. Gordon Gecko is no longer a role model; red braces are now as obsolete as red politics. All around, in the English speaking cultures, postmodernism apparently reigns. Few and faint are the voices which point out the occasional uncanny echoes of totalitarianism and social democracy in certain postmodern claims, which all too often both show contempt for the modernity which allows us to speak and the residual liberalism upon which radical culture draws.

The discourses called postmodern, of course, preceded the recent global events. Fastening upon the apparent reality of the surreal, Baudrillard gestured to the world of arbitrary, uncontrollable signs and drove across America to find paradise in Disneyland and good sex in the arms of various admirers. Readers of his work could be forgiven for imagining that they had somehow warped onto the set of *Paris, Texas*, with the boring and pathetic bits left out. Lyotard, for his part, constructed the grand metanarrative against all such metanarratives in *The Postmodern Condition*. Many were happy to take the cue, to identify the idea of totality with the political strategy of totalitarianism, knowledge with the will to power, intellectual influence with good marketing and glitz. The devastating broadside incipient in this reading was hardly noticed: for if the most pervasive of ideas have no claim to influence other than the noise and glamour of their promotion, where then does that leave postmodernism?

Postmodernism, and arguably also its recent accomplice, postcolonialism, both raise a whole series of entirely legitimate criticisms of certain ways of thinking and being which are allegedly commonplace in the west. But they also become new orthodoxies, to the extent that those who now speak differently are marginalized as intellectual pariahs. Postmodernism and postcolonialism both appeal deeply as intellectual trends to the profound sense of guilt harboured by the generation of '68, for whom changing the world ought, in principle, be as straightforward and as regularly entertained an activity as interpretation is. Western radical intellectuals have always demonstrated a vocational vulnerability to fellow travelling. From the communists who followed the red star, to the Fabians who weakened for Stalin and then Mussolini, from the various admiring Fiends of the Soviet Union the world about to Sartre photographed with Castro and Khruschev, and keen for Mao—and Fanon— western radicals have often elected to wallow in bad faith rather than become more localized and reflective. Failure to engage in ordinary politics at home has for long run together with support for tyrants abroad and defenses of all kinds of abominations in the name of state power—from the Moscow Trials of the 1930s to the imprisonment of Cuban poets and Trotskyists. Academic promotion, beachhouses and guru-status seem only to have inflamed the vehemence of these apologisms.

Now, while the Russian masses still queue poignantly across the television screens, it would indeed well be time to apologize. Beyond the tears and recriminations, however, there also needs now to be a more thoroughgoing consideration of what this whole experience has meant. Some of this process has begun, in the reconsideration of the hype and aura constructed around the experience of the 1960s. The larger issue, making sense of the spell of Jacobinism and of its Bolshevik episode, remains more elusive, perhaps because of the enormity of the task, perhaps due to the awkward sense of relief which can be encountered in various quarters of the left intelligentsia. Very few remaining radicals seem to mourn the loss of the Soviet Atlantis, except for those few remaining Deutscherists who inhabit positions of influence and those actual travellers and time-travellers whose own biographies personally intersected with the October Revolution, in ways which have marked their characters indelibly. For others, the spell is now broken, and the feeling is like that of an unintended *Katzenjammer*—a sense of disbelief that we could have aided and abetted communism so completely to form the ether of contemporary radical thought and practice.

The extraordinary influence of communism and Trotskyism among western radicals remains a major phenomenon of modern history. Alongside the Soviet tradition, however, the German current was also of widespread influence. Social democratic intellectuals left a clear imprint on liberal and Jewish arguments for interpretation and change. Sidney Hook, Karl Korsch, Irving Howe, the Frankfurters—Adorno, Marcuse, Horkheimer—Walter Benjamin and Hannah Arendt all in different ways brought these kinds of influences to bear in North America and elsewhere. German Social Democracy had already begun to work in less apocalyptic, and more appropriately pragmatic registers with Kautsky and Bernstein, who together with the Austro-Marxists saw Marxism fulfilling its historic role by taking its turn back towards the radical stream of liberalism from which it had earlier, perhaps unnecessarily departed.[1]

The task of making sense of the Bolshevik episode brings with it the necessity of a further reconsideration of Marxism. While it is far too easy and misleading to dismiss Marxism as coextensive with communism, the precise nature of the Marxian project often remains elusive. As Louis Dumont has shown in his study, *From Mandeville to Marx*, Marx was in many ways bound into not only the economic premises of classical economics, but he also took on its anthropological individualism.[2] What Dumont misses in this context is Marx's roots in the philosophical individualism of the romantics, from Rousseau to Schiller. Marx's own thinking is, finally, itself insufficiently social. The incredible ambivalences of Marx's theory show that he was simultaneously excessive in his individualism and in his collectivism—as if society could ever reasonably be imaged as the realm of the associated producers and them and it alone. All this has yet fully to be problematized. Marx leaves us, after all, with a utopia of individual, not social differentiation, and yet it is social differentiation which is such a prominent vice and virtue of modernity. The irony then appears, that postmodernists happily replay the narcissistic motifs of romanticism, weeping like the confessional Rousseau in tragic self-pity while they also scorn the Marxism which also takes on this very same attitude. Their focus on suffering is often exactly that kind of lonely individualistic lament, that others fail to take *me* seriously/recognize me for the talented subject *I* am.

Part of this issue, as preposterous as it may seem to name it in this way, is the failure of radicals to think sufficiently in a way that is social, sociological or for that matter historical. Recent witty arguments concerning the alleged end of "history" or of the impossibility of the "social" thus need to be read in the same way as Heidegger's declamations against "humanism"; the problem is less in the categories than in their hypostasization, certainly less in the ideas than in the way in which we use them.[3] Much of what is celebrated as postmodern, in this regard, consists merely in the rediscovery of what was known before but has not been recognized as knowledge concerning the human condition. Postmodernism, in this way, warns against excess—but so did Diderot and Voltaire, Montesquieu and Montaigne—and postmodernism, too, in its turn becomes excessive, bad mannered and intolerant.[4] The postmodern obsession with novelty is part of the deal; from the outside, it is reminiscent of other attempts at respoking the wheel, or at least at rewriting wheelness. Yet Marxists, too, typically failed to observe that if in fact there were nothing new under the sun, then the worshipping of the fetish of Marx was no more emancipatory an act than kneeling at the crypt of Foucault. Only recently, for example, has the significance of Engels's role in the story and his own, German and English context been acknowledged.[5] The problem here, in modern and postmodern thinking alike, is that since the existence of anything like mass communications intellectuals must claim novelty for their own views if they are to be noticed and applauded. Marx and Engels performed an innovative job of this act already in *The Communist Manifesto* in 1848. Here they combined rhetorical tropes from Goethe and Carlyle together with working class and utopian claims in order to announce the arrival of the allegedly new paradigm of scientific socialism.[6] Foucault, for his part, was more self-reflective and modest than this. A sense of limits, then, also sometimes indicates a sense of contexts and traditions.[7] And so Castoriadis returns to the wisdom of the Greeks, and Habermas to Weber.

The cult of Foucault has nevertheless grown to Jim Morrison dimensions—basement tapes keep coming, fragments and laundry lists, we hang upon every word. This is another old problem: postmoderns can learn to live without social hope, but not without heroes. The pursuit of the hero, notwithstanding the cult of subjectivity, now represents a failure to look inward. Heroes become projections of the narcissistic personality. What might postmodernity then put in place of socialism? The answer is obvious, and even if it is not very satisfactory—it is the same answer given by socialists now—democracy. Socialism gives way to democracy, or is reduced to democracy (perhaps it is *expanded* to democratic visions).

The residual utopia of postmodernism is democracy, or at least democracy defined by default as liberalism in the minimal sense—leave me alone, relativistic liberalism, "social conscience", self-regarding liberalism. Socialists, unfortunately, are not a great deal better off. Socialism has always, for the orthodox, been defined in default: socialism from 1917 to 1987 was defined by default as planning, Eurocommunists bucking the system from the late 1970s bleating that socialism would be democratic or not at all (i.e. not at all; no telos left). Here the postmoderns reinvent Weber, now also being read for the first time in Russia: spheres of value and of existence, difference and differentiation, arguments found in more recent writing across Walzer, Rorty, Fehér and Heller. But where does this leave us? If socialism dissolves into democracy, and democracy practically means liberal democracy, has not the whole Marxist experiment been in vain? Are we not back to square one? Such a conclusion only follows if we define liberalism negatively—a widespread radical predilection—as a thin tradition obsessed with the property rights of men. This is a sign of the world-weariness of the age, which the 1990s now exemplify. Historically, liberalism has more often and more usefully been defined combatively, against the blockages and obstructions which power, property and status have placed in the paths of human beings who cannot help but grapple with forces of reason and freedom. As Fehér points out in "The Left After Communism", though, the challenge to social democrats here looms even larger. This is not simply an issue of socialism's liquidation into liberalism, however defined; it is also an issue of the utopian horizons of social democracy itself. After the cult of planning in the 1930s, the widely observed response of Stalinism, Fascism and the New Deal to the proclivity of capitalism to collapse, democratic socialists came generally to view state planning as the solution to all social ills. The social democrats backed into a mortal imaginary embrace with communism because they shared at least some fundamental constituent parts of its utopia. Hostility or indifference towards politics, weakness for administration in its stead, refusal to take seriously political difference and social differentiation, vulnerability to notions of compulsory consensus and economic conceptions of social contribution and right became part of the social democratic world view. Socialisms of all kinds, of course, had parted from radical liberalism around the time of Saint-Simon. It was Saint-Simon who enshrined politics as economics and identified social citizenship with economic productivity. These ideas then permeated Marxism, Bolshevism, Fabianism and finally social democracy. The mechanical conception of society as an economic firm (*sans* class struggle) then surfaces both in Lenin's utopia—socialism as the postoffice in *The State and Revolution*—in the imaginary cornucopia of Crosland in *The Future of Socialism* or the program of the German Social Democrats after Bad Godesberg. Socialisms merged around the state, whether welfare state or central planning, under the sign of the administered society, for this was, historically, the source of their origin.

Concerns with freedom and reason also run through the various socialist traditions—in Fourier, in the romantic writings of the younger Marx, via Kojève's Hegel, through de Beauvoir, Jessica Benjamin and elsewhere, through Lukács to the Budapest School, past Merleau-Ponty to Castoriadis and Lefort, through Weber to Habermas.

The difficulty for socialists, in one sense, has been to pursue the ethics of ultimate ends and of responsibility in tandem, to encourage radicalism to take root in the empirical reality of modernity without simply succumbing to its immediate demands and dissolving under the force of its imperatives and logics. The encounter of socialism with problems of the prerational and irrational, too, remains frequently announced but somehow still unedifying, for problems of reason and regulation still necessarily surround us, alongside questions of action, consequence and intention, recognition and reciprocity.

The legacy of Saint-Simon, through Marx to Bolshevism here rests upon the coupled dreams of transcendence and transparency. Marx, for his part, was too much a creature of modernity to recognize the significant imponderables of the human condition, from antiquity to ourselves, and now magnified into postmodern times. In more conventionally sociological and political terms, it remains the case that socialism (or what remains of it) has not yet taken the problem of democracy to heart. Democratic political will-formation will always give space to all kinds of idiocy, as well as to the inertia and sense of exhaustion of moments such as the present.

The momentary enthusiasm of the 1980s for the radical potential of social movements is one indicator of what for some was still a redemptive hope for politics; where parties failed, there mass movements could surely succeed. Succeed at what?—at gaining access to state power, at which moment social movements cease to be what they were. What is striking looking back on these various, often confused hopes is again the absence of a sufficiently historical or social vision. The fixation upon novelty again resulted in fantasy, this time the fantasy of the so-called new social movements: whereas there have always been social movements in modernity. The vital point is that which has been signalled already: how social movements relate to state power, which has always been the goal, certainly for socialists, Bolsheviks and Social Democrats alike. Some currents in, for example, German Social Democracy differed: they sought, and created, a social-democratic state, but they were swamped by the more boisterous initiatives of communists and Nazis.[8]

The ethical bind for social movement enthusiasts, meanwhile, is to be located in the wish-desire of imputation. Feminists who insist that theirs is the real feminism, and the correct consciousness for the women's movement remind us of certain Marxists who earlier advanced similar cases, and of others for whom, say, the presence of Catholicism in the Polish or Australian labor movement represents just another refusal of history to get it right. But while movements may on occasion choose ideologies, ideologies do not choose movements, except from the comfort of the beachhouse. The hopes of salvation thus projected by radicals onto social movements are bound eventually to pass, as the movements will. As the young Lewis Mumford aptly put it, there is no realistic hope of escape from the human condition, or from modernity: the better utopia is that which posits as its goal social reconstruction.[9] If postmodernity is to be the name given to this project, its attitudes and constituent terms are nevertheless irredeemably modern. If democracy is the name given to this prospect, then the socialist traditions are still among the lines of its vista.

*   *   *   *   *

Part One of this reader opens with Peter Murphy's reflections on "Socialism and Democracy". Working on a global canvas, Murphy draws to our attention the fact that socialism, like liberalism, precedes democracy; these days, when even Pol Pot is a democrat, it is worth untangling the story whereby democracy becomes adopted and co-opted by the various ideological and political traditions. The logic of Murphy's argument cuts deep: democracy, like politics as such, was adopted by socialists as a strategy rather than as a norm. Marxists, of course, exemplified this, and openly, as in the old Trotskyist claim that elections were useless except perhaps as barometers of the real or approaching class struggle. More reformist kinds of socialists became too caught up with the goal of social security to take democracy seriously: they linked ideological arms with the Bolsheviks in that they constructed socialism primarily as a matter of the stomach. It is this minimalist reading of socialism as *eudemonia* which has now completely collapsed; the social problems which elicited it, of course, both remain and fester. Murphy's argument, in any case, makes it clear that critics of communist history should never have been surprised; socialism and democracy have had a far more contingent bond than many would like to think.

Beilharz takes a different approach in "The Life and Times of Social Democracy". The routine tendency to collapse and syncretize concepts and traditions, to crush nuance and difference, often means that socialists miss what is available to them in their own heritage. "Social democracy" or liberalism, in its North American reformist inflexion, becomes a euphemism for welfarist politics, which drives radicals elsewhere to invent or discover "new" solutions. Yet social democracy—like Fabianism—also contains all kinds of insights and arguments, radical democratic in the hands, say of guild socialists such as G. D. H. Cole, closer to the politics of citizenship in the case of Bernstein in the German tradition. Bernstein and Kautsky, like Beatrice and Sidney Webb, did actually recognize that modern utopias needed to specify their dependence on social differentiation. Lenin's postoffice is not postmodern, but premodern. Classical social democracy remains, by comparison, a storehouse of possibilities.

Julian Triado pursues these themes further in "Corporatism, Democracy and Modernity". The spectre of Saint-Simon and the "politics" of productivity haunt modernity. Like the Fabians, Saint-Simon set his project against the idlers, whether plebeian or aristocratic. Social contribution and identity were to be conferred by claims to economic productivity. Politics, not least of all for Marxism, was always subsumed to economics, citizenship to class, democracy to notions of function. Too often viewed narrowly as a technical category in recent political sociology, corporatism refers more broadly to the economization of politics which is one dominant trend in modernity. Viewed institutionally, corporatist decision-making is perhaps now in decline, though the 1990s may well signal attempts at its revival. The theme of Triado's work is, however, more cultural than institutional: for administration will continue to work against democracy in polities which are dominated by economics.

The idea of the administered society developed by the Frankfurt School indicated that totalitarianism could equally as well be democratic-liberal as fascist or Soviet in political form. Totalitarianism, in its strict sense, however, signals what T.H. Rigby in turn called the mono-organizational society; whereas liberal-democratic societies contain a formal plurality of parties, and rest upon diverse and voluntary organizations in civil society. A long lineage of social thinking, which goes back to Max Weber, makes the point that while capitalism is typically historically related to liberal democracy, there is no essential connection here. Edgar Morin begins from the same observation in his essay on "The Anti-Totalitarian Revolution" which spread across eastern and Central Europe: antitotalitarian, but not thereby definitionally democratic. That sense of contingency which postmodernists tend to claim as novel here returns again: for the antitotalitarian revolutions may be one condition of possibility for democracy, but only one, and absolutely no guarantee of positive outcomes. In what remains of the old Soviet Empire, even the socialism of the stomach remains an unfulfilled dream. Now socialists, needless to say, have never had any monopoly on arguments and policies directed toward material need: Fascism developed its own appropriate vocabulary, and liberalism could always draw on its own utilitarian legacy to address these kinds of needs. Plainly there remain limited grounds for optimism.

Yet the simultaneous sense of release from the communist hegemony cannot but result in some hopes. As Fehér puts it in "The Left After Communism", the old regimes have left bankruptcy and chaos of such a magnitude that even old-time critics of the Soviet Union are left flabbergasted. Talk of the "triumph of capitalism", however, simply begs the question, for even as we survey the west this mode of production still seems to generate certain problems. Now responsibility knocks at the doors of the social democrats, who postponed thinking about politics and instead alternatively chastized and revelled in glorifying the achievements of Soviet socialism.

As Gunnar Skirbekk suggests in "A Brief Aggiornamento for Leftist Intellectuals", it is probably reasonable to presume that most radicals today would imagine socialism as resting on the planned markets which the Hungarians earlier advocated. As he observes, the wild card in this post-Soviet setting is nationalism. The newly emerging global system is both more integrated and more particularistic in terms of cultural and political identity. Diversity and particularity, as well as universality are also modern traits. One substantive problem which issues from the coming-of-age of radicalism, in its embracing of representative political forms, however, is the likelihood of corporatist organizational forms canvassed by Triado. Skirbekk offers a Habermasian discourse-reading of democracy as one possible corrective to these obstructions in the path of some reasonable sort of social democracy. His paper also opens the question, whether postcommunism is any meaningful way described as postmodern. For while communism is plainly in some senses a constituent part of what we experience as modernity, it could also be explained as contemporary rather than modern. This part of the volume closes with Johann P. Arnason's considerations on "The Theory of Modernity and the Problematic of Democracy", which also sets the scene for Part Two of the book. As Arnason shows, democracy is a vital thread in modern social theory, even though it is typically undertheorized. Not only Marx, but also Weber and Durkheim missed the chance to develop more muscular normative arguments for democracy. By their times, direct democracy had been transformed into syndicalism, while representative forms simultaneously emerged as largely untried and yet popularly discredited. Whether viewed in a projectual or in a personal way, the prospect of autonomy still lies before us.

Notes

1. Peter Beilharz, *Labour's Utopias—Bolshevism, Fabianism, Social Democracy* (New York, Routledge, 1992).
2. Louis Dumont, *From Mandeville to Marx—The Genesis and Triumph of Economic Ideology* (Chicago, Chicago University Press, 1977).
3. Martin Heidegger, "Letter on Humanism", *Basic Writings* (London, Routledge, 1977).
4. Peter Beilharz, "Back to Postmodernity", *Thesis Eleven* 29 (1991).
5. Geoffrey Claeys, *Machinery, Money and the Millenium: From Moral Economy to Socialism 1815–60* (Cambridge, Polity, 1987); *Citizens and Saints: Politics and Antipolitics in Early British Socialism* (New York, Cambridge, 1989).
6. Beilharz, *Labour's Utopias,* ch. 1.
7. Didier Eribon, *Michel Foucault* (Harvard, Harvard University Press, 1991).
8. Vernon Lidtke, *The Alternative Culture: Socialist Labour in Imperial Germany* (New York, Oxford University Press, 1985).
9. Lewis Mumford, *The Story of Utopias* (New York, Viking Compass, 1962).

SOCIALISM AND DEMOCRACY

Peter Murphy

Democracy is a difficult concept to tie down. Its meaning is slippery and allusive. To different people it can imply, and conjure up, very different ideas. We can probably agree upon a minimal content for the idea of democracy: *viz.* that it means that all persons have a share in government; that no class or party or group monopolizes the state, etc. We can usually recognize a democracy when we see one. But any minimal definition we care to give is only a part, a small part, of the story. For a democratic regime also implies a political and social regime, and a rich substratum of attitudes, practices, aspirations, ideals, and, indeed, utopias.

Democracy carries with it, always, an immense amount of baggage. Everybody today is a democrat, with the exception of a few Jacobin types, and even they usually feign a respect for democracy. But while we are all democrats, we are not all democrats in the same way. When we invoke democracy, we invoke various hidden curriculums. We tacitly refer to ideal worlds of action and behaviour.

Because democracy is what we all, today, more or less, agree upon, it is what we talk about. It is what we proclaim. It is what we enthuse publicly about. It is easy, relatively unproblematic, to do that; everybody else can nod their heads in fraternal recognition. *But* all of us, when we talk about democracy, have in mind a definite political and social regime. And on the substance of this regime, we will *not* necessarily be in agreement. Nor are we likely to be as forthcoming about it.

This is the ambiguity, the allusiveness, of democracy. It refers us to different kinds of social and political regimes. There are, in other words, different kinds of democracy. This is not to say that there is an infinite multitude of kinds. Just a few kinds. But enough to cause us political heart-burn; enough, in practice, to disrupt, irreparably, the chummy and illusory fraternity that we might imagine ourselves to be part of when we declare ourselves, one and all, to be democrats.

We can reasonably distinguish five major kinds of democracy: liberal democracy, social democracy, civic or radical democracy, romantic, and corporatist democracy. These roughly correspond to the major traditions in Western political thought and practice. The great ideals and commitments of Western politics are the ideals and commitments of liberalism, socialism, republicanism, romanticism, and christianity. These represent the great political cultures embodied in the Western tradition. Each of these cultures is the bearer of a distinctive image of politics and society, and distinctive ideals of human association. And each has come to terms with, i.e. made its peace with, democracy. Democracy is what all the great political cultures of the Western tradition now share in common—probably the only thing they all share in common. But each, of course, *understands* democracy in a different way. Democracy invokes, for the bearers of each of these Great Traditions, a fundamentally different image of the good political and social regime. This conflict of interpretations is inherent in the fact that each of these Great Traditions has had to *come to terms* with democracy; each of them had to search for reasons latent in their tradition as to *why* democracy was a good, or at least an acceptable, thing.

Democracy is *not* a free-standing political culture. It is not an ideology-in-itself. There is not a democratic ideology, like there is an ideology of liberalism or socialism or republicanism. The closest we will probably ever come to the formulation of a specifically democratic ideology is Habermas's theory of domination-free communication. But the ultimate barrenness of Habermas's world-view is an object lesson in the fact that we cannot formulate democracy as an independent ideology. A purely self-referential theory of democracy will be unable to answer all kinds of crucial questions about the human condition: about appetites, desire, happiness, justice, value, etc. Democracy can only be a manifestation of more fundamental cultural and philosophical ideals. We cannot live a democratic form of life in the same way that we can live a liberal, or republican, or socialist, or romantic form of life.

In practice, we have only ever come to democracy through the cultures of liberalism, socialism, and so forth. We are first liberals, and then democrats; we are first republicans, and then democrats. Each of the five great political cultures of the Western Tradition has provided *internal justifications* for the embracing of democracy. Each of the five great political cultures has also, in the past, rejected democracy as well. Each of the great political cultures give us *reasons* why we should be democrats. But they don't give us the *same* reasons. Indeed, the liberal's reasons are, intuitively, an anathema to the socialist; the socialist's reasons cause the liberal to squirm. So it goes. The civic democrat eyes with suspicion the corporatist democrat, who returns the favour.

I

In short, none of the ideologists—none of us—can agree why democracy is a good thing, although we do think it is a good thing. Does this matter? Well, yes, it does. Because, to prefer one kind of democracy is to prefer one kind of political and social regime as well. It is to choose one kind of culture to inhabit. When we choose, for example, a social, as opposed to a liberal or civic democracy, we are choosing democracy for one set of reasons as opposed to some other set of reasons. Take, as a starting point, the *liberal* democrat. Liberalism embraced democracy quite late in the piece. For a large part of its history, liberalism was quite at home with princely-autocratic governments. It was reconciled to these regimes as long as it thought its chief values and concerns could be respected by such governments. These values and concerns are summed up in the word *liberty*.

The idea of a relatively autonomous, dynamic commercial economic sphere was crucial to liberalism's eventual acceptance of democracy. In the end, liberals came to believe that democracy was the form of government that most accommodated a dynamic economic order. For the liberal, the individual was born to run, and to run on infinitely. The liberal believed that felicity of life lay not in a contented life, but, as Hobbes put it so well, in the continual progress of desire from one object to another. The liberal personality was restless, always ready to move on, never still. Many 19th century liberals decided that the best chance for such a dynamic order lay with democracy. John Stuart Mill is prototypical in this respect. Mill saw a close connection between the preference for an *enterprising society* and the preference for *political democracy*.[1] He also saw a close connection between an *enervated society* and *political despotism*. Different types of character, different kinds of action (or inaction) are favoured by one kind of government, as opposed to the other. Despotism favours a passive type of character. In despotic states, subjects abdicate their own energies, they leave things to government. This is the cultural presupposition of despotism. It looks for quiescence and submission. Democracy, on the other hand, is much more likely to favour, and encourage, an active kind of character. Democracy, in the liberal interpretation, promotes enterprising behaviour by its citizens—and Mill was quite clear—by enterprise, he meant that peculiarly modern restlessness: the desire to keep moving and to be trying and accomplishing new things for our own benefit or the benefit of others.

Democracy seemed to create the right environment for this modernist agitation to flourish, the right environment, as the liberal utopia promised, "for the person bestirring himself with hopeful prospects, to improve his circumstances..." Little bestirring went on in despotisms. There was little encouragement, in the despotic political environment, for people to put energy into striving, or to exert themselves. Despotism encouraged somnolence. Mill pointed out that those societies which had arrived, or were on the path to political democracy—the United States and England—had a "go-ahead character". These nations were full of energetic, enterprising characters; full of people intent on improving their circumstances, struggling with natural powers, and not just giving way to them,[2] while in despotic states, people submitted to, rather than fought against the vicissitudes of the world.

Liberty is the supreme value of liberalism. It gives rise to a kind of action that is not defensive or necessitarian in character, but is instead a kind of action characterized by *endeavoring* or *striving*. The liberal actor endeavors or strives after ends. These ends are given, or are already present in, the economic and social environment of the actor. They are *objects* of the actors' desire. Liberalism defends the right (freedom) of the individual to *deliberate between*, and *choose*, options or ends that are present in the economic and social environment. Liberalism presupposes the right (freedom) of the individual to move from one object of desire to another, and assumes that persons will desire different things (they will have *different* ends). In a liberal society, each person has the right (if they can afford it) to enter into voluntary, contractual arrangements with others to secure the materials or labour-power they may need to attain their ends, as well as the right (if they are suitably and relevantly qualified) to enter into the various (public and corporate) offices which acquire and dispose of resources (wealth) and co-ordinate labour-power in an "organized" non-contractual manner. Liberty is the sum total of these various rights.

Liberty implies the development of a dynamic economic order in which nothing is fixed or frozen, in which barriers to trade and exchange are removed, in which individuals can "go after" objectives, moving forward rather than standing still, and in which careers are open to talent. *Liberty* does not provide the only reason, however, for choosing democracy. The *civic* or radical democrat, for example, is moved by a much more classical idea of (*public*) *happiness*. In modern constitutions, this was formulated as the right to the pursuit of happiness. This was the freedom to appear in public spaces, to leave the shadows of the household, and enter the public realm. Freedom was the right to participate in all kinds of public realms—in politics, in education, in science, art, etc. These public realms (or value spheres) were not places for people trying to "get ahead"—people who were *dissatisfied* with what they had and who were striving for yet-to-be-realized goals. In public realms, what is done is done for its own sake, not for the sake of personal "advancement" or "getting on" in the world. Public personalities are "active" rather than "busy" or agitated. Public realms offer the possibility of satisfaction (happiness)—job, personal, community satisfaction—in the modern world. The liberal economic realm, by contrast, is a realm of dissatisfaction. It is fuelled by the discontent of individuals with their present position, and by their desire to advance towards some (material or intellectual) goal they set for themselves, i.e. by their desire to improve their lot. Public personalities (civic personalities in the specific case of politics), by contrast, seek only to "improve" (enrich) the *practices* they are immersed in. Their lot is inextricably tied to the value-rational practices (the *praxis*) they are involved in, and from the mastery of whose complexity they draw immeasurable satisfaction. The public kind of energy is the energy of performance, the energy exhibited in associating, speaking, and acting in public. It is not the breathless, restless energy of the liberal, pursuing the phantoms of opportunity. (And they are phantoms. As Lukács once observed: it is the liberal's sad fate to dwell with fascination on the innumerable abstract potentialities that can be imagined, only to fall into a melancholic recognition that most of those possibilities can not be realized.) The liberal, drawn simultaneously in different directions by possibilities, falls foul to short attention span, shallow and frivolous passions, manic fits of enthusiasm, and apathetic resignation in the face of overwhelming options. The liveliness of the liberal ends in exhaustion, in disintegration, in incoherence, in restless, crushing dissatisfaction, as the phantoms of desire stretch out on the horizon, in more and more unattainable forms.

Socialism never suffered from this. By contrast with the liberal, the socialist offered a vision that was more focused, and less intoxicated. Instead of the headiness of *opportunity*, the vision of the socialist was concerned with *security*—i.e. securing society against the multitudinous threats of this world to life. Out of the imperative of security grew the *Social Objective*. The Social Objective was grounded in the *value of life*. The social objective was social security or social immunity. The method of its realization, the *form of rule* in the social security state, was *administrative rule*. And the key to the sustaining of administrative rule was *democratic sovereignty*. The history of 19th and early 20th century socialism is the history of the convergence of the idea of a Guaranteed Society with the Rule of Knowledge and the Democratic form of Sovereign Power.

Like liberalism, socialism was not, in its beginning, especially attracted to the idea of democracy. Liberalism made its peace with democracy in the wake of the French Revolution. Jacobinism's terrorist pursuit of liberal ideas—and the self-destruction of them—was scarifying enough to push liberals into a reconciliation with democracy. Likewise, the defeat of the 1848 Revolution, and the evident failure of the insurrectionary mentality, was the springboard for the emergence of a social, as opposed to liberal, kind of democracy. By the turn of the 20th century, the intellectual foundations for the Great Reconciliation of socialism and democracy had been securely laid. A key to this reconciliation was the preparedness of political thinkers, like Eduard Bernstein, to take up the key themes of the *social* thought of the 19th century, but to argue for reformist and democratic, rather than insurrectionary or revolutionary, i.e. despotic, political means for obtaining those social objectives. I say political *means* quite deliberately because, as I shall argue later on, social democracy, unlike civic democracy, never did, and still does not, see democracy as an intrinsic value, but rather as the most favourable political grounds on which to realize the social objective—i.e. the objective of a Guaranteed Society and an Administered Society.

The social objective was, initially, developed in separate traditions of socialist thought. The first of the strands internal to socialism was the idea of *ascetic socialism*—i.e. the treatment of poverty and "welfare" as a kind of utopia. The second strand internal to socialism developed the idea of an administered society.

II

The ascetic strand of socialism had as its central value the idealization of poverty, the poor, and the propertyless. Alleviation of their plight was its central concern. The social objective, in its ascetic guise, was born of hunger, of overwhelmingly *urgent need*, as Hannah Arendt put it. It was born of the paradoxical, even perverse, *idealization of necessity*. The civic tradition—the Aristotelian tradition—had always argued for the pushing-back of necessity, the shrinking of its province, in favour of freedom. In ascetic socialism, necessity is idealized and praised. The value of freedom is displaced by the value of life. Politics, animated by the value of freedom, is threatened with being swamped by society, over-run by bio-centric preoccupations, by the preoccupations of the everyday world, of mere existence. The goods of life—those of food, shelter, a benign environment, health, safe working conditions, etc.—are goods born of necessity; they displace the goods of freedom—those of public appearance, performance, and engagement. And what a dismal prospect this is!

Society, ironically, is a "social construct". It does not exist before the idea of the social objective. It does not exist until the *needs* of the poor became the benchmark of a good society. I mean "need" in the strong sense of that word; "need" in the sense of necessity, contrasted with liberal choice, romantic contingency, or with the classicist's acting-for-its-own-sake. The political idea of Society did not exist until alleviating the needs of the poor, and the anguish that attends them, became the *telos* of political association. *Civitas* was subsumed by *societas*. The good citizen became the defender of the hungry and the needy. The freedom promised by the *civitas* was buried beneath an avalanche of bio-centric concern.

Yet, ascetic socialism didn't mean simply the alleviation of the pressing needs of the poor; it also represented a profound suspicion of wealth. Ascetic socialism is egalitarian. It wants to *level* wealth—not in the name, either, of eradicating domination, but because it despises richness, of all kinds. It hates voluptuousness. It believes that everybody should have "enough", but not more than "enough". It believes that the acquisitive spirit is the antithesis of liberty. It especially dislikes the "idle" rich. For it, the science of politics is the art of inhibiting the passions of avarice and ambition.

How is ascetic socialism to be realized?

In the case of *the welfare component of ascetic socialism*, it can be achieved:, firstly, by treating part of the wealth of the nation as common property—that part that can supply the pressing needs of people; secondly, by instituting factory laws to guarantee workplace safety and the physiological viability of the labouring population; thirdly, by removing food and other essentials like housing from the sphere of free trade; fourthly, by providing social assistance or social insurance, to compensate victims of misfortune, infirmity, old age, etc.

The aim of the social welfarist is to ensure the right of the poor to their physical existence; to guarantee to all persons the necessities of life. This vision is hardly an elevated one. Its horizon is, in fact, anchored in the most dismal, the most miserable necessities of everyday life. It offers access neither to the value spheres of Morality, Culture, Work, or Politics. Yet even if this social welfarist vision is not an elevated one, it is, on the other hand, not a self-consciously levelling ideology either. By contrast, the *egalitarian component of ascetic socialism* is levelling. It insists that there should be neither rich nor poor. No one should be more or less rich than anyone else; no one should be more or less esteemed than anyone else. Nor should there be differential rewards on the basis of ability. For the egalitarian socialist, equality means, firstly, *equality of property*. This can be achieved by breaking property up into small units; by abolishing inheritance; by limiting the amount that can be owned; by introducing wealth taxes. Equality of property can also be achieved by placing property in a common pool, either for the state to periodically redistribute, or else for the state to manage. For the egalitarian socialist, equality means, secondly, *equality of esteem*. Persons should not be distinguished from one another—either on the basis of knowledge, or leadership, or goodness, or civic performance. And neither material rewards nor honours should flow to persons as a result of such distinctions. Finally, and above all, the egalitarian socialist values *equality in consumption*, i.e. the equality of the stomach. This is assured by laws which forbid ostentatious living and luxury; by measures such as luxury taxes. It can also be assured by the state organizing the production and especially the distribution of consumer goods. Under this arrangement—essentially a dictatorship over needs—all production is planned and then sent to state stores, to be distributed in putatively equal, rationed and above all, paltry shares.

Ascetic socialism only recognizes the satisfaction of "real needs", physiological needs, the needs of the stomach, of the body. It offers the *social guarantee* that these needs will always be satisfied—i.e. it offers "freedom from want". This is the *social* utopia. This utopia of the stomach reserves some of its greatest venom for traders, and for commercial society. Traders inflate prices, hoard, deceive; the labour market depresses wages. The enemy of the ascetic socialist is the liberal market-place with its greed, avarice, and, also, its *unrest.* Modern, commercial societies are full of the agitation and flux that liberals so admire; they are opportunity societies. This the ascetic socialist hates—the perpetual anxiety about our fate; what the egalitarian looks to is a state of "staple felicity" and unalterable "sufficiency".

III

Ascetic socialism was essentially a *distributive kind of socialism.* It was concerned not with the production of goods, but with the satisfaction of needs especially with dictating what needs could and should be satisfied.

The second kind of socialism, productivist socialism, regarded the question of poverty as a secondary question. It had a different way of understanding what the social question was. It was, of course, antiliberal. But its objection was to the unregulated, unorganized nature of liberal economic life. The liberal celebration of economic dynamism struck it as a celebration, so often, of wasted and misdirected energies. The improvement of the lot of the poor was not its special objective; rather such an improvement would be a consequence of the social regulation of economic activity—i.e. it would be a by-product of socialism. The *primary concern* of productivist socialism was not the system of needs, and attendant commercial life, but rather the system of production, and attendant industrial life. Industrialism was counterposed to feudalism. In the industrial regime, feudal and religious power had to yield to scientists and producers. Saint-Simon, the great originator of productivist socialism, interestingly however, recognized a third option, caught in-between feudalism and industrialism; i.e. caught in between the priests and landlords on the one hand and the scientists and industrialists on the other. This was the *juristic path*, represented by the class of lawyers in the practical realm and by metaphysicians in the spiritual realm. As Saint-Simon observed quite sharply, the metaphysicians wedged themselves between positive science and the clergy, inspired at once by the spirit of both. The culture of jurisprudence and the culture of metaphysics was, essentially, an extension into the Renaissance and the Enlightenment of the tradition of Civility. It carried the values of the *civitas* into modernity.

Saint-Simon was not unsympathetic to the historical role of the jurists in liberating science and industry. But once the midwife had done her job, she was to be dismissed. The lawyers and metaphysicians only knew about *limiting* Government Power, courtly and landlordly despotism, and priestly ignorance. The jurists couldn't bring themselves to a conception of a "social" order different from the one they had helped destroy. Saint-Simon objected that the theological spirit continued to animate them. Crucially they pressed forward a theory of the Rights of Man and Citizen. This was the foundation for their political conception. It retained a sense of sacred order, of something that was not a product of human artifice; a sense that man was not the measure of all things. The question of the best government, the civic theorists thought, could be handled as if it were a question of jurisprudence and metaphysics. Saint-Simon found this obnoxious. Administration and science, not jurisprudence and metaphysics, was the *key* to the new politics of industrialism. True, the jurists contributed to the development of new legal forms for commerce under the old regime and this should be recognized, but, essentially, Saint-Simon thought, the jurists had no place in industrial society.

Saint-Simon, in a similarly double-edged manner, was an admirer of the liberal contribution to the liberation of industry from its subjection by the old "feudal/military" system. Socialism promised to extend this emancipation to its logical and absolute conclusion. It promised that industry would, finally, be able to freely realize its own nature—industry would no longer serve as the instrument for ends which were not its own. Socialism was the *intellectual correlate par excellence* of industrial society. Its utopia was the utopia of industrialism. The old, pre-industrial society was aggressive and war-like; industrial society was, by contrast, pacific—it viewed other people not as enemies, but as collaborators in a common enterprise. Neither the martial virtues, nor religious asceticism had a place in industrial society. This socialism also promised the triumph of the utilitarian mentality—the eradication of the old aristocratic love of the useless. In an industrial society, the *production of useful things* was the only reasonable and positive end political societies could conceivably set themselves. They would devote themselves to increasing the power of man over things. *Society* would be a vast production company.

But couldn't we have got all this with liberalism? Didn't liberalism stand for cosmopolitan—commercial—peace? Didn't Bentham give us a liberal utilitarianism? Why wasn't *that* sufficient? The socialists argued that liberals could not divorce productive management of enterprise from parasitic ownership, from "owners living like nobles". Nonproductive, non-managerial owners fell into the despicable category of the useless, the idle. The contractualism of liberalism made ownership respectable. Liberalism was not technocratic or managerial in its ethos. Liberalism was commercial, not industrial in its spirit. The formation of an administered society was alien to its contractual mentality. Liberalism saw only the interaction and combination of individual interests in the market-place, albeit restless, agitated, dynamic, mobile, lively interests. Liberalism praised activity, it was an activist philosophy; but so did productivist socialism—there was nothing it despised more than idleness and laziness. Yet the liberal, it complained, denied individual activity a "social" character. Liberalism failed to "reinterpret" the good things in the old regime—the passion for national glory, the respect for common beliefs and ends. Liberalism thought only of things and feelings that belonged to a private-market-exchange order. It had no feeling for social harmony or national objectives.

The productivist socialist did not want to abolish private or individual enterprise, just to "socialize" it—i.e. to regulate it, to bring it into connection with the state, to restrain it in conformity with the general interests of society, etc. The productivist or technocratic socialist wanted to (i) reduce the influence of lazy, incompetent owners in favour of a regime of hyper-productivity; (ii) introduce codes of rules for private industry so it would be productive as possible; (iii) provide *uniform* instruction for all members of society; (iv) provide *public works* to enhance *national* wealth; (v) *utilize* scholars for research to enhance *technological* development.

This Saint-Simonian vision of society has been a remarkably influential one. It, of course, drew upon many of the elements of enlightenment rationalism. But it adapted these, in surprising new ways, to promote the rise of industrialism. Industrial society is an *administered* society. In its ascendancy, private property and contracts diminished in their importance as forms of wealth and power. In their place, the resources and offices of organizations (both state and corporate organizations) were substituted for them. The market never disappeared, but its influence was hemmed in by "legal-rational" administration. The face of liberal society was transformed, irredeemably. In classic liberal society, the cooperation of others (access to others skills, abilities, efforts, energies, property, information, etc.) was achieved through the system of contracts. Such access was crucial for liberal (purposive-rational) actors to achieve their ends—i.e. succeed in their enterprises. Individuals entered into (short-term) voluntary arrangements with others. A person could place skills, labour, goods, or information at the service of other's ends in exchange for money—at the same time their own ends (acquiring wealth, exercising abilities) could be reciprocally achieved by this exchange. Of course, for the exchange to take place, the person offering the contract needed to have property or income (wealth) commensurate with their ends, while potential parties to the contract needed to have marketable skills or property. These conditions (the conditions of *effective* liberty) were not always met.

In industrial society, by contrast, individuals rarely pursue just their own ends. The majority of actors are engaged in seeking more or less collective ends—either corporate or governmental ends. Their private aims (or "wants")—their *careers*—are subordinate to these collective ends. In this setting, the attainment of goals is dependent not on personal wealth or marketable skills, but on access to organizational resources and the (meritocratic) occupation of offices. Offices, in "legal-rational" organizations, give persons access to the pooled or common wealth of shareholders or tax-payers. Some of this pooled or common wealth of organizations normally brings together a variety of skills, labour, factors of production, etc., on a more or less permanent basis. To occupy an office means not only having access to resources that one does not personally own, but also means being able to rely on, and call on, the efforts of others. Relations between persons in organizations are not arranged contractually. Most common is a "bureaucratic" ordering of relations (which the Saint-Simonians had in mind). Less common (because these are, in a crucial sense, pre or post industrial) are collegiate, democratic, or consultative patterns of coordination.

IV

But what has the Social Objective of an *administered* society to do with Democracy? What caused the Great Reconciliation between socialism and democracy? What produced social democracy? My pre-supposition is that there is no immanent, no *internal* connection between socialism and democracy; just as there was no immanent, no internal connection between liberalism and democracy. The connection had to be argued for, fought for. Indeed, the democratic impulse amongst the first generations of socialists was weak, or non-apparent. The ascetic-egalitarian socialists, when they weren't dreaming of an insurrectional grab for power, advocated a "direct" democracy that was a kind of communal surveillance, a politics of suspicion. In the Western Tradition, the great embodiment of public and discursive politics has, unquestionably, been parliamentary life. Parliaments have been the repository of civilized, urbane, friendly argument. "Direct" democracy is hostile to these civic values. It is militant, anti-parliamentary, and above all, suspicious—suspicious of representatives and their judgement. The key plank of "direct" democracy is always the subordination of representatives to the strict control of the electorate, which, in practice, means to its zealous part.

Yet, the ascetic-egalitarian socialists, no matter how much they were attracted to the Spartan-Rousseauist-Calvinist-paranoid version of democracy, were, because of their *ethos*, also quick, in practice, to ditch it as well. Their overwhelming sense of mistrust extended to "the people" as well—suspicious of their lack of sacrifice, lack of assertiveness. What was needed was a vanguard—courageous, clear-sighted, self-sacrificing, which would usher in an epoch of equality, would fight corruption, ostentatiousness in the name of simplicity. This could even, in a semantic sleight of hand, be squared with the idea of democracy, because democrats were those who were repulsed by the misery and ignorance of the poor; democracy was the process of restituting what had been extracted from the poor by the rich; it was the process of elevating the poor—but not too high. True popular sovereignty—the putative aim of the ascetic egalitarian—could only be obtained when "the people", those-who-had-been-poor, could truly exercise sovereign power; and this was possible only under *conditions of perfect equality*. A virtuous dictatorship to level wealth, to simplify manners, to wage war on the voluptuous, was *a condition of the possibility* of true democracy. For the productivist socialist, on the other hand, the utopic component of politics focused not on the poor, but on industry. A good politics was a politics that fostered industry. Politics—as Saint-Simon said—was the science of production.[3] This didn't lead evidently or necessarily in the direction of democracy. It was certainly not Saint-Simon's belief that every citizen had the right to interest himself in public affairs without the proof of ability. The political ambition of productivist socialism was, in essence, that representatives of industry be admitted to government councils; that they acquire a greater share in determining the course of society. We might say that this amounted to the industrialization, rather than the democratization, of politics. It was a class and sectorial program, rather than a universalistic one. Its intention was to install the "producers of useful things" in positions of power and influence. It was only "useful" people who should make law, or counsel government, or regulate the course of "society". The flip-side of this social utilitarianism was the desire to *exclude* "the useless", the representatives of pre-industrial, theological, juridical, or feudal cultures. The regulating organs of society *must* be composed *exclusively* of the representatives of industrial life. As for the scourge of productivist socialism, *viz.* the idlers, the unproductive minority—they should, Saint-Simon proposed, lose their possessions if they didn't work, be placed in a state of legal tutelage, or be given the status of aliens in their own country—whatever it took, the idle had to be *removed* from political life. Yet, like the liberal, but unlike the ascetic-egalitarian socialist, the productivist socialist *was* interested in demolishing despotism. And, as I shall be arguing, it is this impulse which represents the important source of Socialism's reconciliation with Democracy. The new industrial politics was explicitly contrasted with despotic politics. Despotism operated on a "governmental" model of order-giver and order-taker, superior and subordinate. Productivist socialism sought quite specifically to escape this. Not to escape domination, as such, but to escape "governmental" domination. Governments, Saint-Simon argued, have always been made up of individuals who dictate to other individuals. The will of one person is subjected to the will of another person. Government has all the marks of despotism. Governmental action is necessarily arbitrary, because the men who govern, command as they wish. The sovereign's will, to which others are subjected, Saint-Simon observed, twists and turns in any direction it pleases; the very essence of despotism is will.

A jurist, a metaphysician, a civic thinker like Montesquieu would have absolutely no argument with this. But, unlike civic thought, the Saint-Simonian did not turn to constitutionalism, the idea of rights, or to parliament and public life to check governmental despotism. Indeed, Saint-Simon suggested, the arbitrariness of parliamentary majorities was no better than that of monarchies.

What Saint-Simon argued was that governmental despotism could be replaced by the rule of administration. The contrastive of the despotic state was the administrative state. The rule of administration was not governmental. It was not the rule of strongest or the most wilful, rather the rule of those *most capable in science and industry*. Administration was the *rule of knowledge*, unlike either government which was the *rule of power*, or juristic constitutionalism, which was the *rule of law*. Governmental rule involved the exercise of will—the dictating of orders to subordinates. It was personalized. Administration, on the other hand, was neither volitional or personalized. It consisted not in saying what was wanted, but what was known. Administrators, so the proposition went, didn't dictate orders, they just declared what conformed to the nature of things. It is no longer men controlling men—Saint-Simon suggested—it is the uttering of truth. It is not capricious, not arbitrary, not despotic. In the old regime, society was governed by men; in the new system, it is only governed by principles. Principles, to be obeyed, don't have to be articulated with the tone of command. Conformance to them doesn't have to be coerced. One submits voluntarily to the enunciated principles because they are *the truth*—because one doesn't want to act except in conformity with the nature of things.

Saint-Simon envisaged a state in which governmental rule would progressively shrink to the point where only the police and military acted governmentally (and then only against the idlers of the old system). Administrative rule would prevail. In many respects, Saint-Simon's vision has come to fruition. Despotic rule, which was always embattled in the Western Tradition since Aristotle, has been pushed back, even further, in favour of the administrative state. De Tocqueville, a brilliant observer of the modern political condition, recognized this in his analysis of the *European* state system.[4] He called this new administrative state, the tutelary state. He recognized that this state had a certain resemblance to the despotic state, yet belonged to the democratic age. He even suggested—although he then pulled back from the suggestion—that it might be possible to speak of a democratic despotism. The tutelary state was the product of the democratic age, and the democratic age's passion for equality. Equality, as a value, was shared by all the kinds of democracy: American, French, and English; civic, social, and liberal democracy. Equality in this context was a negative value: it was not the levelling or absolute equality of the ascetic socialist; it essentially represented opposition to the old hierarchical order. The idea of equality expressed the abhorrence of hereditary ranks and distinctions. In its liberal guise, this idea of equality was closely bound up with the modern notion of individualism. In a ranked society, persons were bound to one another in a great chain of being. Each had duties to the other. Liberal equality tore human beings asunder. It meant they were no longer united by the firm and lasting ties of the old hierarchical order. They found themselves isolated from each other. They found that, in the new democratic societies, the notion of human fellowship was faint, and persons seldom thought of sacrificing themselves for others. Equality made men independent of each other. Self-reliance, self-direction came to be valued above bonds of solidarity.

Ironically, it was this *liberal* equality that led directly to the tutelary state— i.e. to the administrative, and ultimately to the *social* democratic state. Let us follow the logic of this. With the destruction of the old regime's hierarchies and ranks, individuals were separated, and ties of personal dependency shrank. Individuals began to relate to one another at a distance; they were unconnected by common ties; they were indifferent or inconsiderate to each other. The mutual ties of deference and protection, of client and patron, evaporated, which left persons to their own devices, i.e. to look after themselves. They could enjoy personal and economic liberty, but they were left exposed to the vicissitudes of an often-time malignant world. The tutelary state arises out of this circumstance.

The tutelary state is a protective and regulatory state. As De Tocqueville argued, the independent persons of the democratic age, when they find themselves vulnerable, look outward for assistance. They can't receive it from their equals, who are disinterested, so they look for it from the state. Yet the idea of equality forbids, absolutely, this state providing social guarantees in a politically despotic manner. That would re-introduce personal dependency in a new guise. Clientelism, patrimonialism, patronage would be returned. So a new kind of state is required. This is the administrative or tutelary state. It instantiates a new kind of rule—the rule of knowledge—and as we shall see in a minute—also a new kind of power or sovereignty—*viz.* Democratic Power or Democratic Sovereignty.

Rulership in this new state involves a new kind of *impersonal* domination. It is a procedural, rule-bound kind of domination. It rests on knowledge, not on volition. It also instantiates a new kind of equality, a social or administrative kind of equality. In De Tocqueville's words, it standardizes norms of behaviour, it destroys the arbitrariness of personal rule; it destroys all individual instances of authority; it appears to belong to no one except the people in the abstract. This power is not despotic; it is not cruel, it is not arbitrary. It is "regular, provident, and mild". Of course, it is also methodical and minute. It spreads everywhere, carefully, thoroughly, with an eye to every detail. It has the capacity to take control of every aspect of people's lives. As De Tocqueville observed, the administrative state can cover the entire surface of society with a network of small, complicated rules. The tutelary state doesn't tyrannize— it rather compresses, enervates, extinguishes, and stupefies. It promotes a servitude of a regulated, quiet, and gentle kind.

De Tocqueville was right to draw a parallel, and also a distinction, between the despotic and administrative state. The administrative state certainty is not the embodiment of political freedom—as De Tocqueville and Aristotle understood it—i.e. the freedom to speak, and act, and associate in public. Yet it *does* lack much of the caprice and personal subordination that is central to despotism. More difficult is the question of whether De Tocqueville was right to see the tutelary state as an expression of the democratic age. On the surface of things, this offends common sense. Yet, in a strictly qualified sense, De Tocqueville was right. The tutelary state had none of the features that one would associate with modern civic democracy—universal suffrage, parliamentary elections and debate, a public sphere of association and influence. But, remember De Tocqueville had *already* extensively examined a democratic state founded on civic lines—*viz.* the American Republic—when he came to examine the tutelary state at the very end of his two volumes of *Democracy in America*. What he had started to come to grips with, although he did not and could not fully explore it, was the emergence of a European *social democracy*, different in ethos from American *civic democracy*, or for that matter from English *liberal democracy*.

The civic kind of democracy emphasizes public participation, public appearance, public debate, parliamentary discussion. It regards speaking, acting, and associating in public as valuable in its own right. Both liberal and social democracy only begrudgingly concede to this. Social democrats, we know, today, *prefer* to act administratively, rather than publicly; yet they were also *long ago* reconciled to a certain kind of public—i.e. a democratized public—a public sphere of open and contested elections, public campaigning, and parliamentary opposition. In other words, social democracy accepts a certain kind of *strategic* public life as a necessary corollary of democratic sovereignty.

V

But what explains socialism's reconciliation with democracy in the first place? Why did socialists like Eduard Bernstein come to the conclusion that parliament was the best ground for socialist prospects? Obviously the failure of insurrectionary political methods played its part in the shaping of this conclusion. But I want to argue that something more is involved.

Socialism reconciled itself to democracy because democratic sovereignty offered the best chance of realizing the socialist dream of administrative rule in the state. Social democrats had to reject the insurrectionary tradition because it led to the dictatorship over needs, and, to *political despotism*. And whatever else it stood for, the mainstream of Western socialism *did* reject political despotism. It *did not* do this in the name of civic freedom, and it certainly did not accept or envisage democracy in the strong, i.e. civic sense, of the word. It accepted rather something in-between despotism and civic democracy. It was this "something in-between" that De Tocqueville devoted his great talent to trying to understand. The genius of De Tocqueville is that he recognized this "something in-between" virtually at the moment of its birth. What he recognized was the emergence of a new kind of rule in the state—the emergence of what we today know as the administrative state or regulatory state. De Tocqueville called it the tutelary state. The name is not significant; the phenomenon is.

Typical of this new kind of administrative rule were the Factory Acts and the labour legislation that were produced in the 19th century to regulate the new factory system. Both liberals and socialists welcomed the collapse of the old master-servant relationship, with its tissue of personal domination and dependency. Liberals believed that contractual relations alone were sufficient for a good society. Socialists, however, were aware of the loss of protection against exploitation and the catastrophes of everyday life that the old rank-ordered society, the *Gemeinschaft*, offered. In a rank-ordered society, protection is offered by superiors to subordinates, in exchange for deference to them personally. In the new contractually-ordered liberal market society, such an exchange of deference for immunity was impossible. The ascetic socialist viewed the inequality of wealth in the same light as the inequality of ranks. Equality meant the abolition of socio-economic classes as well as ranks. But this was only possible with political despotism, a dictatorship over needs, and a kind of "satisfied society" that were an anathema to the productivist mentality of Western socialism. The mainstream of Western socialism, however, adapted to ascetic socialism in one crucial respect—*viz.* its sanctification of the poor. The Saint-Simonians lost this point. The trickle-down effect of hyper-productivity would not solve the question of the poor—instead the techniques of the administrative state were applied to the question. And so the two strands of European socialism were united. Socialism, although stripped of its egalitarian aspect, accepted a version of the idea of a guaranteed society— immunity for the weaker and more vulnerable against the various forms of social catastrophe (illness, accident, malnourishment, exhaustion, inadequate shelter, overcrowding, disease, etc.). This was the social welfarist vision. But socialism was not, in the name of welfare and life, prepared to countenance either the Tory option of the resurrection of the society of ranks (which liberal-capitalism had fundamentally eroded) nor was it prepared to contemplate the kind of egalitarian-despotic state that was eventually to usher in a guaranteed society in the Communist East. Socialism chartered a difficult middle course between contractualism and despotism. Acting in the name of "need", in the name of the value of "life", socialism looked to administration—to the rule of truth—to supervise, regulate, temporize exploitation, to anticipate threats to life, and to institute a system of immunities.

It is no accident that *both* Marx *and* Bernstein lauded the English Factory Acts, and the Factory Act inspectors. Bernstein drew the obvious conclusion from this. The path to socialism was legislative. He expected that socialism would diminish the rights of the capitalist proprietor through legislation—i.e. reduce the proprietor to the role of a simple administrator. Factory despotism would be replaced by social administration. It must be stressed that neither Bernstein nor Marx meant legislation in the civic or juristic sense of Law, but in the administrative sense of Regulation. Such legislation was *the effect* not of the sense of justice, certainly not of justice as dignity, but the result of the knowledge of truth; it was the result of science, of calorific tabulation, of methodical assessment, etc. It *aimed* not at the end of domination, not at the reign of dignity on this earth, not at the prospect of all human beings standing tall; but at securing of immunity against exploitation, at shelter for the miserable and outcast, and social insurance for the rest against the prospect of immiseration. Socialism acted in the name of life, not in the name of freedom and dignity. It acted out of a social, rather than civic, sense of justice.

So why democracy? Surely a system of social-insurance provided by an autocratic-Bismarckian political regime would have sufficed to have satisfied the core aspirations of socialism. I would argue against this interpretation because central to socialism was the idea not just of "society", but of an *administered* society. Socialism sanctified *not just* immunity against the risk and jeopardies of a liberalized world, *but also* the rule of knowledge. It stood for not only the value of life, but also the regime of truth. It looked to a new kind of rule through which to realize its social objectives. Socialism pioneered this new kind of rule. Saint-Simon gave it a name: administration. But along with this new kind of rule was required a new kind of Sovereignty. The authority (the rulings) of Knowledge had still to be complemented by Power. Saint-Simon denied this; it was a reality nonetheless.

The riddle of what kind of Sovereignty, of what kind of Power, was solved by social democracy in the latter half of the 19th century. Socialism needed democracy, because democracy answered the question of "what kind of sovereignty" in a way which was compatible with socialism's preference for an administered society and for administrative rule. Democracy answered the conundrum of socialism: how to find a form of Sovereign Power consistent with the Rule of Knowledge, i.e. consistent with the tutelary state and its pattern of impersonal organization, technical co-ordination, and rule-bound action.

Democracy was the kind of Sovereignty that suited the Rule of Offices. Monarchy too often fell back into bad old patrimonial habits of rule, or it indulged itself in forms of magnificence that were the antithesis of administrative economy. Aristocracy, on the other hand, tended either to juristic forms of rule or to gross forms of oligarchic landlordism, clientelism and patronage. The jurist's respect for argument, for "putting up a case", and for deliberation, for prudential judgement, and for collegiate self-government, held little attraction for the scientistically and positivistically minded socialist; while oligarchy and clientelism were merely despotism by another name. So that, more or less, left democracy. But what kind of democracy? Certainly not a civic kind. That would have supposed the resurrection of juristic mores that positivistic socialism couldn't abide. Such a juristic or civic democracy conflicted with socialism's reliance on knowledge, and its elevation of the truth-values of exactness, precision, and method: the values of an administrative culture. What was worked out, instead, was a *social* form of democracy.

At the heart of this form of democracy was the idea of a political party which was organized and disciplined, yet which was capable of assertiveness and leadership. This was what the new Social Democratic Party combined; and Robert Michel's pioneering study of it in *Political Parties* has never been surpassed. The Party exhibited the promptness of decision, unity of command, and strictness of discipline typical of the administrative spirit. Yet it *also* demonstrated the directive impulse, the tenacity, persistence, incessant effort, indefatigable agitation, and wilfulness of the Prince, as well. The real significance of the Party is that it is the crucible for the emergence of a new kind of Sovereign. The sovereign, in Max Weber's terms, acts politically, not merely bureaucratically. It exhibits *political leadership* as opposed to the rule-following and know-how—i.e. the expert knowledge of the rules and of technique—that typifies modern administration. As Weber stressed, in the modern state the actual *ruler* is necessarily and unavoidably the bureaucracy. The *ruler* is neither feudal, nor patrician, not patrimonial, but bureaucratic. This is well known. Less well known is Weber's trenchant insistence that this is not enough, and that administration must be complemented by political leadership—i.e. administrative rule must be complemented by the will-to-Power, by the preparedness of political leaders to act in a *sovereign* manner, to *direct* the state; to provide, in other words, "substantive rational" direction to orientate "legal rational" administration. A political sovereign gives the state its "directing mind", or "moving spirit", which the professionally-trained, specialized, and duty-bound administrators could not, and cannot, provide. Weber, of course, in his essay, *Parliament and Government in a Reconstructed Germany*, bemoaned the failure of monarchic government to do just that—*provide direction in the state.* So who could do the job? Where would the political leaders, moved by the will-to-Power, come from? Weber answered this in two ways—from Parliament and from the Party system. When he speaks of Parliament, Weber gives voice to a civic concern that politicians should act *responsibly*, and should check and control, examine and supervise the bureaucracy. But political leadership, for him, was more than restraining run-away administration. The political sovereign or leader operated with an existential or romantic wilfulness alien to the civic model. Civic responsibility exercised in Parliament and Sovereign Power are two different things, although Weber does not always see this. Parliament can, at best, be a display case for political leadership knocking on the doors of Power. But the incubation of that Leadership, and its springboard to Power, is the Party—i.e. the democratic Party in competition with other Parties. It was, of course, the Competitive Party System that replaced the Monarchy, in Germany and elsewhere in Europe. Weber in some sense hedged his bets. He talked of Parliament as the ground for the growth and selection of political leaders, yet recognised that these would, inevitably, be Party leaders. Moreover, he also recognized the *weakness* of the Germany party system, including the Social Democrats. Although the Social Democrats were clearly much more robust and tightly organized than the liberal parties, and although the Social Democrats were the pioneer of the idea of the modern political party, they suffered too often from an un-sovereign-like timidity and lack of elan; they focused on their own weaknesses; they preferred too often the swamp of perpetual opposition or wartime co-operation, no matter how destructive this might be. They were, when it came to the crunch, *unwilling* to take the reigns of Power, in the dying days of Imperial Germany. Their wilfulness failed them.

All the same, monarchical sovereignty had been exhausted. Democratic party sovereignty lay on the horizon. This new Sovereign, this collective Prince—the Party—was eminently suited to the administrative form of rule in the modern state, in a way in which monarchy or aristocratic councils were not. The Party was itself *a kind of administration*, so it understood the administrative spirit. The modern mass electorate required *organized* political canvassing, budgeting, fundraising, and the administrative offices to do this. *But* the Party was not merely a bureaucratic machine. The Party, above and beyond all, was a *strategic institution*. It fought, metaphorically, with other parties, other collective Princes, on the terrain of civil society. In this strategic, public environment were fostered the traits of modern sovereignty—will, initiative, flexibility, goal-rationality, tenacity, etc. Weber emphasized that *struggle* is the essence of the politics of modern sovereignty. But the fight is a relatively civilized one; the aggression highly sublimated, highly symbolic. It is a politics of competition, not conquest. Power, in the final hour, is handed over in a routine bloodless manner from one party to another. This is the democratic struggle. It is conducted under the civil constraints of broad, or universal, suffrage. Political leaders, as Schumpeter put it, acquire the *power to decide by means of a competitive struggle for the people's vote*. The competitive element is the essence of democracy because it is in the *electoral context* that the substantively rational or existential-wilful traits of political leadership are fostered and displayed.

Such an arrangement is a necessary corollary of the fact that Power in the modern state, as Claude Lefort has argued, cannot be appropriated by, or embodied in, any one person or group. Power loses its visible representatives; it becomes decorporealized. The places of Power can no longer be permanently occupied. This *also* is the necessary corollary of the administrative form of rule, for where Power is monopolized by one Party, inevitably administration descends into the mire of patrimonialism, cronyism, patronage, nepotism, corruption, and capriciousness. The regular interchange of Power-holders, the regular turn-over of the Parties, of the Collective Princes—democratic practices, in other words—are needed to ensure honest and efficient and "legal-rational" administration. *The fate of one is bound up with the other.* So it made sense for those socialists who believed in the idea of an administered society to, in the end, turn to the democratic circulation of Party elites, and the constraints of universal suffrage on Party sovereignty. For without them, the socialist dream of just rule in the state—i.e. their dream of impersonalized administrative rule—could not be sustained. The administered society requires democratic sovereignty to survive and prosper.

Notes

1. J. S. Mill, *Considerations on Representative Government.*
2. Of course, as Mill freely admitted, with absolute honesty, there was a certain liberal cant in all this. We might from a distance admire energetic characters, but we *prefer* neighbours who are acquiescent and submissive people, because their passiveness increases our sense of security. Something of the corroded underbelly of the liberal utopia is revealed here. A dynamic society—the liberal utopia—is fine as long as it doesn't imperil our basic sense of security—as long as it doesn't jeopardize our place in the world. Yet, implicitly, it does and it must. As we know from the wild-fire spread of the liberal-commercial economy, little can be immunized from the agitation of an enterprising society. Everything is caught in the spin of this washing machine. The liberal would scoff—this is a defence of passivity as against activity. But, as Mill also pointed out, we *also* like our neighbours to be passive because it plays into the hands of *our* wilfulness. Passive characters are less of an obstacle in our path— they don't get in our way—they don't impede our liberty. A passive character, as Mill observed, is not a dangerous rival. And a dangerous rival will turn an energetic character quite possibly into a nervous wreck. For the liberal, passivity is a kind of hypocritical virtue. To be decried publicly, yet privately applauded, because a fully liberalized world, full of energetic improvers, might degenerate into a Hobbesian war of all against each, as one enterprising character clashed with another. Better entirely that one's neighbour be lethargic; and let you alone carry the burden of activity.
3. The best account of Saint-Simon's views remains Emile Durkheim's *Socialism.*
4. Alexis de Tocqueville, *Democracy in America*, vol. 2, part IV.

THE THEORY OF MODERNITY AND THE PROBLEMATIC OF DEMOCRACY

Johann P. Arnason

The dominant paradigms of the sociological tradition are not simply alternative images of man and society; they are also selective interpretations of modernity, and while some of their built-in biases set them against each other, others are shared in common. The "structured disagreement" (J. Alexander) of conflicting theories is thus compatible with a general tendency to emphasize and theorize certain components of modernity at the expense of others. Anthony Giddens has tried to show that the formative phase of modern social theory produced two particularly seminal interpretations of the new social order which was being consolidated and contested at the same time: it could be defined and analyzed as a capitalist society or as an industrial society. Although the classical models of theorizing are probably better understood as different attempts to clarify the relationship between capitalism and industrialism and determine their relative weight, it is in any case beyond doubt that these two dimensions of modernity were much more extensively thematized and systematically explored than the problematic of democracy. Democracy remained, in others words, an under-theorized component of modernity. On the other hand, this neglect may have facilitated the development which Peter Murphy describes as a background to his discussion of democracy and socialism, i.e. the proliferation of incompatible versions of the idea of democracy, as a result of its appropriation by incompatible political cultures.[1] Under-theorization and over-interpretation would thus seem to be two sides of the same coin.

It might be objected that recent efforts to reconceptualize the foundations and developmental trends of modernity have changed this picture. But

Thesis Eleven 26
©1990 *Thesis Eleven*

although it is true that a stronger interest in democracy is one of the more recurrent traits in the otherwise highly diversified spectrum of new images of modernity, the equally widespread tendency to reduce the problematic of democracy to that of its preconditions or co-determinants—or at least to subordinate it to a supposedly more fundamental category—should not be overlooked. The focus may be on the anthropological presuppositions of democracy, as in Habermas's attempt to reconstruct the democratization of the modern state as a progressive articulation of the rationality of the lifeworld against that of the system. Alternatively, the emphasis can be shifted from the more innovative aspects of modern democracy to its historical background, which is then analyzed in terms of a long-term redistribution of social power. Norbert Elias's theory of "functional democratization" is a case in point, and the concept of "polyarchy", at least as it is used by Anthony Giddens, seems to have similar implications. A third approach tends to collapse democracy into its social context, more specifically into the constitution of civil society and its emancipation from the state. Finally, Castoriadis's analysis of the vision or the project of autonomy is the most convincing account of the cultural horizon of democracy, but it does not cover the broader range of questions which arise in relation to the combination of autonomy with other aspects of democracy, and to the interaction of democracy with other components of modernity.

The most obvious exception to this pattern is the work of Claude Lefort. His stated aim is to develop a complex interpretation of democracy that would do justice to its multiple aspects, to the connections and tensions between them and to their joint transformative impact on the modern constellation as a whole. The primary task is, as he sees it, to make sense of the radically new relationship between law, power and knowledge. But the central role which he attributes to democracy obscures the problems and dynamics of other formative factors to such an extent that modernity can no longer be seen as a multi-polar and multi-dimensional context. Moreover, the absence of clear contrasts with other structural principles blurs the contours of democracy itself and leads Lefort to define it in primarily negative terms—as a rupture and as a permanently self-questioning form of political life, rather than as a project or a positive reorientation.

Despite recent progress and new beginnings, it thus seems difficult to balance the tasks of a comprehensive theory of modernity against those of more specific interpretations of democracy, and any attempt to do so should begin with a closer look at some preliminary questions. The following discussion will be limited to three such issues: the conceptual obstacles and reductionist biases inherited from the formative phase of modern social theory (I); the particular problems inherent in the relationship of modern democracy to its pre-modern antecedents (II); and the most general requirements for a conceptual framework that would allow us to relate democracy to other components of modernity (III).

I

If a tendency to neglect or simplify the problematic of democracy is common to the most influential classics of social theory, it should also be noted that this is in each case the result of a specific theoretical strategy. Marx, Weber and Durkheim can—in retrospect—all be accused of not taking the question of democracy seriously enough, but their ways of defusing the issue vary as widely as any other aspects of their work.

One of the most decisive turns of Marx's intellectual trajectory is the early shift from a democratic critique of the modern state to an anthropologically grounded critique of the modern economy. This change reflects the gradual crystallization of an implicit—and never fully conceptualized—image of man and society that proved more conducive to the latter approach than to the former. But our present concern is neither with the underlying reasons for the change of direction nor with the fragmentary insights which survived it.[2] The main point is, rather, the result which opened the way towards further simplifications of the Marxist tradition. The initial reference to democracy as a latent essence and a normative horizon of political life is replaced with a very different version of the critical perspective; as Marx now sees it, the overcoming of alienation would entail a de-differentiation and re-absorption of the political sphere, and the democratic imperative gives way to the vision of a "free association of the producers". The whole problematic of democracy and its anthropological implications is, in other words, overshadowed by an enriched and radicalized image of economic man.

As the later history of Marxism shows, this was a very ambivalent position: it could be reactivated against more reductionistic readings of Marx, but it also obstructed the road towards a radical democratic "recovery of politics", even for those who were otherwise trying to move in that direction.

Marx's way of marginalizing the question of democracy is thus inseparable from a more general relativization of the political sphere as a whole, backed up by an anthropology which centres on production and a social theory centred on economic structures. By contrast, political themes are much more prominent in Max Weber's work, and the political dimension is much more central to his image of man and society, but the conceptual framework which he develops leads to a fragmentation of the idea of democracy and thus prevents him from exploring this side of modernity as thoroughly as the capitalist economy and the bureaucratic state. The pattern of legal-rational domination, i.e. the institutional complex of the *Rechtsstaat*, is separated from the more radical implications of the democratic transformation and reduced to the legitimizing basis of a bureaucratic apparatus which tends to outdistance and overshadow it. This separation obviously reflects the historical experience of Germany, but it does so from a particular angle that is linked to more distinctive aspects of Weber's political sociology and more extreme results of the fragmentation referred to above. The conceptual segregation of radical democracy is only the first step of an argument which goes on to underline its internal inconsistencies and paradoxes. Weber constructs a typology of the basic forms of political life—from his specific point of view they appear as forms of legitimate domination—which includes legal-rational domination, but contains no reference to democracy as such; he then tries to show that more radical democratic projects are the result of inherently unstable and ultimately untenable deviations from the fundamental patterns. In the first version of his sociology of domination, written before 1914, the starting-point for this argument is the close but problematic relationship between domination and administration. According to Weber, "every domination expresses itself and functions as administration" and "every administration needs domination".[3] The mutual dependence is double-edged: on the one hand, it is only when the principles of legitimacy and the corresponding patterns of power set their stamp on administration—Weber is obviously using this term in the broad sense of ensuring the everyday continuity and reproduction of social life—that they can be regarded as constitutive of the social world; on the other hand, the exercise of power at the level of administration also involves its adaptation to social needs, and this can give rise to demands for a more far-reaching subordination that would—as Weber puts it—transform the rulers into servants of the ruled. Weber describes this attempt to minimize domination through "direct democratic administration" as a typological limiting case, rather than a primitive condition, and as self-defeating in the sense that it leads to an irresistible redistribution of social power in favour of those who are—for a variety of historically changing reasons—particularly well situated to carry out administrative tasks. The result is what Weber calls "the domination of notables"; while the first "notables" were the elders, economic and social differentiation becomes progressively more important in the course of later developments.

If direct democracy is thus always threatened by "social alienation", this trend becomes more pronounced in larger and more complex societies: "As soon as mass administration is involved the sociological meaning of democracy changes so radically that it no longer makes sense to look for something homogeneous behind this collective name".[4] Since the problems of mass administration are inseparable from the broader context of the rationalizing process, the metamorphoses of the democratic project can be regarded as an aspect of the latter. This becomes even clearer with the shift to another line of argument in the last version of Weber's sociology of domination, written after 1918 and posthumously included in the first part of *Economy and Society*. In this text, the analysis of direct democracy as a utopian vision of administration without domination is recapitulated in more succinct terms, but it is preceded and overshadowed by a section on "the anti-authoritarian reinterpretation of charisma". This is Weber's most original—and most problematic—contribution to the theory of democracy; it concerns the very foundations of domination, rather than its relationship to administration. As he sees it, the original meaning of charisma is authoritarian, but inasmuch as its real force is a matter of performance and acceptance, it is open to a reinterpretation which makes the legitimacy of the leader depend on the recognition by the followers. Democratic legitimacy is thus a derivative inversion of charismatic legitimacy. As such, it is vulnerable to a reinterpretation of the reinterpretation which gives rise to the phenomenon of plebiscitarian democracy. The genuine content of the latter (which for Weber includes revolutionary dictatorships, but also the less extreme forms of "caesaristic" leadership that can develop within the framework of mass democracy and bureaucratic organizations) is a new type of charismatic domination which hides behind the form of democratic legitimacy. The anti-authoritarian reinterpretation is thus formally retained, but it takes a turn which leads to the reaffirmation of the original meaning of charisma. This analysis adds further weight to Weber's remark on the multiple sociological meanings of democracy: they range from an attempt to minimize domination through techniques of administration to the use of an apparent delegitimation of domination to consolidate its less manifest but more essential aspects. Both ends of the spectrum are related to the rationalizing process; Weber explicitly refers to a rationalized modern version of direct democracy, and the anti-authoritarian interpretation is one of several transformations which accompany—and counterbalance—the retreat of charisma before the advance of rationality and discipline.

Although the fragmentation of the problematic of democracy is the most obvious implication of Weber's approach, another aspect should not be overlooked. The original meaning of charisma—as a generic term for phenomena which transcend the horizons of everyday life—is linked to an archaic context, and later sublimations could not halt its long-term decline. Weber's account of the origins of democratic legitimacy thus leads to what we might call an "archaization" of democracy which further attenuates its connection with modernity.

Durkheim's conception of democracy in relation to modernity seems at first sight very different from Weber's. His most detailed discussion of this question leads to the conclusion that democracy is the political form through which society becomes most clearly conscious of itself; he also associates democracy with a more rapid and more consciously accepted social change and emphasizes its close links to the modern idea of the individual as well as to the modern form of the state.[5] If such connotations are to be taken into account, definitions of modern democracy must go beyond vague notions of self-government or unrestricted participation and avoid the widespread but misleading conflation with political forms of primitive societies. Against the idealization of archaic models, Durkheim stresses both the more radical implications and the more complex procedures of modern democracy. His comments on the former aspect contain a clear reference to the idea of autonomy: "In principle, we lay down that everything may for ever remain open to question, that everything may be examined, and that in so far as decisions have to be taken, we are not tied to the past".[6] As to the latter point, Durkheim's main argument is that if the state is to fulfil its specific tasks as a centre of reflection and deliberation, it must not be reduced to a simple expression of the more diffuse levels of social consciousness. On this view, the coordinating role of the state depends on effective communication with its social environment, but also on a cognitive autonomy that is incompatible with the misguided utopia of direct democracy. This is one of the reasons for Durkheim's strong interest in intermediary organizations, such as—most importantly—professional groups: in mediating between state and society, they defend the autonomy of each side against the other.

These ideas would seem to add up to a full recognition of democracy as a key component of modernity. But in the overall context of Durkheim's work (and even more so in the later Durkheimian tradition), they were overshadowed by a much more one-sided and restrictive conceptual scheme. In *The Division of Social Labour*, Durkheim had developed a theoretical model of modern society which went beyond Spencer-style functionalism in its emphasis on normative structures and it refusal to collapse the social bond into the rationality of cooperation but neglected the political sphere and thus lacked an essential prerequisite for thematizing the self-constitution of society. Durkheim's critique of Spencer had a lasting impact on later attempts to analyze modern society in terms of functional differentiation and integration (Parsons is the most obvious example), and while the fusion of functionalism with a normativistic image of society did not preclude a less dismissive approach to political forms in general and democracy in particular, the limits of such improvements were a priori determined by a frame of reference which reduced the political sphere to one functional subsystem among others and its transformations to correspondingly localized processes. If the more radical interpretation of democracy, summarized above, failed to develop into a plausible alternative, this was not simply because the most relevant text was not published until 1950; the decisive obstacle was, as another look at that very text will show, a conceptual impasse.

As the shortcomings of Durkheim's first synthesis—centred around the key concept of the division of labour—became more obvious, they prompted him to explore several new areas; his reflections on democracy are a major step forward, but they were never brought into closer contact with other similarly innovative themes. In particular, the understanding of democracy as a new and superior form of the self-thematization of society was not linked to later insights into the creative and self-creative character of social life. That would only have been possible on the basis of a reconceptualization of the core element in Durkheim's image of society: the collective representations. Despite various additions and reconsiderations, the emphasis on their cognitive aspect remained dominant, and when Durkheim refers to a clearer self-consciousness in connection with democracy, the connotations are those of cognitive adequacy, rather than creative capacity or interpretive potential. This limitation leaves the whole argument open to a functionalist turn: "The more societies grow in scope and complexity, the more they need reflection in conducting their affairs".[7] And the cognitivist bias is brought to bear on the general idea of autonomy: "To be autonomous means, for the human being, to understand the necessities he has to bow to and accept them with full knowledge of the facts".[8]

It might be objected that the most penetrating and emphatic interpretations of modern democracy are to be found in the works of outsiders or unjustly neglected theorists rather than in those of the generally recognized classics. Tocqueville is undoubtedly the most striking case. But Raymond Aron's attempt to extract from his writings a paradigm of democratic society, comparable to Comte's vision of industrial society or Marx's theory of capitalist development, is not fully convincing.[9]

This is not to deny that the analysis of American democracy and the reconstruction of the background to the French Revolution resulted in some major contributions to social theory, but Tocqueville's argument is too fragmentary and inconclusive to add up to an alternative paradigm of modernity. His use of the concept of democracy is—as Aron admits—inconsistent, and the relationship between its social and political connotations remains unclear. More importantly, the two main themes of his work—the fully-fledged democratic regime in America, which had taken shape without a revolution and hence without a clear awareness of its own revolutionary implications, and the unfinished democratic revolution in France, which misunderstood itself because it had to cast its absolutist precursor in the role of an antagonist—were never integrated into a more balanced and comprehensive account. Each of them was, on its own, of limited value as an interpretive key to modern societies. Because of an exceptional historical and geographical conjuncture, the American version of democracy had matured before a corresponding unfolding of other components of modernity; as for the finished part of the projected critical history of the French Revolution, it throws more light on the genealogy of modernity than on its structure. Further progress would have entailed the introduction of a third theme: that of the democratic *question*—in the sense of the institutionalized self-questioning of society—as distinct from the democratic *condition* and the democratic *revolution*.[10] Claude Lefort notes Tocqueville's failure to confront this issue: ". . . his exploration mostly comes to an end with what I would call the obverse of each apparent characteristic of the new society, instead of going on to look for the obverse of the obverse".[11] What Lefort has in mind is Tocqueville's diagnosis of a self-destructive dynamic that would replace the spirit of individualism and innovation with conformity, consumerism, and the despotic power of an anonymous collective; the missing part of the picture is the counter-trend which gives rise to new forms of individualization, differentiation and contestation. It is the complex interplay of both aspects that justifies the description of democracy as "the historical society par excellence, a society which, in its very form, accepts and preserves indeterminacy ... "[12]

Another outsider deserves at least a brief mention. T. G. Masaryk was not primarily a social theorist, and if his legacy in this area has been neglected, that is at least partly because of the fragmentary and protean character of his work. The idea of democracy in a very broad sense—social, political and intellectual—is central to his cultural and political project; it is thematized in different contexts and from diverse points of view, but never systematically elaborated. His vision of the modern world, however distinctive, also falls far short of a comprehensive theory. A certain conception of the relationship between democracy and modernity can nevertheless be extracted from his writings, especially from his critique of Marxism and his attempt to spell out the historical meaning of the First World War.[13]

Masaryk accepts—as a starting-point—the notion of democracy as self-government, but adds that this principle should be extended beyond the political sphere and manifest itself in social and economic institutions as well as in a general pattern of conduct and outlook ("democratism" is the term he uses to refer more specifically to the latter aspect). The reference to the public sphere is as essential as the grounding in autonomy; hence Masaryk's insistence that democracy presupposes not only equality, but also a dialogue between equals, and not only liberty, but also a public deliberation of free citizens. This complex and radical idea of democracy is for Masaryk the most fundamental normative orientation of the modern world. As such, it stands in sharp contrast to two interconnected but not fully interchangeable patterns that were predominant in traditional societies and are still capable of reproducing themselves in more or less modified forms in the modern context: those of aristocracy and theocracy. Masaryk's use of these terms is somewhat irregular, but the general thrust is clear. Both concepts are used in a broad sense that goes far beyond their conventional meaning and links their political models to cultural horizons; the constitutive characteristic of aristocracy is a monopolization of social power, associated with the devaluation of work and everyday life, whereas the notion of theocracy refers to a sacralization of power that tends to go together with a disregard for the finite character of human reason and experience. The strength and flexibility of the forces opposed to democracy explain the need for a correspondingly strong defence. While democracy is for Masaryk indisputably the normative core of modernity, he also tries to show that its logic can be grounded in other aspects of the modern world; conversely, the reference to democracy helps to separate their genuinely modern implications from deviations or misinterpretations that are more reminiscent of pre-modern patterns. The spirit of modern science is an indispensable ally of democracy in its struggle against theocracy and its mythological accompaniments, but the scientific subculture also needs democratic principles—those of public debate

and critical examination—to protect itself against its own absolutist tempta-
tions. Although Masaryk did not see the elective affinities with science as a
substitute for the religious foundations of democracy, the latter—i.e. first and
foremost, Christian ideas of individuality responsibility and solidarity—had to
be made compatible with modern attitudes and conditions, and that could only
be done through a "struggle for religion", i.e. a permanent effort to separate
the core of religion from mythological and theocratic admixtures. But the most
interesting part of Masaryk's attempt to contextualize democracy is perhaps
the close association with work and the use he makes of this connection in his
critique of Marx. The recognition of the human dignity and paradigmatic significance of everyday work is seen as an essential precondition of democracy,
especially in the context of its struggle against aristocracy, and Marx is credited
with having oriented the science of society towards "the world of work", but
his reductionistic approach to ethical and political questions led him to misun-
derstand his own discovery and translate it into two fatal shortcuts: the labour
theory of value and the myth of the proletarian revolution. Masaryk sees both
of them as relapses into an aristocratic way of thinking. The aristocratic spirit
in philosophy manifests itself in a preference for speculation at the expense of
empirically grounded reflection; Marx is following this line when he deduces
value from labour and dismisses the complex interaction between production,
exchange and consumption. Similarly, the misguided view of revolution as a
royal road to social change is influenced by a tradition which tends to model
political action on sport and warfare rather than work.

It seems clear that Masaryk moved—on the whole—from a strong emphasis on the problematic structure of modernity to an increasingly harmonizing
image.[14] No doubt this is partly due to religious—more precisely Christian and
primarily Protestant—presuppositions which remained intact and reasserted
themselves. But the lack of an adequate frame of reference on the level of
social theory may have been more decisive. In this respect, Masaryk's position
is paradoxical: he saw more clearly than most other critics at the turn of the
century that Marx's work had a philosophical and a sociological dimension,
but he had only a limited grasp of the shift towards a less reductionistic image
of society that was taking place at the time—often in the work of authors with
a more superficial understanding of Marx than his own.

II

All components of modernity have their pre-modern analogies or antecedents, and in each case, the analysis of contrasts and similarities has some
paradigmatic examples to draw on. In some of the most extensively explored
areas, the comparison with non-European civilizations has proved particularly
fruitful. As far as capitalism and industrialization are concerned, China is now
generally recognized as the most interesting counterexample: at the beginning

of the second millennium AD, it was—with regard to technology, economic organization and bureaucratic administration—so far in advance of the rest of the world that some historians have described it as an early modern or proto-modern society, but for a variety of complex and controversial reasons, this progress did not lead to a definitive breakthrough, and when China faced a direct threat from the expanding West, it had fallen so far behind that the result was a cultural and structural crisis that has yet to be overcome. The comparison with India can—as Max Weber showed—throw light on both universal and specific characteristics of the religious traditions involved in the Western road to modernity; moreover, some recent interpretations have revived the Weberian idea that the differentiation of socio-cultural spheres was particularly pronounced in India, but took a direction which sets it apart from the modern pattern of differentiation (on one view, the latter represents a higher degree of systemic interpenetration, but it would be more in line with Weber's suggestions to describe it as more conducive to productive conflicts). Islamic civilization shares with its Occidental counterpart the constitutive link to both Greek and Judaic origins, and the problematic relationship between these two sources was thematized in Islamic thought earlier than in the West, although the overall development of the Islamic world prevented the interaction between them from reaching the same level of dynamism and cultural productivity as in the West. Finally, Japan is the only non-Western society that has gone through a modernizing process comparable to that of the West but specific enough to result in an alternative version of modernity; it is therefore uniquely relevant to a comparative analysis of the modern constellation as a whole.

But in the case of modern democracy, the most significant pre-modern analogy is a part—one of the most formative parts—of the early history of the West. The question of the relationship between ancient and modern democracy (with regard to the former, it concerns not only the character and significance of Athenian democracy, but also the reasons why the democratic transformation progressed much further in some Greek city-states than others and why it was so successfully blocked in the Roman republic) is thus much more closely linked to the origins of Western modernity and more crucial to its self-understanding than the comparison of its other aspects to their respective counterparts can ever be. More specifically, this confrontation differs from others of the same kind in that it raises at once the issue of relative merits and demerits on both sides. Both the idealization of ancient democracy because of its more authentic content and the defence of modern democracy on the basis of its more universal principles are recurrent answers to this question. A detailed evaluation of the debate is beyond the scope of the present paper; the following remarks should be read as an attempt to clarify some preliminary hermeneutical points and underline the complexity of the problem. The hermeneutical "fusion of horizons" involved in the comparison of ancient and modern democracy was, as I hall try to show, not easy to achieve; it took a long detour and focused on misleading examples, but this was to some extent a productive misunderstanding, which helped to develop perspectives that would otherwise have been blocked. On the other hand, the rediscovery and recognition of the most decisive historical landmark—the experience of Athenian democracy—does nothing to defuse the conflict of interpretations: those who insist on the enduring significance of ancient democracy do so for a whole range of different reasons, and each of them is open to specific objections.

Early modern attempts to thematize and justify the political self-constitution of society reflect a new historical experience and interpret it in the light of classical precedents, but their lodestar is the idea of the republic, rather than that of democracy, and they generally prefer Sparta or Rome to Athens. As J. G. A. Pocock has shown, the key characteristic of this tradition is an internal tension: while its successive reformulations of the classical models of citizenship and the *vita activa* are a major contribution to the political culture of modernity, it is at the same time involved in a permanent "quarrel with modernity", more precisely with the economic mainstream of the modernizing process. " 'Bourgeois ideology', a paradigm for capitalist man as *zoon politikon*, was immensely hampered in its development by the omnipresence of Aristotelian and civic humanist values which virtually defined rentier and entrepreneur as corrupt, and... if indeed capitalist thought ended by privatizing the individual, this may have been because it was unable to find an appropriate way of presenting him as citizen. 'Bourgeois ideology', which old-fashioned Marxism depicted as appearing with historic inevitability, had, it seems, to wage a struggle for existence, and may never have fully won it".[15] The conflictual relationship to modernity was probably the main reason for the dismissive attitude to Athens. In Benjamin Constant's well-known essay on ancient and modern liberty, which can be read both as a postscript to the republican tradition and as a paradigmatic statement of the case for modern liberalism, Athens is described as the most modern of the ancient republics, because of its commercial spirit and its individualism.[16] Its legacy was, in other words, too ambiguous for those who wanted to oppose political autonomy to modern individualism and its economic foundations. On the other hand, the republican point of reference—the Machiavellian moment, as Pocock calls it—was open to a wide range of variations. The idea of the republic could be detached from its classical background and used—as in Kant's political philosophy—to define a new form of government, irreducible to the traditional typology of autocracy, aristocracy and democracy, but compatible with more rational and rigorous criteria of legitimacy. This shift paved the way for later invocations of the republican project as a corrective to impoverished or superficial versions of democracy. But the orientation towards the Greco-Roman world—and the above-mentioned choice of models within it—could also facilitate an innovative approach to modern problems. Rousseau's rehabilitation of democracy as a legitimate utopian perspective, even if not a practicable form of government for human societies, is closely linked to his image of Sparta (Castoriadis may be right in describing the latter as utterly aberrant, but the imaginative effort involved in putting it to this use can perhaps be seen as the beginning of a quest for new historical models).[17] The experience of the Roman republic, as interpreted in Machiavelli's *Discourse*, was particularly relevant to the search for a political form that would be capable of recognizing division and conflict as essential to social life and transforming them into sources of strength rather than weakness.[18]

The growing interest in and preference for classical Athens after 1800 was, to begin with, based on its apparent affinities with liberal democracy. But in the present context, our main concern is with a critical counter-perspective which developed later and was more sensitive to contrasts between ancient and modern democracy. From this point of view, the merits of the former are not simply those of direct democracy in contrast to representative forms of government, and although that aspect is too massive to be overlooked, it is not always regarded as the most important one. The lesson that is still to be learnt from the experience of Athenian democracy may have more to do with the unique combination of progress towards political autonomy with an outburst of cultural creativity; the main emphasis may, as in the work of Hannah Arendt, be on the pioneering and paradigmatic construction of a public sphere that stands in sharp contrast to the modern tendency to collapse this dimension of the human context into the socio-economic infrastructures; alternatively, the return to the Athenian source may—as in Cynthia Farrar's recent work on the origins of democratic theory—be motivated by the hope to find a closer connection between the theory and practice of autonomy and to use it as a corrective against the mutual insulation that prevailed in later epochs.[19]

Castoriadis's analysis and defence of Athenian democracy is undoubtedly the most complex argument of this kind.[20] His emphasis on direct self-government, as practised by the Athenians, is closely linked to a radical questioning of the forms of political division of labour taken for granted in the modern world: the distinction between the state and the political community, between the sovereign people and its representatives, and between laymen and experts. Political autonomy in the full sense is inconceivable without a permanent problematization (not to be confused with a definitive abolition) of the barriers imposed by these dichotomies, and it can at least draw inspiration from the example of the political community which most successfully neutralized them. But it is the combination with other aspects of the Athenian experience—and the interpretation of this combination in Athenian thought—that makes the Athenian version of direct democracy particularly significant. Pericles's "Funeral Oration", which Castoriadis regards as the most condensed expression of a whole political culture, emphasizes the freedom of choice and the tolerance of diversity in the private sphere; individual autonomy is thus recognized in principle as a necessary complement to collective autonomy. This presupposes an institutionalized distinction between three spheres, clearly separated for the first time in classical Athens. Castoriadis defines them as the private sphere of the households (the oikos), the public sphere for private activities and exchanges (the agora, including the market), and the public sphere for collective deliberation and action (the ecclesia). Although the last one is the political dimension par excellence, Athenian theory and practice link it to the "love of what is beautiful" and "of the things of the mind"[21] i.e.—as Castoriadis sees it—to cultural creation and appreciation as a collective task of the polis. Finally, the question of self-limitation, crucially important for a community that recognizes itself as the source of its own laws and seeks protection against collective hubris and self-destruction, was taken very seriously by the Athenians, as both their institutions and their cultural legacy show.

It is absurd to accuse Castoriadis of glorifying classical Athens as an absolute model; he rejects this view as emphatically as the opposite tendency to treat ancient Greece as simply a particular society among others. His alternative to these two misconceptions is summed up in a biological metaphor, somewhat surprising in the context of a work which otherwise insists on the ontological originality of the social historical and the inapplicability of models derived from other regions of being: Ancient Greece—and ancient Athens in particular—is described as a germ, rather than a model. A closer look at the analogy suggests some disturbing—more precisely: de-contextualizing—implications. A germ is something that can—and can be expected to—grow into a fully-fledged organism; the Greek breakthrough would thus be an embryonic version of the pattern that reaches full maturity in the modern project of autonomy (the project as such should not be confused with its limited and inconsistent realization in the institutions of modern democracy). But for an analysis of the role of autonomy and democracy in the constitution of modernity, the question of their intrinsic logic and its more or less adequate expressions is inseparable from that of their contextual determinants; the latter include not only capitalism and industrialization, but also nationalism and state formation, to mention only the most conspicuous cases. The distinction between the project of unlimited rational mastery and the project of autonomy is thus only the first step towards a more complex contextualization. As for Athenian democracy, the cultural orientations which Castoriadis rightly emphasizes were only a part of the context which gave it its distinctive meaning, and the more regressive and repressive aspects should not be overlooked. It is true that the connection between democracy and slavery was not nearly as close as some earlier historians of the classical world assumed; the growth of slavery did not necessarily strengthen democratic forces or tendencies (in the Roman republic it had the opposite effect), and the specific radicalization of Athenian democracy certainly cannot be explained in terms of any concomitant development of slavery. But it is also true that—in more general terms—the progress of democracy was conditioned and circumscribed by slavery: "the advance, hand in hand, of liberty *and* slavery" (Moses I. Finley) was characteristic of Greek history. In the case of Athens, there are further factors to be noted. The golden age of Athenian democracy was also that of the Athenian empire, and while the latter helped to construct a more solid material base for the democratic *polis*, it also led to a self-destructive struggle for hegemony in the Greek world. Finally, the ethnic exclusivism of Athenian democracy—manifested in its attitude to foreign residents—became more pronounced during its classical phase.

If the limits as well as the specific accent and direction of a shift towards autonomy are always co-determined by a historical context, this can even result in a radical—and paradoxical—reorientation; and if we reconsider the contrast between Athens and the early modern paradigms of republicanism from this point of view, it may seem less absolute. The institutions of Sparta were very different from the Athenian pattern, but the problem is more complex than an unqualified distinction between autonomy and heteronomy suggests. Sparta was not simply a heteronomous society; rather, her social regime was the result of an early—and in many ways obscure—reorganization which was made possible by the indeterminacy and transformative potential characteristic of the *polis* from the outset, but turned the logic of this new form of social life against itself in such a way that it was effectively immunized against further change.[22] An elementary form of autonomy thus took a self-negating turn. As for Rome, its initial marginality (in relation to a more advanced system of city-states) and ethnic heterogeneity set the scene for further developments; an indigenous aristocracy retained (or regained) its dominant position within a complex political framework that was designed to limit the scope of conflict and contestation, rather than suppress them altogether, and to control the absorption of foreign influences and communities, rather than enforce ethnic closure.[23] Both these aspects proved conducive to—and were in turn consolidated by—an exceptionally sustained and successful dynamic of expansion. A limited and ultimately deceptive concession to autonomy thus facilitated the transformation of the city-state into an empire.

From this point of view, it would seem that the republican interest in Sparta and Rome was not wholly misguided. The idealizing vision was backed up by a sound intuition which can now be expressed in more moderate terms: even the institutional patterns which were designed to exclude democracy or block its development presupposed an elementary—and malleable—autonomy that sets the world of the classical city-state apart from its more traditional antecedents and surroundings.

III

The reference to ancient democracy can, as I have tried to show, help us to focus on the explicit self-constitution of society as a background to democratic institutions (in contrast to the elementary self-constitution involved in all forms of social life). In retrospect, the lack of such a perspective appears as the common underlying weakness of the otherwise divergent trends in classical theory, discussed in the first section of the paper; in this regard, Durkheim came closer to a breakthrough than the others did, but his most basic presuppositions neutralized his most promising insights. A systematic treatment of the problem would have to begin with the distinction between two aspects of explicit self- constitution: the interpretive one, i.e. a distinctive and innovative relation between social consciousness and social being, and the transformative one, which involves the exercise of the self-constitutive competence and a corresponding distribution of power between social actors and agencies. The two dominant but elusive themes of social theory, culture and power, thus remain central to the more specific problematic of democracy. Inasmuch as it refers to a project or a vision of a self-instituting society, the concept of autonomy highlights the cultural dimension, whereas the concept of polyarchy reflects a preference for the theory of power. Other approaches are less directly related to this dichotomy: if the attempt to derive the developmental logic of democracy from the rationality of the life-world can be regarded as a culturalist line of argument, the interest in civil society and its opposition to the state has to do with configurations of social power. But as I noted at the outset, all these points of view are unsatisfactory in that they tend to overemphasize some aspects or implications of a complex problematic at the expense of the rest. Before we can attempt a systematic integration of power-centred and culture-centred perspectives, there is obviously a whole range of preliminary questions to be clarified; the rest of the paper will be devoted to some of them. The Greek experience illustrates not only the contrast between heteronomy and autonomy, but also the importance of the historical context which determines the limits, levels and direction of the latter. Similarly, an analysis of the tendencies and potentialities of modern democracy must relate them to the overall pattern of modernity. In other words: a comparison of the modern project of autonomy with its classical forerunner should take into account the whole spectrum of contextual adaptations and conflicting interpretations that co-determine its historical content. The following reflections will be limited to four particularly salient aspects of this problematic: the institutional conditions and channels of the modern democratic transformation (1); the functionalization of democracy, i.e. the adaptation of its principles and practices to the dynamics of other components of modernity (2); the radicalization of the democratic project, beyond and against the limits imposed by the dominant factors as well as the established patterns of modernity (3); and the totalitarian perversion of democracy (4). In all cases, the aim is to formulate questions, rather than propose answers; this section of the paper should therefore be read as a selective survey of the agenda for a theory of modern democracy, not as an outline of such a theory.

    1. The emergence of modern democracy takes place in a social and historical environment that is already marked and being further changed by the

process of state formation. As Norbert Elias has shown, this process goes back to early medieval origins; it involves the consolidation of territorial units as well as of the twin monopolies of violence and taxation, and it must be analyzed in terms of a large-scale and long-term dynamic of power structures. But it is also accompanied by other developments, about which Elias's theory of state formation has much less to say. The obverse of state formation was the growing complexity of civil society, and the relations between the two poles were co-determined by a tradition that emphasized legal norms and representative institutions. The medieval background of modern constitutionalism and forms of political representation is as important as that of the military and administrative apparatuses of the modern state.[24] Finally, the development of the nation as a new form of collective identity—based on ethnic foundations but going beyond them in different ways, depending on different contexts—increasingly determined the concrete framework within which the other factors interacted. Early modern absolutism led to a one-sided strengthening of the state in relation to its counterweights and co-determinants, but its way of pursuing this goal was internally inconsistent and ultimately incompatible with the most fundamental imperatives of state formation. The absolutist pattern was, in other words, temporarily superimposed on a more complex context and a more diverse historical legacy, and a genealogy of the modern state must take account of this background.

If the democratic transformation is to be analyzed in connection with state formation and its cross-currents, two complementary oversimplifications must be avoided. Modern democracy is not—as the concept of functional democratization suggests—reducible to a functional component or episode in the process of state formation. But the idea of a gradual adaptation of the state to an unequivocal logic of democracy seems equally misleading.[25] The reference to an underlying project of autonomy may help to develop a less reductionistic perspective: the shift towards autonomy adds a further dimension to the above-mentioned historical constellation, but it can also be assimilated and redefined in line with various aspects of the latter. For state-centred conceptions of democracy (Durkheim is the most obvious example), the modern state embodies the principle of autonomy to the extent that it raises social organization to a higher level of consciousness and liberates the individual from restrictive forms of social integration. By contrast, the emphasis on civil society is compatible with a wider range of interpretations: it can lead to the identification of the autonomous society with a market-regulated one (i.e. in Castoriadis's terms, a reduction of the public sphere to a part of the agora), with local or regional self-government—in contrast to the political expropriation of society by the bureaucratic and centralistic state—or with a "network of societal communication consisting of public spheres, associations and movements".[26] Finally, the fusion of popular sovereignty with the sovereignty and self-determination of the nation—prefigured in the 1789 declaration of human rights—subordinates the modern project of autonomy to a supposedly paradigmatic—but only partly modern—form of collective identity.

2. The hermeneutical complexity of modern democracy can be reduced in various ways. One of them is the recurrent polarization of two main trends. John Dunn sums up the contrast in the following terms: "So we have really two distinct and developed democratic theories loose in the world today—one dismally ideological and the other fairly blatantly utopian. In the first, democracy is the name of a distinct and very palpable form of modern state; at the most optimistic, simply the least bad mechanism for securing some measure of responsibility of the governors for the governed within modern states. In the second, democracy (or, as it is sometimes called, participatory democracy) is close to meaning simply the good society in operation, a society in which we produce as profusely as we do today—if less wastefully and with better taste—and in which all social arrangements automatically represent the interests of all persons, in which all live actively and for their society, and yet all remain as free as before (where *before* means roughly as they could urgently and excusably desire)".[27] If we understand the two theories as interpretations of structural and cultural trends and define the latter in somewhat broader terms than Dunn's formulations would suggest, the alternatives correspond—roughly speaking—to the functionalization and the radicalization of democracy.

Dunn first describes the ideological version as "capitalist democracy", but his subsequent remarks underline the affirmative and functional relationship to the modern state. If we also take into account the cultural premises of modern capitalism and the modern state, including—most importantly—the paradigm of rationality which operates on both levels but extends far beyond them, the theory in question would seem to reflect the functional adaptation of democracy to a dominant but essentially and permanently contested pattern of modernity. This entails above all the elimination of the very idea of a democratic project and a corresponding reduction in the meaning and scope of democratic institutions: they are now defined as a set of specific rules within a clearly delimited sphere, without any reference to the partial institutionalization of autonomy (Castoriadis) or the institutional recognition of indeterminacy (Lefort). Schumpeter's definition of democracy as "that institutional arrangement for arriving at political decisions in which individuals acquire the power to decide by means of a competitive struggle for the people's vote"[28] is a classic example. Later variations have adjusted the same idea to different theoretical languages, but whether it is seen as a method, a protective device or a subsystemic code, democracy is in any case cleared of all associations with an unfinished project. Schumpeter's line of argument shows that this position does not necessarily involve an uncritical commitment to capitalism, but it imposes severe limitations upon the search for alternatives. Schumpeter expected "the bourgeois scheme of things", which "limits the sphere of politics by limiting the sphere of public authority"[29] to be replaced by a bureaucratic and centralistic socialism. The latter would not be intrinsically incompatible with democracy, but the extension of public authority could easily lead to an over-extension of the democratic method beyond its proper sphere—the competitive struggle for power—and thus provoke a backlash that would threaten the very existence of democracy. The only guarantee against this is an efficient and independent bureaucracy. By contrast, the attempt to base a socialist order on the radicalization of democracy would—for Schumpeter—lead to their mutual destruction.

3. The radicalization of democracy is a more complex and diversified process than Dunn's account of the "utopian theory" would suggest: it does not always culminate in a global vision of the "good society" as an alternative to the dominant pattern of modernity, and even when it takes this turn, it does not ipso facto side-step the problems of the modern state and the modern economy. The extension of citizenship—more precisely, the progressive incorporation of new social and economic contents into the original legal and political framework of citizenship—draws on the developmental potential of modern democracy and changes its relationship to other components of modernity. This process cannot plausibly be described as the gradual replacement of one paradigm of modernity by another, but it has undoubtedly led to a far-reaching conditioning and modification of the dominant pattern. Some analysts have been tempted to reconstruct it in terms of an evolutionary logic that would both explain past achievements and promise further progress. Such accounts, however, tend to neglect the conflictual and problematic aspects of the process. The extension of citizenship is the outcome of recurrent social conflicts, and it constantly opens up new fronts for social conflicts. Moreover, it gives rise to interpretive conflicts. The predominant point of view focuses on the codification of human rights and the gradual concretization of new rights, but it is contested by the communitarian approach which stresses the primacy of participation. And the very meaning of the idea of rights is controversial: the individualistic interpretation, more or less explicitly linked to a notion of human nature, is rejected by those who insist on the novelty of a socio-cultural construction that changes the status of the individual. For Claude Lefort, who takes the latter view, the institutionalization of human rights marks a new mode of legitimation and bars the way to despotic fusion of power, law and knowledge.

On the other hand, the visions of a global and radical alternative have drawn on the democratic imaginary, given it a specific direction and fused it with other components that often tend to overshadow it. In other words: the utopian model, as defined by Dunn, is not only less exclusively representative of the radicalization of democracy than he seems to assume; it is also less self-contained and less firmly anchored in modern value-orientations. A more concrete analysis of the socialist tradition and its crucial but changing relationship to radical democracy is beyond the scope of this paper. In the present context, its most relevant aspect is the translation of radical democracy into the vision of a self-organizing and self-governing community that can abolish both the state and the market; Marx's idea of the "free association of the producers", discussed in the first section of the paper, was the most articulate version of this project. The historical and conceptual shortcomings of this perspective have been thoroughly exposed: the underlying failure to grasp the complexity of modern society leads to a de-differentiation of the political and the economic sphere which obscures the problematic of modern democracy and misdirects the critique of modern capitalism. But as long as the idea of collective self-determination is not completely absorbed by the shifting balance of state and market, it can be used as a guideline for distinguishing emancipatory intentions of the radical socialist project from its archaic frame of reference. Such an immanent critique of the socialist tradition points to a redefinition of democratic socialism as a permanent corrective, rather than a global alternative, but it also raises fundamental conceptual questions. In a recent essay, Habermas summarizes them in roughly the following terms: in what sense can we still defend the idea of self-constitution or self-organization, when the traditional models of macro-subjectivity—the sovereign people or the revolutionary class—have been discredited, and when the theory of self-referential systems is proposed as de-radicalized alternative?[30] Habermas's own theory of communicative action is obviously—among other things—an attempt to answer this question, and in that capacity, it can be compared to Castoriadis's reformulation of the idea of autonomy as well as to Touraine's work on social movements.

4. The totalitarian regimes of the 20th century have thrown new light on the problematic of modern democracy. To start with, the conflict between totalitarianism and democracy differs from that between the absolutist states and the democratic revolution which overthrew them: it seems both more radical and less external. Talmon's theory of "totalitarian democracy" over-emphasizes the latter aspect at the expense of the former. On this view, totalitarian domination is the logical outcome of a "totalitarian democratic school . . . based on the assumption of a sole and exclusive truth in politics".[31] More specific features, including in particular the synthesis of popular sovereignty and single-party dictatorship, are supposedly derived from this original premise. On the other hand, a closer look at the historical preconditions of totalitarianism shows that its most successful breakthroughs occurred in societies which had gone through a limited and unbalanced modernizing process and resisted thorough-going democratic transformation. It would thus seem more plausible to explain the totalitarian catastrophe as the result of a refusal of the democratic road to modernity, rather than an unfortunate by-product or a basic misinterpretation of democracy.

Both these views are open to objections. Talmon's critics have rightly accused him of short-circuiting 18th century ideas and 20th century practices;

they have also rejected the concept of totalitarian democracy as a contradiction in terms and argued that totalitarianism presupposes a radical break with some structural principles of modern democracy, not simply a misreading of them. As to the other line of argument, the failure to consolidate the social and cultural foundations of democracy does not always lead to a totalitarian backlash and is therefore not a sufficient explanation; a more concrete analysis must—among other things—take into account the ability of the totalitarian projects and movements to turn both the limits and the achievements of an underdeveloped democracy to their advantage.

But it should be possible to relate totalitarianism to the internal problematic of democracy, without reducing the former to an offshoot of the latter and thus obscuring the paradoxical character of the connection, and to acknowledge the durability of traditional obstacles to democracy, without trying to explain totalitarianism as nothing more than a continuation of pre-modern autocracy on a new technical and organizational basis. Claude Lefort's reflections on the first question may help to formulate the second more clearly, and to link both of them to other issues discussed in this paper.[32] For Lefort, the logic of totalitarianism is directed against the most distinctive innovations of modern democracy: it involves the negation of division (i.e. both the division between state and society and the internal division of society) and the rejection of pluralism. At the same time, however, it activates and transforms some aspects of the symbolic framework of democracy at the expense of others. The notion of the "sovereign people" postulates an ultimate unity of society, but in the democratic pattern, it is counterbalanced by other elements: the construction of power as an "empty space" or the "power of nobody", beyond the reach of any individual or collective actor; the institutionalization of social conflict; and, last but not least, the separate and autonomous development of different socio-cultural spheres. The totalitarian project destroys these counterweights and replaces the field of tensions with the symbolic fusion of a unified society and an unrestricted power. The link between these two aspects is established through the embodiment of society in a macro-subject; the latter role can be assigned to the class or the nation, which in turn is represented by the vanguard and/or the leader.

If the symbolic reference to popular sovereignty is central to the functioning of modern democracy as well as to the genealogy of totalitarianism, it should also be the starting-point for a reflection on the broader context of both. From the viewpoint of a theory of modernity which regards the project of autonomy as a key component, the notion of popular sovereignty appears as a secondary signification, superimposed on a more fundamental one. It is, in other words, an interpretation of autonomy from a specific angle: the self-determinative and self-transformative capacity of society is assimilated to the imaginary construction of sovereignty, which first emerged as an attribute of the state. The very possibility of a totalitarian perversion of democracy can thus only be understood in relation to the state, and this connection becomes especially important when a state with imperial traditions plays a dominant role in the modernizing process.

Notes

1. cf. Peter Murphy, "Socialism and Democracy" in *Thesis Eleven*, No. 26, 1990.
2. On these questions, cf. György Markus, "Four Forms of Critical Theory", *Thesis Eleven* 1 (1980), pp. 78–93; Jean L. Cohen, *Class and Civil Society* (Cambridge, Mass., 1983); John F. Rundell, *Origins of Modernity* (Cambridge, 1987).
3. Max Weber, *Economy and Society*, vol. 3 (NY, 1968), p. 948.
4. ibid., p. 951. I have adjusted the translation. In the original Weber refers explicitly to the "sociological meaning" of democracy but this point is less clear in Roth and Wittich's version. More important, Weber seems to be referring not simply to a change of meaning, but to the disappearance of any unifying meaning
5. cf. Emile Durkheim, *Professional Ethics and Civic Morals* (London, 1957), chs VII–IX.
6. ibid., p. 84.
7. ibid., p. 89.
8. ibid., p. 91.
9. cf. Raymond Aron, *Main Currents of Sociological Thought*, vol. 1 (London, 1968), pp. 183–232.
10. On this idea of the democratic question, cf. Ulrich Rödel u.a., *Die demokratische Frage* (Frankfurt, 1989).
11. Claude Lefort, *Essais sur le politique* (Paris, 1986), p. 24.
12. ibid., p. 25.
13. cf. T. G. Masaryk, *Die philosophischen und soziologischen Grundlagen des Marximus* (Osnabrück, 1964; re-edition of the 1898 text); *The Making of a State* (London, 1927).
14. This line of interpretation has been developed by the Czech philosopher Jan Patoćka.
15. J. G. A. Pocock, *The Machiavellian Moment* (Princeton, 1975), pp. 460–461.
16. Benjamin Constant, "De la liberté des anciens comparée à celle des modernes" in id., *De la liberté chez les modernes—Écrits politiques*, ed. ant intr. Marcel Gauchet (Paris, 1980), pp. 491–515.
17. On the Spartan myth and its many variations, cf. Elizabeth Rawson, *The Spartan Tradition in European Thought* (Oxford, 1969).
18. cf. Claude Lefort, *Le travail de l'oeuvre: Machiavel* (Paris, 1972).
19. cf. Cynthia Farrar, *The Origins of Democratic Thinking* (London, 1987).
20. cf. Cornelius Castoriadis, "The Greek *polis* and the creation of democracy", *Graduate Faculty Philosophy Journal* (New School for Social Research) IX, 2, pp. 79–115; and "Fait et à faire", *Revue européenne des Sciences sociales* t. XXVII, 86 (1989), pp. 457–514.
21. Thucydides, *The Peloponnesian War*, II. 40.

22. On the early origins and the innovative character of the *polis*, cf. particularly Anthony Snodgrass, *Archaic Greece—The Age of Experiment* (London, 1980).

23. This interpretation draws on Norbert Rouland, *Rome, démocratie impossible?* (Paris, 1981).

24. cf. Joseph R. Strayer, *On the Medieval Origins of the Modern State* (Princeton, 1970), p. 64; "The idea of political representation is one of the great discoveries of medieval governments".

25. cf. Habermas's account of the evolution of the modern state in *Theory of Communicative Action*, vol. 2 (Boston, 1987), pp. 357–361; on this view, the initial constitution of the modern state during the absolutist era led to an instant functionalization, followed by a progressive democratization.

26. Andrew Arato and Jean Cohen, "Politics and the Reconstruction of the Concept of Civil Society" in *Zwischenbetrachtungen—Im Prozess der Auflkärung* (Festschrift for Jürgen Habermas) (Frankfurt, 1989), p. 58.

27. John Dunn, *Western Political Theory in the Face of the Future* (Cambridge, 1979), pp. 26–27.

28. Joseph A. Schumpeter, *Capitalism, Socialism and Democracy* (London, 1987; 6th ed.), p. 267.

29. ibid., p. 297.

30. Jürgen Habermas, *Die nachholende Revolution* (Frankfurt, 1990), pp. 179–204, especially pp. 195–196.

31. J. L. Talmon, *The Origins of Totalitarian Democracy* (London, 1966), p. 1.

32. cf. Claude Lefort, *The Political Forms of Modern Society* (Cambridge, 1986); *Democracy and Political Theory* (Cambridge, 1988).

THE LIFE AND TIMES OF SOCIAL DEMOCRACY

Peter Beilharz

Social democracy remains a major political current of modernity. Contrary to postmodernists and to certain marxists, modernity is not just *all* about flux. We remain firmly stuck within modernity, and hence within social democracy. Recent events in Eastern Europe would seem to confirm rather than to deny this. Communism now is off the agenda; socialism remains on it. Or has socialism had its day as well? As C. B. Macpherson suggests in his *Life and Times of Liberal Democracy*, which I take here as my frame, the "life and times" approach is by nature suggestive of an obituary. Ideas, however, do not follow the life cycles of mere mortals. They merge into other ideas, recurring unpredictably and often simply refusing to go away. Socialism is one such idea, for as the alter ego of capitalism it changes forms without ever just expiring. All civilizations need their animating narratives; socialism remains one of the narratives of modernity. But with communism in decay, what then of social democracy?

In this paper I argue, in sympathy with Macpherson, that if the formal institutions associated with social democracy are more or less lifeless or decrepit, there nevertheless remains something alive in the project of social democracy. Like the Enlightenment, social democracy has let us down—or perhaps it is more accurate to say that we have let the project down, given that historic responsibility ultimately rests with actors and not ideas. The project, at least, remains to be realized.

In order to put my case, I need first to provide one definition, two premises and one pretext. The core of the argument then takes up the theory of two dead dogs from the history of socialism, Eduard Bernstein and Karl Kautsky, in order to argue that far from being the idiots sometimes thought to be, these central figures of social democracy were both theoretically sensitive and are socially useful today. The argument is staid rather than scintillating, worldly rather than wizardly, and I offer no apologies for this.

First, the definition. By social democracy I refer to the political experience which preceded World War I. The point of this paper is not to defend social democracy since World War II. Though revolutionary marxists would likely be loathe to concede the point, social democracy was transformed by the events of the forties and fifties; it was not always the grey cat that it came to be. The 1945–51 Labour Government, the Keynes-Beveridge consensus, the ideological disputes over socialist platform in the debates over Clause Four and Bad Godesberg all saw social democracy transformed from its earlier project, just as the events of the seventies and eighties have again transformed social democracy, emptying it of all content save the thin gruel of "social justice" or socialist accounting. Thus I define social democracy as prewar, because unlike communism, and relatively speaking, social democracy is inconsistent, its historic path ruptural rather than entirely predictable. Where the experience of communism is in some ways consistent—from the New Economic Policy to perestroika, from Kronstadt to Tien an Mien Square—social democracy has been a more rapidly moving, if simultaneously declining object. Where communism is something of a piece—especially in the Soviet and Chinese cases—social democracy means something completely different before the first war, after the second, and again after the present economic crisis.

Second, the two premises. The argument in this paper is built on the premise that all social and political theories contain utopias, or images of the good society. Here socialism differs from liberalism only in being more fully explicit or more wilfully utopian. But all arguments about how we ought live rest on some utopic sense, however well or little elaborated, which looks romantically backward or futuristically forward (or both). A related premise on which this argument rests is that what we call modernity is in fact an amalgam of modern, premodern and postmodern social forms, beliefs and practices. The significance of this premise, in the present context, is simply that it highlights the way in which not all of our problems are "new". It follows that "old" social theory still speaks to us, today.

My pretext for this case, as I have mentioned, is Macpherson's *Life and Times of Liberal Democracy*.[1] The essential message of Macpherson's essay is that liberal democracy is both alive and dead, simultaneously exhausted and yet capable of addressing the human condition in our times, especially with reference to classical hopes for active citizenship and individual-social self-development. Macpherson for his part thus speaks of the limits and possibilities of liberal democracy. The limits of social democracy are evident, and will not be further discussed here: like other forms of political thinking, social democracy has become fundamentally implicated with the state and its paternalism, and it has refused to take its own professed principles seriously into the realm of policy, hoping rather that socialism might be worked out by others, by civil savants. The main concern of this paper is rather with the discursive possibilities of social democracy, and this relates back to the earlier premise, that ideas matter, that "old" problems still confront us, and that consequently "old" ideas may be helpful in the process of attempting to develop a vocabulary for social change.

The central thinkers of social democracy, for this purpose, are the Germans Bernstein and Kautsky. Neither of these figures is taken sufficiently seriously by socialists, partly because of the tradition's own inclination to ridicule and caricature reformism. Bernstein is typically dismissed as a kind of Ramsay Macdonald in disguise; Kautsky is too frequently viewed as the pedantic pope of marxism, the crepuscular figure displayed by Trotsky, in his slippers, perpetually ready to retire. Bernstein and Kautsky deserve better than this, because they are arguably better sources for rethinking social democracy than the British figures who generate so much enthusiasm today, such as modern medievals R. H. Tawney and perhaps T. H. Marshall.[2] Bernstein and Kautsky are potentially useful because they provide better social theory than the British, partly because they descend from marxism, partly because they develop a kind of weberian marxism, and both dimensions are highly significant. My argument is that Bernstein and Kautsky offer modern socialist utopias—unlike Bolshevism, which via Lenin offers a premodern, one-class proletarian utopia, but also unlike Fabianism, which has a modernist, functionalized utopia. Bernstein and Kautsky are significant because they accept the sober necessities of modern social organization without functionalizing them into necessities.[3]

DEAD DOG I: BERNSTEIN

From Belfort Bax to Helmut Hirsch the question is asked, was not Bernstein merely a Fabian?[4] The answer to this question is no. Bernstein's wife may have translated the Webbs, but so did Lenin. The very idea that someone's cultural location should entirely form them ought to be thrown out together with Robert Owen's other enthusiasm, spade-husbandry. This is not to deny the significance of Bernstein's lengthy English sojourn, but it is to suggest that his incipient revisionism has its own roots as well. We could as well ask why Bernstein chose England as ask what England did to him. Reformism is not a disease, English or other; it is a legitimate socialist response to the problems thrown up by capitalist civilization. Against Fabianism, however, Bernstein had a different utopia, and he was a democrat, not a Democrat.

Part of the issue here is doubtless that Bernstein upset altogether too many good marxists by simultaneously advocating practical reformism and theoretical revisionism. But if this were the only problem, we might still expect today's radicals to take Bernstein's *Evolutionary Socialism* seriously, at least perhaps to read it. Bernstein did, however, also write other things, even less recognized.

Several distinct attributes become clear, for example, in his earlier articles in *Die Neue Zeit* and elsewhere. The first is that, opposed to Bax, Bernstein was a modern romantic. Bax viewed modernity and capitalism as coextensive, and consequently conceived socialism as their negation. For Bernstein, by comparison, modernity contained capitalism, socialism and civilization—the point was thus not to go backwards, but to seek the fullest possible development of social individuals within modernity.[5] For Bax, modernity was all loss, no gain.[6] For Bernstein, capitalist civilization was for all its excesses still civilization, worth defending.[7] Civility thus mattered, for Bernstein; unlike Rosa Luxemburg he translated *Burgerliche Gesellschaft* as civil society, not bourgeois or capitalist society, because again he thought the practice of civility and the institution of civil society worth defending.[8]

The significance of civil society bears emphasizing, here, not least of all because civil society was the primary arena of social democratic activity. When people spoke of the SPD as a "state within a state" their use of language was imprecise—it was rather a matter of a society within a society. In contemporary language, the SPD was indeed a social movement, not a counterstate, and the bulk of SPD effort was expended within its voluntary, cultural associations—bicycling clubs, libraries, singing clubs, smoking clubs, anti-smoking clubs, etc.[9] For this reason I do not find Peter Murphy's particular view of the SPD in his provocative paper "Socialism and Democracy" convincing. The SPD viewed as a movement was incapable of the kind of oligarchy ascribed to it by Michels in *Political Parties*. But more, the ordinary social democrats of Wilhelmine Germany knew something about democracy, and not just that they wanted to practise it in their cultural and associative lives—they also knew that Bismarck would not allow it to them, long before Hitler was to deprive them of it. This does not mean, as Murphy rightly suggests, that the category social democracy can be used to resolve falsely, because semantically, the relationship between socialism and democracy. But it does suggest that social democracy became administrative; social democrats could just as well, in other circumstances, have chosen to become democrats. For democracy, like civility, is surely something not innate, but that we in fact learn.

What attracted Bernstein to England, apart from his freedom from jailers there, was exactly the room to move, not simply to engineer socialism through the state. According to Bernstein, then, socialism grows not out of chaos but out of the "union of the organised creations of the workers in the domain of political economy with the creations and conquests of the fighting democracy in State and community".[10] In a striking anticipation of recent events in Eastern Europe, Bernstein wrote further:

> The socialistic theory of the bolshevists is, as much as it does not offhandishly recede behind Karl Marx, a marxism made coarse, its political doctrine is an overvaluation of the creative power of brute

violence and its political ethics are not a criticism but a coarse misunderstanding of the liberal ideas that in the great French revolution of the eighteenth century have found their classical expression. But just as by the unbending language of facts they have already seen themselves compelled to subject their economic policy to a thorough revision, the time will not stay away when in the face of the rebellion/revolt of the ineradicable striving of the peoples to freedom and right they will also have to fundamentally revise their policy and their ethics.[11]

There are significant marxist critics, such as Guglielmo Carchedi, who would probably view this as further evidence of Bernstein's petty-bourgeois socialism (i.e. not socialism at all). In his important but relatively undiscussed study *Class Analysis and Social Research*, Carchedi analyzes the problem of revisionism via another sadly unnoticed book, Hans Muller's 1892 study *Der Klassenkampf in der deutschen Sozialdemokratie*. Muller's case is that the SPD went rotten under Bismarck's antisocialist laws, as good working class leaders literally became petty-bourgeois, opening shops or workshops because their old employers blackbanned them, denied them work as labourers.[12] The Carchedi-Muller case, somewhat like the Michels-Murphy argument, is effectively that the SPD lived out the contradiction of fighting for democracy by authoritarian means. The significant difference is that where Michels and Murphy view institutionalization, or the state as the problem, for Muller and Carchedi class analysis explains the problem of class slippage—changes in class composition explain the change in, or decline of the SPD.

The Muller case is indeed significant, and Carchedi is correct to observe that its forgetting is symptomatic—the implication is that the revisionism debate began a decade earlier than traditionally thought, but was suppressed by Engels' siding with the elders.[13] Muller emerges from this argument as possibly the primary sociologist of the party, writing as he was before Michels or Ostrogorsky, and well before Gramsci. And yet there is something anthropologically, or sociologically surprising about the sense of surprise in the case—as though the emergence of a division of labour in the party were atypical, and as though class struggle were a legitimate meta-metaphor for social life as such. Unlike Muller, Bernstein and Kautsky saw something to defend in the institutions of socialism, an entirely understandable attitude. In this light, it is worth turning to Bernstein's in/famous maxim about the goal of socialism being nothing, the movement everything. Contrary to received marxist wisdom about Bernstein, I want to suggest that this maxim is hermeneutically meaningful in a positive way. First of all, it should be said that Bernstein's maxim was deliberately hyperbolic; he was the first to qualify it, when it was read as a sign of moral liquidationism.[14] Yet he had, also, at the same time chosen his terms cautiously. In proposing that the goal was "nothing", Bernstein's logic was that socialism was a norm and not a goal, a premise and not a telos, or as he put it, a principle, and not a plan of society.[15] For this reason Bernstein entitled his work *Voraussetzungen des Sozialismus*, principles from which we set out; it was only at Ramsay Macdonald's mischievous suggestion that the title was Anglo-cized as *Evolutionary Socialism* for the British edition. Clearly, then, Bernstein was committed to socialism; the argument from the left should have concerned the nature of this socialism, not its alleged non-existence. Similarly, for Bernstein, the idea that the movement was everything did not simply betray a monolithic institutional bias on his part—he spoke of the movement, not the party, and used the category movement in the dual sense which we today associate with the work of Alain Touraine, to refer both to the idea of the actor and to the fact of the process of movement itself—bourgeois civilization was no solid crystal, rather it moved. Social progress resulted from social struggle, agitation and organization. This process involved the slow transition to socialism, while the "final goal" emasculated such struggles, collapsing socialism into the utopia of dreamers.[16] This was his view, in any case.

The society of the future, for Bernstein, ought thus be complex and differentiated, dependent on social self-help, and given to the development of personality within the division of labour.[17] More, it was dependent on political obligation, a theme rarely discussed by socialists then or still now. Bernstein put emphasis not only on right, but also upon duty—he argued for an active, rather than merely passive or welfarist conception of citizenship.[18] Thus civilization precedes and transcends capitalism, for Bernstein, and citizenship precedes liberalism and contractualism. More than this, Bernstein had a sense of the past, as well as of the future. He discussed the power of tradition and memory and argued for the centrality of the imaginary.[19] He agrees with Weber about the "centrality of interests via-a-vis the ideal" and the "material", and proposes Durkheim-like that morality is even more durable than economic life.[20]

The novelty of Bernstein's thought is equally clear in the much maligned *Evolutionary Socialism*. Here Bernstein discusses socialism in specifically political terms, to do with the citizens of the future. Economy is to be subordinated to politics, not the other way around, as in the tradition of productivist socialism. Bernstein did not succumb to the instrumental conception of democracy, characteristic of social democracy after fascism. Socialism he understands as a movement towards a new order based on the principle of association.[21] He rejects the marxist-syndicalist proposition that unions are somehow the proletarian order *in statu nascendi*. "The idea of democracy includes, in the conception of the present day, a notion of justice—an equality of rights for all members of the community."[22] Democracy, in short, is not the projection but the suspension of class government—class government is a bourgeois practice. The upshot was that "social democracy does not wish to break up this society and make all its members proletarians together; it labours rather incessantly at raising the worker from the social position of a proletarian to that of a citizen, and thus to make citizenship universal".[23] Its purpose is not to set up a proletarian society, but rather a socialist one.[24] Socialism was in this specific regard best understood as the heir of liberalism, for the security of civil freedom is always a higher goal for social democracy than the fulfillment of some economic program.[25] Against Lassalle, and fully recognizing the constraints of his own native language, Bernstein declared that "we are all citizens (*Burger*)".[26] Yet in all this socialism is clearly an "ought", not an "is", even Bernstein's maturational optimism notwithstanding.

DEAD DOG II: KAUTSKY

It is Kautsky, of course, who is more often associated with "maturational reformism", the idea of the great day one day, made by itself and not by a party.[27] The theoretical issue at stake is probably more fundamental than we allow: all socialisms need a telos, a project, a sense of future or utopia. Doubtless Kautsky's real theoretical crime here was that he produced and subscribed to the most influential theory of automatic marxism, that of the Second International itself. But Kautsky was no fool. In fact, his views are interesting, I will suggest, not only in their own right, but also because they illustrate the difficulties of being an orthodox marxist with empirical sensitivities. What is interesting about Kautsky's theory is that he remains committed to a whole series of orthodox premises which Bernstein abandoned, but he did not defend these when they patently flew in the face of the problems confronting him as a social democrat.

There are two central texts here, both of them now, finally by happy coincidence available in English, so that even Kautsky's local opponents may at last finally pay him the courtesy of reading his work. They are *The Agrarian Question* (1899) and *The Materialist Conception of History* (1927).

The Agrarian Question is an extremely interesting work, because it shows Kautsky denying his orthodoxy where it stands to inhibit the analysis. If Kautsky was a shellback, then it cannot be said that he never ventured out of his shell. Kautsky's task here was to illustrate the pertinence of Marx's claims about capitalism—the general trends to concentration of capital, and proletarianization of the mass—to agriculture itself. While Kautsky's own tedious defences of scale now look dated in the face not only of ecological radicalism but also of post-fordist flexibilities, we can nevertheless see him following the footsteps of Marx, freshly imprinted by Bernstein, regarding the so-called idiocy of rural life. Kautsky, like the Webbs and most other fin-de-siecle socialists, defended the ideas of culture and civilization—the task was not to abolish the galleries, but rather to universalize access to them. Scale, of course, meant division of labour, and thus—here perhaps more like Bernard Shaw than the Webbs—Kautsky located the realm of freedom in leisure, the latter to be maximized while the working day was to be minimized.

Yet Kautsky's hope to prove the theses of *Capital* for agriculture was to come up against what sociologists respectfully call "the data". So Kautsky ended up, appropriately, explaining why Marx's theses were unhelpful, and how the peasantry would continue to remain a permanent characteristic of modern class structure.[28] Consequently Kautsky even engages in a half-hearted attempt to wax lyrical about a craft renaissance.[29] Certainly Kautsky's attitude to William Morris was more positive than that of Bernstein to his offsider Bax.[30] To mention their names in the same breath is also, however, to recognize that a word is in order prior to passing on the Bernstein-Kautsky pair itself.

If Kautsky was a pope, a theologue, Bernstein was by comparison an amateur, an artisan. Their approaches to the creation of knowledge were very different, Kautsky's still governed by some kind of pretence to the encyclopedic, Bernstein's more postmodern and fragmentary. But it is not at all clear that they ever disagreed that much. The oft-quoted quip of Ignaz Auer's was that Bernstein had behaved stupidly by wanting to change the rules of marxism theoretically, and not just in practice. As another contemporary saying had it, the SPD was keen on hanging onto the Sunday china, even if it were never used. Certainly Bernstein's epistemology, like his politics, was pragmatic; he had no time for "dialectics" or for the kind of foundationalism characteristic of most marxism.[31] Yet, as I will suggest, Kautsky's practical position did not differ excessively from this; we have to turn to someone like Plekhanov to see the stereotype of marxism more recognizably at work. So that even Kautsky's authoritative chastizing of his friend in, for example his anticritique, *Bernstein und das Sozialdemokratische Programme*,[32] is like the teacher reprimanding his wayward but preferred student. Their major difference here was simply that over the social-democratic or more specifically proletarian telos which Bernstein had rejected. It was no accident that their views then merged after the first catastrophe of Bolshevism. What Lukács triumphally called Bernstein's triumph was no victory at all.

Further evidence of these nuances exists in Kautsky's *Materialist Conception*. The first striking thing about this study is that it opens with a denunciation of materialism, conventionally defined. Historically, the problem has been that no one has read the book, particularly since Karl Korsch sliced it up in the pirouettes on sharpened skates conducted in his 1929 critique of the same title. As one suspects is often otherwise the case, people seem to have read the critique and not the original text: case closed. But if the book is opened we find a defence not of any materialism, but of classical marxism, tempered by an overriding concern with the "developmental history of mankind".[33] Perhaps Habermas was less original than we were led to believe. Like Bernstein, Kautsky viewed modernity as formed by the past, and sees the future as structured by it; the sense of history involved is fundamentally different to that, say in H. G. Wells's *A Modern Utopia* or in Trotsky's *Literature and Revolution*, where it somehow becomes at least implicitly possible to step out of time, tradition, memory, biography, culture.

At the same time, however, Kautsky's work is also postmarxian, in the literal sense, that his utopic vision accepts and develops the distinction between freedom and necessity sketched out in the third volume of *Capital*. Kautsky here specifically rejects the hunter-fisher-cattleperson-critical critic utopia of the *German Ideology*, which had been published in 1926.[34] More, he presumes a kind of scepticism in knowledge and in politics, and argues about the limits to knowledge and to action, even though his frame is encyclopedic in breadth. He argues in detail, for example, about the weight of tradition and the conservative nature of the mind, balancing the romantic component in marxism with the sense that human beings seek self-development, but also stability.[35] An important intellectual source which we find for this disposition in Kautsky is the study of anthropology; it serves as a useful artifact, reminding us that for all their modernism the social democrats did actually take anthropology seriously, and probably there is still no better monument to this than the pages of Kautsky's own extraordinary journal, *Die Neue Zeit*, encyclopedic in interest and enthusiasms yet free of the sense of a governing or incipient synthesis.

Thus, for example, Kautsky discusses the Durkheim-issue of the social construction of morality, the cultural autonomy of morality, and now rejects the Spencer argument central to *The Agrarian Question*, that society is an organism (it is *not*, he says, because it consists of individuals, each of whom is not only sentient but possessing of consciousness).[36] Given that he takes social differentiation seriously, what we end up with is the image of socialism as a society based on differentiation, based practically upon production but not on the image of production. Socialism for Kautsky is rather based on variable forms of activity which work against the syndicalist identity of the tradition; work is central but diverse, and is viewed as a responsibility. These kinds of arguments occur in the context of a discussion which is explicitly sympathetic to Weber and critical of Engels, with whom Kautsky is typically guilt-associated.

The Weber-connection is significant here because Kautsky takes up both Weber's political "realism" and his methodological "idealism". Unlike a generation of marxists more recently, Kautsky duly engages Weber's thought, and not just in the footnotes. Kautsky refers to *Economy and Society* and to the *General Economic History*, and presents the thesis of *The Protestant Ethic* as a complement to that of *Capital*. Kautsky does not seem fully to have understood the argument about rationalization as a social trend.[37] What may perhaps be more a surprise to the marxist shellbacks of my generation is Kautsky's attempt to address the question of politics, as a vocation. Here, again, Kautsky seems to understand the modernizing moment of Weber's thought, and not the fears of cages iron or regulative.[38] His discussion of the limits of charisma is jarring, composed as it was only five years before the rise of the charismatic leader in Germany.[39]

More fruitful, however, are his theoretical affinities with Gramsci. If Kautsky's reading of Weber is one-sided, his comments on intellectuals are more positively reminiscent of *The Prison Notebooks*. Here, like Gramsci, he discusses the universality of intellectual life. The autodidact, the organizer is as much an intellectual as is the critic of opera,[40] Kautsky says, and here he repeats an argument from *The Agrarian Question*, that there is no reason to believe that the possession of academic knowledge elevates the modern citizen over the populace of "primitive" society.[41] Further parallels exist in the shared sense that state and society must be transformed via democracy, and that socialism emerges from order, and not crisis—if at all.[42] However, where Bernstein would place democracy, still, as the central premise of socialism, Kautsky persists in giving this place to the proletariat.[43] Kautsky adds, though, that the theoretical possibility that the needs of the proletariat could be met within capitalism would necessitate the renunciation of socialism, the implicit liquidation indicating one basis in his reunification with the spirit of Bernstein's project. For as he put it, the final goal of the proletariat is not a final goal for the development of humanity. "An enduringly perfect society is as little possible as an absolute truth. And both the one and the other would mean nothing other than social stagnation and death."[44]

This is not, I think, the figure of Kautsky loosely portrayed by Trotsky, in smoking jacket, cosy but terminal both theoretically and practically. Conversely, I do not mean to turn Kautsky (or anyone else) into some kind of new hero for the nineties of our own century. He would have looked ridiculous in hair gel, with a flat top and in black. My argument rather is that notwithstanding idiosyncrasies to do with Darwin and whoever else, Kautsky and Bernstein still talk to us, and in language which is closer than we might at first think. For Kautsky and Bernstein seem to have understood something of the limits on the future (if not its propensity to generate degeneracy and barbarism) and yet to argue for human possibilities within it. My case is not that we should all become Kautskyists, so much as that those who still identify with the aims and traditions of socialism should actually attempt to clarify what those aims are and where those traditions speak, or are silent.

This is not to say, then, that Kautsky (in particular) was not a shellback (though even Rosa Luxemburg was equally crustacean in political economy). It is striking, however, that even when Kautsky ventures out, no one notices, and then we have to suffer the slings and arrows of Althusserian political economy or Poulantzian class analysis in the seventies as a dull replay of some of these earlier, forgotten events. The discovery that socialism has something to do with democracy is then received by us as a great surprise, too great a surprise, as though it is actually invented by Eurocommunists, where Bernstein had already argued the case in *Evolutionary Socialism* and Kautsky taken it further in 1918, in *The Dictatorship of the Proletariat*. The case presented here, then, is that the social democratic project, in contrast to Bolshevism, at least provides a place to start, for it possesses a concrete utopia. Thus, in Weber's sense, social democracy presents itself as one of the warring gods between whom we must choose.

We return here to the idea that the German social democrats engage a kind of Weberian marxism, by which I mean a kind of marxism which is politically realistic, takes ideas seriously, and embraces the postfaustian future. This may be a heavyhanded way of describing a marxism come of age, for certainly I refer to something different than the Weberianized marxism which has frequented sociology since Frank Parkin's "bourgeois critique", and something more pragmatic than Merleau-Ponty's tracing of Weberian marxism via Lukács in *Adventures of the Dialectic*. I refer back rather to the effective location of social democracy in the heart of classical social theory, that theory which sits on the cusp of modernity, and which tells us so much of the spirit, hopes and woes of our time.[45] This locus offers us a view of sober optimism, and a modern sobriety rather than the implicitly medieval sobriety of Tawney's worldview. It reminds us, as well, that as Martin Jay puts it, the *fin* of our own *siècle* somehow compels us to reconsider the *fin* of the previous *siècle*, its hopes and dreams, failures and nightmares.[46]

There is a myriad of possible objections that could be put against this case. The most powerful, I suspect, is that asking West Europeans to revive social democracy is about as futile as hoping that East Europeans might care to revive the imaginary of communism. It is almost certainly true that the persuasiveness of my case will be weak for denizens of cultures that have in any way recognizably been "social democratic" since the war. *Weltgeschichte ist Weltgericht*, as Castoriadis reminds us—if people take the postwar experience to be social democracy, then we have to accept this, and find a new language. These are real claims, which have to be taken seriously, but they in turn raise others, apparently insoluble, about how we transcend liberalism from within a liberal or postliberal culture. My response is that the reception of the present case is likely to be better in Anglo cultures, where social democracy persists in representing a superior project and tradition to that of the local tradition of labourism.[47] Labourism, as feminists such as Marilyn Lake have shown, is in genesis in fact a *rural* utopia, which cannot have adequate purchase on everyday lives lived mainly in the cities of modernity.[48] Until recently, with the miraculous arrival of the ALP-ACTU Accord and particularly *Australia Reconstructed*—so tellingly criticized in *Thesis Eleven* by Kevin McDonald[49]—the Australian labour movement has, with certain syndicalist exceptions, sought the utopia of yeomen, first in the bush, then in the suburbs. Perhaps because the German Social Democrats pitted themselves against the miseries of peasant life, theirs was a utopic vision which was never to reach this far back into history in search of inspiration—or escape (for men).

Social democracy matters, I would argue, because it mediates between social theory and politics, and more, it bridges premodern and modern. Durkheim was not the only one to recognize that communism was premodern, while socialism was modern—so, too, did the dead dogs of social democracy. The issue is significant, because while communism's utopia is premodern, so too is that of ethical socialism. The problem in the latter connection is that while medieval ethics may be extraordinarily valuable—a theme actually suggested by Macpherson himself[50]—medieval social theory will not do. Arguments for the "simple life" romantic-English style do not adequately address the needs-structures of modern citizens, or the peculiarities of postmodern culture, and while these phenomena are obviously socially constructed, we do need some sense of the difference between the way forward and the way back. More, arguments for reviving the past, literally, produce what Michael Ignatieff calls moral narcissism, a sort of middle-class version of the "prolier-than-thou" attitude governed by the misty nostalgia for better days bygone, for 1945–51 in Britain, or 1972–75 in Australia.[51] These may have been better days, but they are no future.

DEAD DOGS, SLUMBERING HOPES

I conclude by returning to Macpherson and to *The Life and Times of Liberal Democracy*. In this presentation I have resisted Macpherson's attraction to model building with reference to the idea of a social-democratic utopia. This is consistent with Bernstein's sense that socialism is to do with norms, not with plans. I leave it to other colleagues and friends to indicate economic directions for the future of Australia. As regards models, however, I share Macpherson's sense that one-class models, whether those of proletarian socialism (Bolshevism) or freeborn English persons with or without spade husbandry (Tawney, Owen) are passed, perhaps even dangerous. The vital point in connection with Macpherson is the idea of uncoupling citizenship and functional status or labour-market status. With reference to the future, however, a possible socialism based on difference as well as on differentiation need not, either, fetishize democracy, any more than it need universalize politics. "Democracy" needs "responsibility", just as "rights" call forth "duties".

There are of course other issues involved. As Beatrice Potter sensibly if wickedly put it, democracy has limits of other sorts—the slogan "the factories to the workers" misses the point that they may possibly not want them, any more than the sewer-workers want absolute sovereignty over their own vocational domain.[52] Democracy is a problem, as well as a "solution".

The logic of my case has been that social democracy runs a line between romanticism and realism, between Bax and Webbs, between anarchism and bureaucracy, between Morris and Bellamy, between moral and mechanical socialism, between the possible dichotomy of the values of freedom and life. This is so because social democracy is simultaneously sociological and ethical. Because sociological, it has a developed sense of some of the ambivalences which characterize modernity. Because ethical, it is able to address some very ordinary questions about our own existence. Among other things, it is a discourse which perhaps helps us better to see that part of our predicament today lies not in the institutions upon which we frequently blame the present impasse, but in our own failure to become more fully human. With that, however, I accept the view—as do Bernstein and Kautsky—that new social institutions will always be necessary, even if we do not yet know what they are. Pierre Rosanvallon may be right to suggest that this project be called post-social democratic.[53] This however reinforces the sense that we ought to take social democracy seriously, especially if post-social democratic means anything like "postmodern" or "postmarxist"—new, yet continuous, for these are still the tracks within which we work.

Notes

1. C. B. Macpherson, *The Life and Times of Liberal Democracy* (Oxford University Press, 1977).
2. See for example N. Dennis and A. H. Halsey, *English Ethical Socialism* (Oxford, 1988); cf. my review in *Australian Society* (September 1989).
3. These arguments are detailed more fully in Beilharz, *Labour's Utopias: Bolshevism, Fabianism, Social Democracy* (London and New York, Routledge 1992).
4. E. Belfort Bax, "Our German Fabian Convert" in H. Tudor and J. M. Tudor, *Marxism and Social Democracy* (Cambridge, University Press, 1988), pp. 61–65; H. Hirsch, *Der "Fabier" Eduard Bernstein* (Bonn, Dietz 1977); see also R. Fletcher, *From Bernstein to Brandt* (London, Edward Arnold, 1987), H. Kendall Rogers, "Eduard Bernstein Speaks to the Fabians", *International Review of Social History* 28 (1983), pp. 320–338, T. Meyer, *Bernstein's Konstructiver Sozialismus* (Berlin, Dietz, 1977), H. Heiman and Meyer, *Bernstein und der Demokratische Sozialismus* (Berlin, Dietz, 1978).
5. Bernstein, "Möglichkeiten Sozialismus" (Bernstein Papers, International Institute for Social History, Amsterdam, E123, n.d.), p. 14.
6. Bax, "Our German Fabian Convert" in Tudor and Tudor, pp. 61–62.
7. Bernstein, "Among the Philistines" in Tudor and Tudor, p. 66.
8. Tudor and Tudor, p. 23.
9. See generally G. Roth, *The Social Democrats in Imperial Germany* (Totowa, Bedminster, 1963); V. Lidtke, *The Alternative Culture: Socialist Labour in Imperial Germany* (Oxford, University Press, 1985); H. J. Steinberg, *Sozialismus und deutsche Sozialdemokratie* (Bonn, Neue Gesellschaft, 1972); R. Fletcher, *From Bernstein to Brandt*.
10. "Evolutionary Socialism: Interview with Herr Eduard Bernstein", *Jewish Chronicle* (24.11.1899), p. 22 (Bernstein Papers, Amsterdam Institute, G462), p. 22.
11. Bernstein, "The Socialistic Theory of the Bolsheviks. . . " (Bernstein Papers, Amsterdam Institute, A123, n.d.).
12. G. Carchedi, *Class Analysis and Social Research* (Oxford, Blackwell, 1987);

H. Müller, *Der Klassenkampf in der deutschen Sozialdemokratie* (Zurich, Verlag-Magazin, 1892).

13. Carchedi, p. 11.
14. Tudor and Tudor, p. 192f.
15. Tudor and Tudor, pp. 193, 215.
16. Tudor and Tudor, pp. 168–169.
17. Tudor and Tudor, p. 151.
18. Tudor and Tudor, pp. 90–97.
19. Tudor and Tudor, pp. 221, 229f.
20. Tudor and Tudor, pp. 233, 240.
21. E. Bernstein, *Evolutionary Socialism* (New York, Schocken, 1965), p. 96.
22. *Evolutionary Socialism*, p. 143.
23. *Evolutionary Socialism*, p. 147f.
24. *Evolutionary Socialism*, p. 148.
25. *Evolutionary Socialism*, p. 149.
26. *Evolutionary Socialism*, p. 148.
27. See generally D. Groh, *Negative Integration and revolutionarer Attentismus* (Frankfurt, Ullstein, 1973).
28. See generally Kautsky, *The Agrarian Question* (Winchester, Zwan, 1988). Some of the antinomies of his position are nicely summarized by the editors, Alavi and Shanin, in their introduction.
29. Kautsky, *The Agrarian Question*, II, p. 443.
30. Kautsky wrote about Morris in *Der Wahre Jacob*, 268 (1896), p. 231f.
31. On dialectics, see especially Carchedi, *Class Analysis and Social Research*.
32. Kautsky, *Bernstein und das Sozialdemokratische Programme* (Stuttgart, Dietz, 1899).
33. Kautsky, *The Materialist Conception of History*, ed. J. H. Kautsky (New Haven, Yale, 1988), pp. 5–6. This is a labour of scholarship and love, and Kautsky's grandson and the publishers are to be applauded for it.
34. *Materialist Conception*, p. 260.
35. *Materialist Conception*, pp. 28, 38–39, 43.
36. *Materialist Conception*, pp. 69, 70. cf. *Agrarian Question*, II, p. 329.
37. *Materialist Conception*, p. 356.
38. *Materialist Conception*, p. 387.
39. *Materialist Conception*, pp. 395–397.
40. *Materialist Conception*, p. 399.
41. *Agrarian Question*, II, p. 362.
42. *Materialist Conception*, pp. 410, 419–421.
43. *Materialist Conception*, pp. 425–426.
44. *Materialist Conception*, p. 464.
45. See generally the useful study by Harry Liebersohn, *Fate and Utopia in German Sociology, 1870–1923* (Boston, MIT, 1989).
46. M. Jay, *Fin de Siècle Socialism* (London, Methuen, 1988).

47. Beilharz, "The Australian Left: Beyond Labourism?" *Socialist Register 1985/1986* (London, Merlin, 1986); "The Labourist Tradition and the Reforming Imagination" in R. Kennedy (ed.), *Australian Welfare Historical Society* (Sydney, Macmillan, 1989); "Social Democracy and Social Justice", *Australian and New Zealand Journal of Sociology* 25/1 (1989).

48. See generally M. Lake, "Socialism and Manhood: The Case of William Lane", *Labour History* (Sydney) 50 (1986); *The Limits of Hope: Soldier Settlement in Victoria 1915–1938* (Oxford, University Press, 1987).

49. K. McDonald, "After the Labour Movement", *Thesis Eleven* 20 (1988).

50. C. B. Macpherson, *The Rise and Fall of Economic Justice* (Oxford, University Press, 1986).

51. M. Ignatieff, "Citizenship and Moral Narcissism", *Political Quarterly* 60/1 (1989).

52. B. Potter, *The Co-operative Movement in Great Britain* (London, Swan Sonnenschein, 1891), p. 75.

53. P. Rosanvallon, "The Decline of Social Visibility" in J. Keane (ed.), *Civil Society and the State* (London, Verso, 1988), p. 218.

CORPORATISM, DEMOCRACY, AND MODERNITY

Julian Triado

Corporatism has emerged as one of the central problems confronting both political theory and critical social theory today. The following reflections are prompted by the emergence in Australia of explicitly corporatist trends with the advent of the Labor government nine years ago.[1] While no attempt will be made to examine Australian corporatism, or its history in Australian labourist traditions,[2] what follows is an attempt to confront the almost universal acclamation extended to corporatist developments by the Australian left with a more general discussion of the problematic nature of corporatism, based largely on extensive studies carried out in England, the U. S. and West Germany, where the reception of corporatist trends is, on the whole, a good deal less enthusiastic, more circumspect and, at times, downright hostile. After locating the development of corporatism within the dynamics of modernity and overviewing trends and the reactions of some observers, I will turn to two central problems confronting the appreciation of corporatism today—namely, the inability of class based action to counter the logic of corporatism and the challenge corporatism presents to democracy.

CORPORATISM AND MODERNITY

The concept of modernity, which has enjoyed a good deal of currency in aesthetics over the past century, has not always proved easy to accommodate within other disciplines. The social sciences have, until very recently, been reluctant to countenance its usage, preferring more 'precise' identifications of the modern world with capitalism (Marx), with industrialism and bureaucracy (Weber), with the emergence of mass society (Tönnies), with the emergence of functionalist societies (Durkheim) or even with the logic of militarization. More recently, several thinkers have sought to develop more complex and more differentiated models of modernity. Thus, while conceding the importance of the rationalizing process of industrialism and the universalizing development-logic of purposive rational forms of thought, Habermas has attempted to prove the centrality of the development of normative structures for socio-cultural evolution, a project yielding a model of late capitalist societies which stresses both systemic imperatives and the normative expectations of the life-world.[3] Fehér and Heller have specified modernity as that region and epoch in which capitalism, industrialism and democracy have emerged as co-present, separate, though interrelated 'logics'.[4] Both conceptions have the advantage over earlier ones of profiling the conflict-ridden and open-ended nature of contemporary societies and of underscoring the centrality of those normative realms of such societies to which critical social theory might appeal as the basis for radical social action. In highlighting the 'hidden logic' of democracy, both conceptions share the view that democracy is essentially normative and cannot be fully functionalized in accordance with empirical and systemic constraints. Both, therefore, hold firmly to the view that the emancipatory possibilities rest in the unfettering of a logic which has become increasingly empirical, though one which, nevertheless, remains co-constitutive of the modern world.

If democracy represents the only legitimate basis for government in the modern world, its relation to 'governability' is problematic; for the governance of contemporary states increasingly takes place in modes not always subject to democratic procedures and norms. The problematic relation between governability and democracy has a long history in the modern world, and touches the problem of how and on what basis interests can be organized outside the formal democratic institutions of the modern state and what relation ought to obtain between organized interests and such institutions. While associability has taken many forms—guilds, workers' councils, corporations, pluralistic interest organizations—the relations between these and the requirements of democracy have usually remained unclarified.

Whilst corporatism is a very old phenomenon reaching back to Roman and medieval times, here we are concerned only with its appropriation in the modern world. That corporatism is a modern rather than specifically late capitalist response to problem solving within differentiated social systems can be seen in the influence it has exerted on political theorists and actors within modernity.[5] Hegel's adoption of corporatism as a solution to governability is, perhaps, the most significant and exerted a good deal of influence, particularly on English 'pluralists'—J. N. Figgis, G. D. H. Cole, M. P. Follet—who drew on the work of English Hegelians like T. H. Green and Bernard Bosanquet. Hegel's corporatist doctrine was formulated against what he took to be the excesses of the French Revolution, which had seen a good deal of Rousseauean thought reach fruition in measures such as the banning of trade unions and professional associations in the Loi le Chapelier (1791). For Rousseau's solution to the problem posed by associability to governability was as simple as it was untenable. 'Partial associations' could, in his view, have no place in the process of democratic will formation and, hence, in the governance of a society. Hegel confronted the relation between associability and government in a more plausible manner, though one purchased at the expense of democracy. For Hegel, the 'concrete person', the particular of civil society, with wants, idiosyncrasies, talents, accidents of birth etc., had to be integrated into the ethical life (*Sittlichkeit*) of the state; the sphere of competition and atomism had to be mediated to the sphere of universality embodied in the state. The corporations of civil society perform, for Hegel, this essentially reconciliatory function: 'the single person attains his actual and living destiny when he becomes a member of a Corporation, a society etc....'[6] The corporatistic organization of the 'business class' (here, Hegel means commercial associations, guilds, unions and professional associations) allows individuals to overcome their particularity, as embodiments of mere abstract rights, without simultaneously denying their particularity as was the case with Rousseau. The purpose of the corporation is wholly 'concrete and no wider in scope than the purpose involved in business, its proper task and interest'.[7] Two questions can be raised here which are of pertinence to the contemporary discussion. Firstly, do corporations function to exclude competing interpretations concerning the ends of production? And, secondly, how can those needs which do not come within the scope of the corporations be organized, represented and educated? After all, Hegel argued that interest associations require state 'authorization' before they can become corporations and participate in the life of the state.[8] Both questions which, admittedly, are of greater significance today than they were at the birth of the modern era, will be addressed below in the light of contemporary corporatist developments.

Marx remains one of the most trenchant critics of Hegel's corporatist solution to the problem. Two aspects of his, often acutely incisive, *Critique of Hegel's Doctrine of State* are particularly relevant here. Firstly, Marx criticizes Hegel's attempt to reconcile the forces of civil society in a substantive unity with the state as being a reconciliation with the 'actually existing' state. Hegel failed to recognize objective freedom (political institutions) as 'the realization and activation of subjective freedom',[9] the 'political state' as the 'self-determination' of the people.[10] Secondly Hegel failed to understand the significance of the so-called bourgeois revolutions which underscored the human authorship of social and political institutions, a view summed up by Marx in the notion that it is man who 'makes the constitution'. Democracy was, for Marx, the key to the modern world and Hegel's corporatist solution merely replayed the unfreedoms of pre-modern societies insofar as political activity was circumscribed by the systemic requirements of rational administration.[11] Membership of the corporations, a prerequisite for political activity, not only excluded those social strata who had no corporate status (the working class, labourers, the poor etc.), but also narrowed the scope of political activity to action in conformity with an already given social- systemic order. The premising of political life on membership of the corporations at the same time subsumes politics to the empirical universality of bureaucratic administration. Whilst the corporations remain organizations of the particular interests of civil society, and thus are formally separate from the state bureaucracy, as integral and functional units of the state a common bureaucratic spirit inhabits both. In a striking anticipation of Weber, Marx writes:

> The *corporations* are the materialism of the bureaucracy and the
> bureaucracy is the *spiritualism* of the corporations. The corporation is
> the bureaucracy of civil society; the bureaucracy is the corporation of the
> state.[12]

Marx resolutely rejected this canalization of political activity into the functional requirements of the state as being contrary to the normative requirements of democracy. Marx's early critique of Hegel thus amounts to a partisanship for a model of society which does not take the functional requirements of an actually existing state as the parameters for legitimate political activity. Far from being an open door to the political and cultural life of modern societies, corporatism operates as a mechanism of exclusion, bracketing democratic participation as a right of all citizens toward goals which ought to be as open-ended as the universal values whose institutionalization defined the advent of the modern world.

At heart, Marxian critical theory rested on a serious conflation between system and class,[13] which was politically disastrous for subsequent Marxists. Having begun with a differentiated social theory which examined the action potential of social actors in terms of normative goals, Marx proceeded to telescope social action into a systems theory, where the mode of production was the single, overdetermining system of modern, capitalist society. All social contradictions were theorized as derivatives of the mode of production. From seeing the proletariat as a social movement and actor outside civil society, Marx's analysis shifted to seeing the proletariat in its functional role in the capitalist mode of production: its potential for social action was then conceived from within a theory which had already narrowed the scope of social action to systemic contradictions. When he turned his attention to a systems analysis in *Capital*, he analyzed all forms of subjectivity in terms of the all-embracing power of the object. Nevertheless, despite the fact that Marx bracketed the possibility of analyzing other sub-systems and spheres of social life, he could still hold out the possibility of emancipation by retaining the metaphysical guarantees of a philosophy of history which posited socialism as the necessary resolution of systemic contradictions. He could not, however, locate the possibility of emancipation within political society because he had reduced social action to struggles within the economic system, and thus made revolutionary action dependent on economic crises. The social democrats who followed Marx formalized the Marxian philosophy of history and thereby justified inaction; while Lenin, confronted with the need to produce a proletariat, resolved the problem of revolutionary action through the vanguard party. Neither resolved the specifically political problems involved; for this, a political and ethical theory, already missing from Marx's own social theory, would have been required. We shall see that the understanding of corporatism today, whether it is positive or negative, suffers from an almost exclusive systems-bound focus and a corresponding inability to take normative questions seriously, features which grow out of earlier social democratic traditions.

CORPORATISM AND LATE TWENTIETH CENTURY MODERNITY

There are many causes for the growth of corporatist forms of the mediation of societal interests within contemporary societies. Nearly all commentators, however, agree on the connection between a modernity in crisis and the developmental trend toward corporatism.[14] The governability problems attending liberal parliamentary systems, the centralization of national trade union organizations, and the incidence of Labor or Social Democratic governments, are all related factors accounting for the graduated, though often varied, 'quiet revolution' which has transformed modes of interest representation and decision-making in nearly all contemporary societies. We will argue here that corporatist developments represent nothing more, and certainly nothing less, than an emergent state form within modern society, rendered possible, even necessary, by the developments of the capitalising aspects of modernity, in crisis, and a concomitant search for solutions to problems of governability through new forms of decision-making and policy formation. The drift of power from representative to executive bodies is a well documented phenomenon within liberal democracies, reflecting not only manifest problems of governability but also a growing disinclination to make public the bases for much state policy formation. The genetic development of an economy in crisis has, in short, given rise to a problem complex which is essentially politico-logical. On the one hand, the crisis potentials of the economic system now require state intervention well beyond Keynesian 'fine tuning', which has resulted in great fiscal burdens being placed on the administrative system; this in turn heightens the need for greater 'supply-side' control over inputs to policy-making. On the other hand, public policy formation takes place in modes which are increasingly instrumental; the strategic goals of state action are becoming more focused on the solution of pressing problems within the logics of industrialism and capitalism. Corporatist arrangements play a central, even crucial, role here. The question of the kind of political rationality employed in problem solving requires thematization. We shall address in the final two sections the systemic nature of this kind of political rationality and its growing distance from democratic expectations, but before turning to these questions, we must first look at the nature of contemporary corporatism.

State intervention, despite free-market zealots, has always provided the stability required for capital accumulation and reproduction, something which an unfettered market manifestly could not achieve. Not only has the state provided for welfare needs but its provision of infrastructural services from urban planning to the regulation of trade is entwined deeply with the needs of capitalist accumulation. Organized labour has been no less implicated; far from being a spontaneous expression of working class interests, unions rely crucially on state intervention for their effectivity. Such measures as the sanctioning of compulsory unionism, provision of legal and quasi-legal modes of conflict resolution, protection from litigation for unintended consequences of industrial action etc. make it difficult to define unionism in isolation from state involvement. The wage labour-capital relation has, then, long been politicized. In exchange for relative industrial stability the "substitute programme" of the welfare state ensured throughout the post-war years economic growth and rising living standards.

With the onset of recession in the early seventies new contradictions began to emerge, presenting new problems for public policy formation and the mediation of societal interests. The structural models of "late capitalist" societies sketched by Habermas, Offe and O'Connor in the early seventies, each stressing new crisis potentials—'legitimation and motivation crises', 'crises of crisis management' and 'fiscal crisis'—are now well known.[15] These models underscore the tension-ridden and often contradictory functions performed by states as they try to underwrite the continued reproduction of a profitable capital base, meet ever-increasing demands for welfare needs and hence a greater share of resources to offset the effects of unemployment, resource depletion, environmental damage and, finally, as they are forced to guarantee the reproduction of "mass loyalty". This delicate balancing of conflicting demands has heightened rather than attenuated and is reflected in the growing literature on the 'crisis of the welfare state', 'post-growth' politics and 'regime ungovernability' on both the left and the right.[16] Thus, on the one hand, an ever-increasing state expenditure on welfare to meet the needs of rising unemployment confronts the threshold limits of taxation levels (the so-called 'tax revolts' are only symptomatic of the more deeply felt hostility of an increasingly privatized and 'narcissistic' middle-class to rising taxation) while on the other hand, the need for industry restructuring, the decline of manufacturing in the metropolitan nations and the onslaught of high technology has heightened conflict between labour and capital both nationally and regionally.

Corporatism arises, then, within this context of growing and conflicting demands. Much recent discussion of corporatism (or neocorporatism) owes a good deal to Philippe Schmitter, who, since the early seventies, has underlined the post-pluralist, corporatist nature of most advanced capitalist societies.

His famous definition, though it can be criticized as ideal-typical,[17] overly-functionalist, and demonstrating an insensitivity to the empirico-historical nature of state power,[18] nevertheless remains the most useful. Thus, in contrast to liberalism (and syndicalism):

> Corporatism can be defined as a system of interest representation in which the constituent units are organized into a limited number of singular, compulsory, non-competitive, hierarchically ordered and functionally differentiated categories, recognized or licenced (if not created) by the state and granted a deliberate representational monopoly within their respective categories in exchange for observing certain controls on their selection of leaders and articulation of demands and supports.[19]

Much in the analyses of Schmitter and others bears out Manoilesco's prediction that this would be "the century of corporatism". Fascist states were avowedly corporatist even if this was a "decorative facade for force";[20] in the post-war period, corporatist tendencies emerged in many societies, most notably Austria, the Netherlands, Sweden and Denmark. In more recent years, corporatist tendencies have heightened across nearly all countries which have experienced multi-dimensional modernisation. Yet, post-war corporatism is vastly different from its nefarious fascist namesake, a difference in part revealed by Schmitter's distinction between 'state corporatism' and 'societal corporatism'— the latter reflecting a pre-history of stable liberal democracy. The social bases of the two forms of corporatism also differ markedly. Fascism relies upon an effective mobilization of the petty bourgeoisie and small capitalist, while with post-corporatism it is precisely these strata who are most uneasy about the proliferation of corporatist institutions. The exigencies of state action also differ markedly. Fascism had a strong ideological motivation to resolve economic and political difficulties by a strong commitment to a *status quo ante*: post-war corporatism, however, issues from societies with strong and organized labour movements and attempts to resolve systemic problems through administrative-rational public policy formation without reliance upon mass mobilization and retroactive ideologies. Indeed, what distinctively marks latter day corporatism is its reliance upon depoliticization and the absence of any corporatist specific legitimation. The attempts made to draw parallels between the latter and fascist experiments are, then, at best misleading.

Post-war corporatist developments then, emerge in a context of economic and administrative (overload) crises; from a recognition of the need for greater state intervention designed to control inputs (wage-bargaining, interest group demands) into policy making, so that greater control can be exerted upon outputs (investment planning, extended reproduction etc.). As Offe has observed, no less than a shift in political rationality is involved here, a shift from demand management (characteristic of more loosely organized pluralist interest

representation) to 'supply-side' restructuring. This has entailed the abandonment of 'conjunctural policies' in the face of economic and institutional crises
in favour of 'structural policies'.

> This shift is from policy output and economic demand management to
> the shaping of political input and economic supply -from 'state
> intervention' to 'politicization'.[21]

Corporatism furnishes the institutional means to mediate the demands of *functional* interest groups of contemporary modern societies, with the aim of developing an administrative *consensus* over resource allocation, investment planning, industry restructuring, the introduction of high technology, economic
performance, full employment (in time!), wage levels, price controls, and various policies designed to augment the 'social wage', all pursued with the aid
of certain ideological and cultural accoutrements stressing the presence of an
overriding 'national interest'. Its principal institutional forms are tripartite government and semi-government bodies, national economic advisory councils,
industry councils, Quangos and commissions of inquiry—all comprising representatives of the three key functional groups of capitalist society: Labour,
Capital and Government. In return for participation in public policy formation,
capital surrenders an untrammelled sovereignty of the market in the interests
of 'capital in general' and unions, having become an 'estate of the realm', not
only gain a share in decision-making but must control their constituencies and
deliver compliance to a nationally adjudicated consensus.[22]

The growth of tripartite, corporatist institutions for public policy formation
has been greeted with varying degrees of enthusiasm. Liberal-conservatives
see it as institutionalizing the altered basis of authority from the market to the
state.[23] On the left, little consensus can be found. Leo Panitch, one of the most
influential left critics of corporatism, sees it as a new form of class collabora-
tion and a further betrayal of the working class by union leaderships. Pahl and
Winkler see it as 'fascism with a human face'.[24] Cawson[25] views corporatism
as a not undesirable development which formalizes an institutional framework
complementary to parliamentary democracy, where reformist politics combine
with trade unionism to produce the highest achievement of social democracy.
Other theorists are even more optimistic about corporatist achievements, which
represent the accession of class struggle to the inner sanctums of the state
apparatuses, pointing to a possible socialist transition through greater control
over investment planning.[26] Observers such as Newman, who sees corporatism
as 'late Capitalism's primary option'[27] and Jessop, for whom it represents the
'highest form of social democracy'[28] and others such as Offe, Schmitter, Lehmbruch and Anderson, are a good deal more cautious and circumspect, though
nonetheless accepting corporatist developments. No attempt will be made to
evaluate these contributions to the growing debate over corporatism; rather, in

what follows, the problems involved in the perception of corporatism from a class-theoretical perspective are examined.

CORPORATISM AND CLASS

The perception of corporatism from a class-theoretical perspective, while prevalent, is misguided. Insofar as corporatist arrangements represent an institutional means to intermediate the interests of functional groups, this inevitably (and justifiably) implicates classes within the framework of analysis—though this ought not imply that classes are the only groups which can be corporatized, only that they are clearly the most significant.[29] From the perspective of class, two evaluations are possible. Either corporatism is seen as a new 'form of capitalist domination' of the working class or as an actual argmentation of the power and influence of the working class. However, both views fail to establish how and on what basis class-based action can today be said to be emancipatory. An unargued assumption that this is necessarily so is hardly adequate. This positive or negative perception of corporatism is inseparable from a recognition of its partisanship for certain bureaucratic, administrative-rational forms of societal control. As a *systemic* response to systemic problems within the logics of capitalism and industrialism, corporatism remains genetically bound to the problem-complexes of these domains. The denunciation and affirmation of corporatist trends are two sides of the same attempt to re-affirm a model of society based on the primacy of class conflict. Those who denounce it seek to retain the erroneous view that the working class is still the subject of emancipation; while those who enthuse about corporatist forms subvert the very possibility of emancipation insofar as they embrace, wittingly or unwittingly, technocratic illusions about the organization and control of social life.

The evaluation of corporatism from the vantage point of class misses two crucial points. Firstly, whatever adequacy Marx's class model of capitalist society may have had during his own lifetime, its claim to provide the key to the more generalized contradictions and different loci of domination within complex modernity is misguided. Such views rely on the assumption that the wage labour-capital relation has explanatory significance for every realm of social life. The complex nature of modernity with its complex and differentiated nature of social conflicts (manifested in various social movements, struggles over social services etc.) are hardly exhausted by the primacy of the wage-labour capital relation as an explanatory key. Secondly, the logic of class struggle needs careful consideration. What precisely is meant by the term? On the one hand it could mean class action with overtly political aims analogous to the struggle waged by the ascendant bourgeoisie against a profligate aristocracy for the control and more rational administration of production and for greater political control of state matters. On the other hand, class struggle could mean a distributive struggle aimed solely at an optimal distribution of the social product. It is almost self-evident that the first form of class based *action* or political class struggle, as it was conceived especially by Rosa Luxemburg, has informed the practices of very few avowedly socialist movements throughout the course of this century. As a normative goal, it may certainly be part of the collective consciousness of many socialists and has been reflected in the ideas of workers' councils, guild socialism, soviets and, within the East European context, in the idea of a "Great Republic".[30] The stricture, nevertheless, remains: it has informed very few broadly based socialist programs. Such ideas have inevitably foundered on the complex nature of twentieth century capitalist societies, on the strategic programs of 'working class' parties (or, in the case of Eastern European movements, on the Soviet army). This is not to say that complexity rules out the possibility for the self-management and self-administration of work places, but that such goals can only be part of a broadly based *political* struggle for democracy aiming at *generalized* self-management. Its guiding principle here would be freedom and the overcoming of the wage-labour capital relation has no monopoly on that principle.

If political class struggle remains a largely counter-factual assumption about the actual operation of class struggle, all the empirical evidence points to the fact that class struggle is indeed systemic; that is, that its logic is distributive, has as its aim only quantifiable gains, and presupposes the central systemic principle of capitalism: the wage labour-capital relation. The actual practice of class struggle has become thoroughly economized, defining itself by optimal bargaining within the parameters of systemic constraints, thus reaffirming the counter-factuality of political class goals. If, however, systemic bargaining is accepted as definitive of class struggle, then it is difficult to see how class-based action can inform any emancipatory project. That is, if class struggle merely re-affirms the capitalization of social life, the emancipatory goals of socialism cannot derive their normative validity from class-based action alone. The emancipatory potential of working class struggles, then, has long exhausted itself (though any emancipatory project must include the aspiration of workers to control their work places within the limits afforded by complex societies). Indeed, as Bauman has argued the language of class struggle is a discourse belonging to the early phase of capitalist development in the 19th century, when class action comprised overtly political goals. His stricture against class theory is clear; the formation of the working class had a political, not economic basis:

> the formation of workers into a class was a response to the advent of industrial society; only obliquely, because of circumstances of time and place, can this formation be portrayed as a reaction to the capitalist form of industrial society.[31]

The political formation of the working class was in Bauman's view, bound up with defensive action against the "discipline power of capital' as it sought to impose its time constraints and factory discipline on labour. The notion of the 'right to the whole product of labour' (which had also informed Marx's own early anthropology), belonged to a context of resistance by the newly emergent industrial worker against capitalist discipline of the body and mind. Early working class action was thus bound up with the normative goals of autonomy and freedom. Once the clock held sway and Foucault's prison society was finally entrenched the logic of collective struggle altered fundamentally, and a normatively grounded political struggle gave way to an "economized politics" of wage bargaining.

The wage labour-capital relation was, then, infused from the beginning with a political content which, once dissipated, transformed the relation into an economic one, reflecting the supremacy of the capitalist aspect of modern society—for without a political and moral basis (against injustice, discipline, enclosures etc.) class bound struggle could only be *systemic*, that is, a struggle based upon the prior acceptance of the wage labour-capital relation. The emergence of an economized class struggle cannot, however, be explained in terms of 'false consciousness' or 'trade union consciousness', or other sleights of hand against the empirical working class. The logic of distributive struggles derives from a system in which the struggle over production has never been at issue, at least since the entrenchment of capitalist discipline within the dynamics of modernity. Once the issue of control over the products of labour has receded, the only question was one of the better management of production, paving the way for the true inheritors of the capitalists' mantle: the technocrats. The extent to which class struggle has entrenched itself within the systemic constraints of advanced capitalism is indicated by the depth and range of administrative control over wage labour-capital relations, as the state assumes greater control over the conditions for capital accumulation.

That working class representatives are inducted through corporatist arrangements into the administrative complex (the notion of 'class struggle within the state') does little to bolster the subverted emancipatory potentials of an already economized class struggle, even if it does satisfy the technocratic aspirations of some of its representatives. It should by now be clear that the negative or positive assessment of corporatism in class terms is drastically misconceived on two counts: class conflict does not account for the complex and varied sites of domination in advanced capitalist societies and an economized class struggle in part and parcel of a system whose own administrative logic comes into conflict with 'vital areas' of the life world. Corporatism must therefore be understood as an administrative rational response to the systemic logics of capitalism and industrialism, reflecting the altered focus of *state* action within advanced capitalism. Corporatism thus represents the highest achievement of an economized class struggle thoroughly emptied of any normative goals, and guided only by the performance principle of the economic system.

How then is corporatism to be evaluated? Again, a partisanship for or against misses the essential point: corporatism is symptomatic of a thoroughly

modernized, though hardly emancipated, society. It is an inevitable development, given the logics of industrialization and capitalization and in some senses
is even defensible—the prepolitical power of the working class, after all, has
every right to be institutionalized in national policy making bodies. What has
to be shattered, however, are the illusions that it represents any more than a
systemic adjustment within late twentieth century modernity and that it carries
with it a necessarily progressive or emancipatory promise. Modernity, after all,
moves along three axes of development, each competing with the other and
each promising vastly different forms of societal organization. Democracy,
for reasons to be explored, receives short shrift within a corporate society
and all too little attention from the thoroughly economized existing socialist
movement and parties. And yet, if class struggle moves only along the axes
of capitalism and industrialization, emancipation is necessarily premised upon
the greater democratization of society. Socialism today, following Feher and
Heller, can only be understood as 'radicalized democracy'. It is not empirically
derivable from qualitative adjustments in consumption or in a numerical, even
preponderant working class presence within administrative bodies controlling
production. Socialism is essentially normative, questioning the basis of a societal organization in which power is institutionalized in administrative rational
forms and in reified social relations of which the wage labour-capital relation
is only one. To take democracy seriously today as a normative goal is to be
truly radical, in that democracy challenges the very roots of a society in which
all political questions and vital human needs are treated as problems requiring
administrative solutions, that is, it calls into question the basis of society which
subordinates democracy to empirical systemic imperatives and it holds out the
promise that it is the latter, which ought to be, as far as practicable, subordinate
to the former.

CORPORATISM AND DEMOCRACY

The relation between corporatism and democracy is one of the least developed and least explored areas within existing areas within existing discussions of corporatism.[33] In part, this has to do with the pragmatic nature of
the adjustment of contemporary societies towards corporatist arrangements.[34]
Not only are the substantive ends of public policy (economic growth, industry
competitiveness and restructuring, high technology etc.) simply assumed to
coincide with the 'common good', but key functional groups are identified as
embodying the capacity for achieving such ends. The minimum requirement
of a democratic society is the safeguarding of negative liberties (the protection
of civil liberties, and the freedom to vote in regular elections). The exercise of positive freedoms (to participate in decision-making processes), however, falls unequally upon particular groups, classes and individuals within
all existing democracies. Such inequalities were justified by liberal pluralists

through their market-theoretical assumptions of free competition between interest groups. Under corporatist arrangements, the problem is compounded; formalized, functional participation by some groups in public policy formation brings into sharper relief the problem of how privileged participation of *some* can be justified. Clearly, it cannot, and this is precisely why the 'logic' of democracy implies its own radicalization; that is, positive freedoms must be generalized.[35]

There are today, three major conceptions as to how a democracy ought to function. Liberal pluralism relies on the first two, which can be characterized as elite theory—a view holding that democracy is realized in a 'competitive struggle' amongst elites for the people's vote and that, once elected, the business of government rests solely within the competence of such an elite — and the theory of responsible government — the view that governments ought to be responsible to people's needs and that they should be removable by electoral decisions. Both conceptions are plebiscitarian and rest on the principles of the sovereignty of parliament and territorial representation. Both are also empirical conceptions of democracy. The third conception, which places a premium on participation, is typically identified in the theories of "classical democracy" (Rousseau, J. S. Mill and G. D. H. Cole).[36] Democracy here is conceived in normative terms. In contrast to the first two, democracy is not adapted to the requirements of systematic stability, but rather is evaluated in terms of its ability to promote certain normative ends (participation, political inequality, self-development, freedom etc.). In the first two theories, democracy is conceived as a 'method', while in the third its status as a regulative principle is upheld.

Schmitter has argued that the democracies of complex modernity have exhibited a 'shift' away from participation and the accessibility of state institutions towards government which operationalizes the principles of accountability and responsiveness, and further, that the presence of corporatist arrangements is instrumental in such a shift.[37] However, such a formulation is misleading insofar as it implies that such democracies have relied, at least in the past on the participation of citizens in the political process. In fact, the opposite has been the case, and in this liberal pluralist theory has played a crucial part, by reducing democracy to empirical parameters and thus subordinating it to the systemic requirement of economic performance. This necessitated, above all, rule by competent elites, and in the process, as Macpherson noted, "democracy is reduced from a humanist aspiration to a market equilibrium system".[38] Corporatist tendencies heighten the trends in the political processes described by the pluralists. The "attribution of public status" to certain functional interest groups with formalized access to state policy-making bodies raises, as Anderson, Offe, Schmitter and others have pointed out, crucial problems for democracy. The growth of functional representation is accompanied by a diminution of institutional spheres governed by the procedural norm of majority rule, while the functional nature of representation in corporatist bodies entails the exclusion of non-functional and dysfunctional interests from authoritative decision-making.

Political institutions based on territorial representation generally operate in accordance with majoritarian norms. The procedural norm, which governs policy formation within the framework of functional representation, is *consensus*. The process of consensus formation however, presupposes a commonality of purpose, certain shared assumptions about the conduct and performance of argumentation. Those who are invited to dinner must dress accordingly. Offe has put this problem well:

> At the very least, corporatism in order to be stable, must not only
> continually *generate* consensus, it must first of all pre-suppose
> consensus, that is, a solid and undisputed acceptance of a certain mode
> of interest representation and accommodation.[39]

Corporatist bodies share basic assumptions concerning the primacy of systemic considerations (growth, economic performance, industry restructuring etc.), so that policy formation within the framework of such bodies both presupposes and generates consensus. Let us be clear: what is at issue here, is not consensus formation as such, but rather the assumption that authoritative institutions can generate public policy according to the procedural norm of consensus. Once this is accepted, politics becomes 'metapolitics' as conflict not over the definition of claims but over the definition of legitimate claimants.[40] Yet politics ought to have as its goal the good life, and require that public policy formation include all societal interests and that conflicting interests be articulated in accordance with democratic norms. Clearly, antisystemic interests cannot be thematized, let alone represented within corporatist bodies. Yet many societal interests are affected by the public policy formulated by such bodies. It would take us too far afield to discuss how conflicting interests can be resolved, though we should at least indicate that this is possible. If the interests of, say, the unemployed, conflict with systemic imperatives, then clearly there must be some appeal to higher principles, for instance, the citizenship principle, which is clearly at odds with the presence of a permanently marginalized strata of the population. The same could be said for a whole range of interests and needs, which conflict with the imperatives of the economic system. We do not question the norm of consensus as such; after all, a consensus must exist on certain fundamental values in any community (principally the values of life and freedom, though also on normative principles which derive from them, such as political equality, citizenship, etc.). Consensus can also take place within institutions which share certain (empirical) principles, such as systemic stability, though such institutions must be subordinated to higher order values. In short, the principle of democracy requires that corporatist institutions, at best, be subordinated to the institutional framework of society.

The second, though related issue, concerns the exclusion of nonfunctional and dysfunctional interests from authoritative decision-making. The organization of functional interest groups in corporatist bodies (which are designed to reduce the conflict potential between participating parties and to restrict the range of societal inputs into public policy formation), inevitably entails the marginalization of 'vital areas' of social life reflecting important, at times compelling, needs of the life-world. New "conflict zones" based on ethnicity, environmental concerns, government secrecy, urban planning, peace, feminism, health, education, unemployment, poverty etc., which have given rise to social movements, often fail to gain public status and representation in policy formation. These conflict zones and the needs they reflect cannot be handled as administrative problems requiring solution, for they call into question precisely such systemic incursions into the life-world. They suggest, rather the finite limits to the administrative organization of social life, for as Habermas has observed, there can be "no administrative production of meaning".[41] Above all, though, they suggest the depth and breadth of the impulse for the radicalization of democracy.

If then, corporatism is seriously at odds with the principle of democracy, can the democratization of corporations, as Cawson and Anderson suggest, solve the problem. Many left enthusiasts for corporatism (Esping-Andersen et al, Clegg et al, and Higgins) insist that the maintenance of links between the leadership of trade unions and their constituencies can not only enhance working class interests, but actually broaden the scope of public policy formation. Leaving aside the question as to whether this reflects an emancipatory logic anyway (a view already rejected), certain organizational features of corporations sketched in Schmitter's model, and which are *presupposed* by the successful operation of corporatist arrangements, suggest otherwise. As 'the bureaucracies of civil society', corporations are necessarily hierarchical and non-competitive. Only the pious hope that leadership concerns accurately reflect the interest of their constituencies could hide the view that compliance to a nationally adjudicated consensus is bought at a significant cost: the de facto loss of the right to strike and to bargain collectively for certain ends, both by individual workshops and less advantaged unions. Corporatism, as we have already suggested, is two-sided.

CONCLUSIONS

Let us then briefly summarize the argument. Corporatism represents an emergent state form within advanced complex societies, reflecting systemic imperatives within the modernizing logics of capitalism and industrialism. We have argued against the possibility that corporatism carries with it certain progressive, even emancipatory promises. We have also argued that the positive or negative understanding of corporatism from a class theoretical perspective

misses the essentially system-bound nature of corporatist modes for the intermediation of societal interests. A political and theoretical agnosticism is hardly
appropriate either. The questions posed by corporatism to democratic theory
are deep and unresolvable. An empirical conception of democracy which un-
derpinned liberal-pluralist plebiscitarian theory reaches its apotheosis in the
corporatist state-in-the-making with the privileged attribution of public status
and the granting of representational rights to certain key functional groups,
largely, but not exclusively class based, under the guidance of systemic imperatives. The marginalization of 'vital areas' of social life is only indicative
of broader politico-logical problems posed by the 'quiet revolution' which a
burgeoning corporatism has spawned. Participation and accessibility to state
institutions have been achieved by certain functional interest groups to an
extent hitherto unknown while the accountability and responsiveness of governments to societal needs has been circumscribed by the systemic objective
of achieving a workable administrative consensus in policy formation. Such
developments suggest a more significant and perhaps long-term threat to the
citizenship principle which underlies any democracy; for the principle entails,
even demands, equal treatment of all individuals. The permanent sacrificing
of the unemployable, the poor, welfare recipients and other disadvantaged
groups to systemic imperatives is hardly consistent with the citizenship principle. Coupled with the proliferation of social movements, these developments
also suggest a limitation which attends all contemporary discussions of corporatism; that is, the extent to which so much corporatist theory accepts these
and other phenomena as problems requiring resolution is indicative of the prior
acceptance of a focus implicitly or explicitly systems-theoretical or at the very
least functionalist.[42] A model of society based upon the adaptation of the system to its environment screens out the originary of 'historicity'. The norms and
values which lead social actors to contest society's self-conception, to fracture
the multiple representations of power embodied in state institutions and social relations suggest a different model of society's 'self-production', one which
gives attention to the conflictual and contestatory nature of a heterogeneous
range of social movements as they seek to 'conquer new territory'[43] through
a revitalization of political culture and the creation of public spaces beyond
the 'simulated politics' which narrow the scope of political activity and the
possibility of articulating radical, even compelling needs. The universal norms
and values embedded in our pluralistic culture demand that all needs other
than exploitative ones be publically articulated with institutional and procedural norms adequate to the highest expression of the promises held out by a
democratic culture. Democracy is not a method which can be flexibly adapted
to changing circumstances as Schmitter suggests; democracy as a rational and
normative principle carries with it implications for the organization of society,
implications which today must be heeded urgently.

Notes

1. The Hawke Labor government came to power in March 1983 with an 'accord' sealed between the Labor Party and the trade union movement, and immediately put into motion a National Economic Summit to which key economic spokesmen of the new government, the leaders of the State governments and the principal representatives of the trade unions and business were invited. The Summit communique saw general consensus for the policy direction to be pursued by the incoming government. Such policies included a commitment to growth, the containment of wage levels, low interest rates, tight fiscal policies and an (implied) acceptance of high levels of unemployment. More significant than the presence at the Summit were those groups who were absent; women, the unemployed, environmentalists and the aged. All social security recipients were tokenistically represented by one participant. The National Economic Advisory Council set up by the government continues the process of consensus formation on public policy, while various industry councils examine the restructuring of particular industries. For a variety of reasons the Australian left has on the whole watched far too uncritically the development of explicit corporatist trends in Australia. For some of the Very few exceptions see Peter Beilharz and R. Watts, 'The Discovery of Corporatism', *Australian Society*, November, 1983.

2. cf. R. Watts, 'The Light on the Hill. The Origins of the Australian Welfare State 1935–45', Unpublished Doctoral Dissertation, Melbourne University, 1983.

3. See Jurgen Habermas, *Legitimation Crisis*, Boston, Beacon 1975 and *Communication and the Evolution of Society*, Boston, Beacon 1979, Chs. 3–5.

4. Ferenc Feher and Agnes Heller, 'Class, Democracy and Modernity', *Theory and Society* 12, (1983). See also their *Eastern Left, Western Left*, Cambridge, Polity, 1987, and Agnes Heller, 'Marx and Modernity', *Thesis Eleven* 8, (1984).

5. For an excellent discussion of this see Philippe Schmitter 'Still the Century of Corporatism?', *Review of Politics* 36, (1974), Leo Panitch 'The Development of Corporatism in Liberal Democracies', *Comparative Political Studies* Vol. 10 No. 1, April 1977, and also N. Harris, *Competition and the Corporate Society*, London, Methuen 1972.

6. G. W. F. Hegel, *Philosophy of Right*, trans. T. M. Knox, London, Oxford 1964, S 182–7.

7. ibid. S 308.

8. ibid. S 253.

9. 'Critique of Hegel's Doctrine of State' in K. Marx, *Early Writings*, Harmondsworth,Penguin 1975, 125–6.

10. ibid. 89. See also 87.

11. ibid. 106.

12. ibid. 106.

13. Jean L. Cohen, *Class and Civil Society: The Limits of Marxian Critical Theory*, London, Martin Robertson 1983, esp. Part Two passim.

14. A. Shonfield, *Modern Capitalism*, London, Oxford 1965; Otto Newman, *The Challenge of Corporatism*, London, Macmillan 1981; Schmitter op. cit.; Panitch op. cit. and Panitch, 'Trade Unions and the Capitalist State', *New Left Review*, 125, 1981.

15. Habermas, *Legitimation Crisis* op. cit.; C. Offe, " 'Crises of Crisis Management":
Elements of a Political Crisis Theory', *International Journal of Politics*, Fall 1976,
and James O'Connor, *The Fiscal Crisis of the State*, New York 1973.

16. G. Esping-Andersen, 'The Incompatibilities of the Welfare State', *Thesis Eleven* 7,
1983; 'Competitive Party Democracy and the Keynesian Welfare State', mimeo;
A. Wolfe, *America's Impasse*, New York 1981; Daniel Bell, *The Cultural Contradictions of Capitalism*, New York, Basic Books, 1976.

17. Panitch, 'The Development...', op. cit.

18. Bob Jessop, 'Corporatism, Parliamentarism and Sochl Democracy', in P. Schmitter
and G. Lehmbruch, *Trends Toward Corporatist Intermediation*, London, Sage 1979,
185–190.

19. Schmitter, 'Still the Century...', op. cit., 93–94.

20. Harris, op. cit., 72.

21. C. Offe, 'The Attribution of Public Status to Interest Groups: Observations on the
West German Case', in Berger, op. cit., 127.

22. Newman, op. cit., 127.

23. See e.g. David Kemp, 'The National Economic Summit: Authority, Persuasion and
Exchange', *The Economic Record*, November 1983. Sir Keith Joseph put it more
bluntly: 'Corporatism and Liberty do not go together'. Quoted in Alan Cawson,
'Functional Representation and Democratic Politics: Towards a Corporatist Democracy?', in G. Duncan (ed.) *Democratic Theory and Practice*, London, Cambridge
1983.

24. R. E. Pahl and J. T. Winkler, 'The Coming Corporatism', *New Society* 10, October
1974, 73.

25. Cawson op. cit. See also his 'Pluralism, Capitalism and the Role of the State', *Government and Opposition* 13, 1978.

26. S. Clegg, G. Dow and P. Boreham, 'From the Politics of Production to the Production of Politics', *Thesis Eleven* 9, 1984. While they use the concept 'political
class struggle', Higgins and Esping-Andersen et al. fail to specify how this differs
from corporatism and precisely what is political in their notion of class struggle. See
W. Higgins, 'The Corporatism Thesis and Political Unionism', mimeo and G. Esping-
Andersen, R. Friedland and E. 0. Wright, 'Modes of Class Struggle and the Capitalist
State', *Kapitalistate* 4/5,1978, esp. 197 ff.

27. Newman, op. cit., 221.

28. Bob Jessop, 'Capitalism and Democracy: The Best Possible Political Shell?' in G. Lit-
tlejohn et al. (eds.) *Power and the State*, London, Croom Helm 1978, 45.

29. Offe has distinguished between 'market participants' who include not only classes
but also status and professional associations from 'policy takers'—taxpayers, welfare recipients, public hospitals etc. as potentially or actually corporatized. Cf. 'The
Attribution...', op. cit.

30. Cf. F. Feher and A. Heller, *Hungary 1956 Revisited*, London, George Allen and
Unwin, 1983.

31. Z. Bauman, *Memories of Class*, London, R.K.P. 1984, 19 .
32. ibid. 1–24 and Ch. 2–4.
33. The only exceptions here are Cawson, "Functional Representation...' op. cit. C. W. Anderson, 'Political Design and the Representation of Interests', *Comparative Political Studies*, Vol. 10 No. 1, April 1977 and the excellent attempt made by Philippe Schmitter to spell out the tensions between corporatist practice and democratic theory, 'Democratic Theory and Neocorporatist Practice', *Social Research*, Vol. 50 No. 4, 1983. The argument which follows owes to this and other works of Schmitter's, despite the fact that he is unable to theorize democracy in other than its infinitely adaptable, empirical forms. This, in our view, runs counter to the normative requirements of democracy, which he himself alludes to.
34. Andersen, ibid., 142.
35. For a discussion of this, see F. Feher and A. Heller, 'Forms of Equality', *Eastern Left, Western Left* op cit.
36. Carob Pateman, *Participation and Democratic Theory*, London, Cambridge 1970.
37. Schmitter, 'Democratic Theory...', op. cit., 920.
38. C. B. Macpherson, *Democratic Theory: Essays in Retrieval*, Oxford 1973, 78–9.
39. Offe, 'The Attribution...', op. cit., 151.
40. ibid., 132.
41. Habermas, *Legitimation Crisis*, op. cit., 70.
42. For a critique of Offe's radical functionalist standpoint along these lines, see Cohen, op. cit.
43. J. Habermas, 'New Social Movements'. *Telos*, 49,1981.

THE ANTI-TOTALITARIAN REVOLUTION

Edgar Morin

Even if we can guarantee nothing about the short-term future of the USSR we can be sure that those who have always been mistaken in their forecasts will continue to be so. Moreover, what is considered impossible by those feebleminded people who are incapable of seeing, let alone forecasting, is what is most likely to occur, for whatever the future of the USSR will be, whether militarist, bourgeois, or socialist, it will invalidate the myths of both Soviet communism and anti-communism. The future of the USSR will put the lie to all those who think they can enclose it in their rigid formulas; in short, those who would like to live with the illusion that there is no future.

(E. Morin, *The Future of Communism*, 1962)

The year 1989 has been characterized by a revolution which began in the USSR and was carried out in Poland, Hungary, East Germany, Czechoslovakia and Romania. It is not yet certain that this will lead to a firm basis for a democratic system, even though this revolution was inspired by a desire for democracy. Therefore, although the phrase is accurate, it does not go far enough to call this a democratic revolution. We can call it anti-totalitarian, however, insofar as it is overthrowing not just a dictatorship or tyranny, but the whole totalitarian system. So if we want to understand the revolution which is taking place it is essential to understand the variety of totalitarianism known as "communism".

WHAT IS TOTALITARIANISM?

What is totalitarianism? It is a system based on the monopoly of a party which is unique not only because it is the only party allowed to exist and to have power at its disposal, but also because it is a most unusual sort of party. It is a party in which all spiritual and temporal powers are concentrated in the apparatus which governs, controls and administers. (We may recall the cybernetic definition of the apparatus as a mechanism which controls a system without undergoing any reaction.) This apparatus can do anything and knows everything. It is a disciplinarian, an activist, a soldier, a director and a policeman, all rolled up into one. At the same time it is the sacred bearer of an absolute truth which has two grounds for its self-assurance. The first of these is the clear and visible scientific basis which is the knowledge of all truth concerning the world, especially the laws of history. The other is the deep hidden basis of religious conviction with its promise of earthly salvation revealed by these "laws of history".

With Stalin, the apparatus absorbs the party by exterminating the political leaders who had previously dominated it. He eliminated internal political debate by destroying the left and the right of the party, thereby making it "monolithic". Then, after the party is swallowed, the apparatus can speak on behalf of it, the proletariat, the people, the nation, humanity, science and history.

This apparatus-party is at the same time a party of the masses in the typical Leninist-Stalinist sense, which is to say that it is spread out into all the divisions and parts of society. The party of the masses means that all the blue and white collar workers, intellectuals, women, youth, children, housing, workshops and offices are controlled by the all-pervasive party. The party, being both of the apparatus and the masses, is doubly totalitarian. It controls all, knows everything, and is everywhere.

It is a mistake to imagine totalitarianism as the omnipotent power of the state. The state is completely dominated by the party-apparatus and hence becomes the instrument for the enslavement of all society. The state is not omnipotent but is subjected to the omnipotence of the party while at the same time enhancing it. That is why one of the main aspects of the anti-totalitarian revolution is the revival of the autonomy of the state and the corresponding withering away of the party's domination, right up to the point where it loses the political monopoly which guaranteed its totalitarian power.

The circular linkage of one control to another in the totalitarian system appears perfect: the party controls the state, the party's police controls the party, but the party controls the party's police. This all-too-perfect system can go haywire, however, as happened once in 1937–38. Nothing could stop the series of arrests until Stalin eliminated the major liquidator, Yagoda, and his successor, Yezhov. This loss of control looked like recurring a second time in 1953 until Stalin's death stopped the lunacy. On the other hand, this ultra-security-minded system has often gone astray on the occasion of crises of succession when it risks becoming two-headed. This occurred after Stalin's death when the head of the secret police, Beria, made a bid for supreme power and was eliminated by the rest of the party. Then, after Brezhnev's death, it was the policeman Andropov who gained control. This shows that the antitotalitarian revolution must abolish not only the omnipotence of the party, but also that of the secret police, which remains an enormous power in the heart of the state even after the party has withdrawn from the state.

What is also important with regard to totalitarianism is the need for the complete control of communication in order to have a monopoly on information and truth. This system is not only one which enforces censorship to stifle the explosive force of information, as other dictatorial systems do. It is also a system which presents the image of the blissful, unanimous, enthusiastic and transparent world of "really existing socialism". In this world there are no rail or air disasters, no catastrophes, certainly no strikes, no struggles and no conflict. If any faults or defects appear they are blamed on enemies, agents of capitalism, saboteurs, traitors or spies. The totalitarian control of the media also involves the control of vocabulary, and of the meaning of words and things. The party alone has the power to give names to things to identify good and evil. Its truth is presented as a reflection of how things are. This is the significance of "socialist realism", that things are as they should be. Moreover, official language via the media dictates to the reader and the viewer what people must say, as well as what must not be said if they wish to avoid denunciation and arrest. Hence the subjects of the system are forced to participate in an enormous farce and end up finding it natural to repeat this wooden language like zombies. For a long time this farce was very effective, as the majority of foreign visitors allowed themselves to be deceived, being unable to perceive that the unanimous consent of the "Soviet people" was a generalized lie.

Totalitarianism is a system which wants to become self-contained and to prohibit questions, and in addition it needs the gulag to eliminate not only different beliefs but also any possibility of their arising. The system is obsessed with being self-contained because, as I said in my book *On the Nature of the USSR*, this is precisely what it cannot fully be. Totalitarianism cannot be completely self-contained or else it would destroy itself by destroying its subjects, since "no-one is perfect" apart from the highest leaders in the party, and then only during their periods of supposed omnipotence.

There are always gaps and openings, but the system maintains its totalitarian character precisely by constantly acting to close them. This brings us up to the Gordian knowledge of totalitarianism which I defined in 1983 just when totalitarianism seemed all-powerful: it is a system which derives its enormous strength from its enormous weakness. The weakness is enormous because the system produces an economy which is both ultra-bureaucratic and ultra-anarchic; because it sustains a wide diversity of potentially divergent nationalities under an artificial constraint; because in the name of the working-class it prevents the working-class from expressing itself in unions, grievances and strikes; and because it is not able to tolerate political pluralism or to allow free elections.

Its weakness lies in its use of force to carry out its economic plans and thus to maintain an inefficient economy. But this force preserves the power of the repressive apparatus of totalitarianism. The weakness is that this force must tolerate a basic economic anarchy which is a manifestation of the population's resistance to the system; yet at the same time this resistance makes the system work, hence the impossible economy becomes possible. This impossible economy is the only one which allows the "Soviet" system to work. It becomes even less feasible when the ratio of force to anarchy is changed, and an attempt is made to introduce the freedom of the market. Herein lies the tragedy of perestroika, a tragedy which worsened during 1990: the impossible economy is losing what made it possible while the new possible economy is still impossible.

There is an enormous weakness in a system which claims to be the mouthpiece of the proletariat while not being able to give it the right to express itself, to strike and to form unions. However, this is also the strength of the system because it has at its disposal the force to forbid self-expression, strikes and unions. Moreover, thanks to the silencing of the proletariat, totalitarianism was able, for half a century, to convince a large part of the world, including capitalists and the majority of intellectuals, that it was really a proletarian government.

It is essential for totalitarianism to always censure; this is both its weakness (it changes the smallest critical remark into a treasonable crime), and its strength (it prohibits expression of even the smallest critical remark). It is a system which has its strength in its weakness in another sense in that it is not capable of becoming democratic without destroying itself. (Gorbachev's miracle was that he undertook a process of democratization and did it so slowly that the apparatus was not able to immediately perceive the deadly threat to its power and thus to destroy this process. Yet at the same time he did it so swiftly that the system was not able to suppress the change.)

Totalitarianism, therefore, is a system which has developed a tremendous strength because of its innate and infinite weakness. From the years 1920–24, the last years of Lenin, all the Bolsheviks understood that the world revolution would not break out in the immediate future; that Russia was in a terrible state; that there was no socialist culture; and that life there was unbearable. From this failure was born the success of the Stalinist myth of socialism in one country, which contradicted classical Marxism, but which shaped the creation of a pseudo-socialism as well as of a great industrial power. The attempt to create a socialist culture and society failed and it is this failure which led to the successful creation of an enormous industrial power.

The second great failure was that of Khrushchev who was unable to complete a process of real liberalization in the USSR, and who repressed this liberalizing process in its satellite countries by crushing the Hungarian revolution (1956). The failure of his reform brought about the hegemonist solution, namely the development of the military industrial complex. The system, incapable of self-reform, looked for salvation in global domination. Starting in

1962 (the Cuban missile crisis), and continuing until 1985, a politics of global expansion developed, taking advantage of the opportunities afforded by Latin-American, African, and Asian situations. We can say that the dialectical interplay between the enormous weakness and enormous strength of the system worked in favour of power from 1919 to 1985. Everything that should have brought down the system turned out to be useful for it. Of course there was an historic opportunity, brought about by the failure of the German offensive against Moscow in 1941, Hitler's strategic errors, and some political aberrations germane to Nazism, such as the politics of colonization of Eastern Europe which brought enslavement to the Ukrainians (who had previously welcomed the Germans as liberators) and hence transformed them into opponents of Hitlerism.

The difference this time lies in the transformation of this dialectic at the very centre of the enormous strength, the Kremlin, and not at the outskirts. It was however in the outskirts, the captive nations (where totalitarian power was the instrument of a foreign force), that the revolts had first broken out, showing the enormous weakness of the supposedly indigenous communist power in East Germany, Poland, Hungary, and Czechoslovakia. This first began in 1953, with the uprising in East Germany crushed by the "Soviet" tanks; then in 1956, the Hungarian revolution was also crushed by the "Soviet" tanks; the same year revolution was prevented in Poland solely because of the intervention that had taken place in Hungary; and in 1968 the Prague Spring was crushed, once again by "Soviet" tanks. All these revolts were on the way to success and it is precisely for that reason they were crushed, their fate determined by the enormous concentrated central power in Moscow.

THE BREAKING OF THE VESSELS

By the end of the 1950s we had come to the conclusion that the system could only be reformed from the centre. But at the same time reform seemed even less possible because we could only see the enormous strength emanating from the Kremlin and we could not take into account that what was the centre of strength was also the centre of weakness. For we must not forget that the events of Hungary, East Germany, Czechoslovakia and Romania in 1989 were only made possible because revolutionary reform had begun in Moscow with perestroika. Of course, it was not Gorbachev who instigated the collapse of the system in Berlin, who inspired the emancipation of Prague, or who prompted the explosive events in Romania. However, if there had not been the great beginning of the democratizing process in Moscow in Spring 1989, these upheavals would never have taken place, or if they had, they would have been bloodily put down.

Nevertheless in the 1980s Poland and Hungary had ceased to be orthodox "people's republics". In Poland the Solidarity Union had driven a wedge into the system, dug itself in, and had been able to win a small symbolic victory with the installation of a military man (no longer the General Secretary of the party) in the most powerful position. However, although Poland was the country furthest along the path of anti-totalitarianism in June 1989 (when elections took place which were half-rigged but half-free), the heroic Verdun of Solidarnosc meant that the country remained temporarily backward while the offensive for liberty broke out everywhere else. On the eve of 1989 in Hungary, the system was becoming more relaxed and open. This factor was crucial for the unleashing of the revolutionary wave in the "people's democracies". Hungary's decision to lift the tiny fragment of the iron curtain which separated it from Austria had an extraordinary thermodynamic effect. With this unexpected break occurred the even less foreseeable flood into the neighbouring republics of holidaying East German youth. Then, due to a veritable chain reaction, the tiny break in the Hungarian barbed wire made the collapse of the Berlin Wall possible within a few weeks, and this led in turn to the downfall of the Prague Kafkaesque castle. So we can see that 1989, which was an amazing year for Eastern Europe, benefited from special conditions, from fortuitous coincidences, and from unexpected events. The gradual course of events could only have begun in the Muscovite capital, and could only have spread as it did because Hungary, already on the path of liberalization, suddenly opened a crack which released a torrid flood. This then changed into the huge historic whirlpool of the anti-totalitarian revolution.

Let us reject the absurd determinism which believes that the *fait accompli* is inevitable and that the unleashing of a revolution is controlled from a distance by "historical necessity". The anti-totalitarian revolution was not inevitable in 1989 or even in the 20th century. Totalitarianism, in the decisive year 1934, could have diminished instead of growing had Kirov and his allies removed Stalin from his throne instead of being destroyed by him. Today people try to forget the extraordinary characteristic of this event by *a posteriori* rationalization. An economistic commonplace tells us that perestroika is an inevitable consequence of the USSR's economic failure; up to recently it was these failures that had determined the movement of the USSR into hegemonism. The economic failure was a failure that was not a failure, since, although the economy's mixture of bureaucracy and anarchy worked rather poorly, it did in fact continue to work, while at the same time the military-industrial complex developed rather well and continued to do so. Perestroika was not the outcome of a short economic crisis; on the contrary, it was perestroika which precipitated a crisis in the authoritarian/anarchic economy. Of course there had been a deep hidden crisis which the intelligentsia, the technical experts and a part of the party were becoming aware of, namely the crisis of "really existing socialism" which was incapable of arranging the future politically, socially, and of course economically, although it had been promising to do this since 1924. The reformer, Khrushchev, was still able to naively believe that it was enough to deStalinize in order to achieve a rational economy of abundance under the wise guidance of the party. Thirty years later, this illusion had disappeared.

A CHANGE OF DIRECTION

It was under these conditions that Gorbachev made a choice. An historic change of direction, imposed by one man and a very restricted group of people, was able to be enforced because it had key military support for key positions from the beginning. Another General Secretary, his predecessor for example, would not inevitably have made this choice, the proof being that there were in the political system some very powerful enemies of the reform when it showed its true face. So Gorbachev's decision was truly momentous and offered an extraordinary historic opportunity.

Why did it start at the head of the system? We must begin with the initial choice which was economic and technocratic, and whose consequences Gorbachev could not weigh.

The reformers were people who deplored the fact that their civil economy was weak in relation to the capitalist countries, despite the enormous wealth of the USSR. They wanted to be modernizers and renovators, wanted to bring in reforms, sports, oil, machinery and new opportunities. This became all the more desirable since they had lost faith in the economic efficiency of the ultra-centralized/planned/bureaucratized system called socialism. These reformers had time to become informed and reflect during the "stagnation years" of Brezhnevism. They were able to acquire information and see the economic success of the "capitalist" market economy. They had lost their faith in the future of their bureaucratic economic system and the only faith in the future that they could now maintain depended on the success of their reforms. They were also reformers in the sense of a lost faith in the supposed superiority of so-called socialism over so-called capitalism in the areas of humanity, society, and culture; they had lost faith in themselves as bearers of the salvation of humanity; and they had lost faith in the idea that they had a monopoly on the meaning of history. This loss of faith is inseparable from the withering away of Marxism, accompanied by an internal secret rot which sets free something in these reformers that has nurtured Marxism from its origins, that is, European humanism. Marxism was nurtured on great ideas which were expressed in the philosophy of the Enlightenment, in the French Revolution, and in German philosophy. The idea inherent to Marxism, that we must work for the improvement of the fate of humanity, had been turned away from this goal by the apparatus in order to justify all its acts. This notion appears revitalized in the universalist idea of belonging to a common human civilization without any appropriation of the destiny of humanity by the party. As a supporter of perestroika told me in Moscow in 1988, "We are all in the Titanic rushing in the night towards the same iceberg". All this surfaces in Gorbachev's "new way of thinking".

When did it begin? How did the intellectual evolution of this person develop to the point of becoming a "new way of thinking"? Let us note that the Number One apparatchik, Gorbachev, was not alone; he had a wife, Raisa, who was cultivated and had no doubt been open for a long time to the ideas expressed by writers banned during the Brezhnev era. There were also young people in the families of these apparatchiks who, by enjoying such privileges as being able to make tiny acts of non-conformism, with impunity, could express their criticism and desires. Thus there is through women and the young an umbilical cord to the Russian intelligentsia, whose samizdats had been expressing the need for freedom. As a result, a tiny intellectual milieu was formed around a modernist elite of apparatchiks and constituted a favourable cultural environment in which the "new way of thinking" could develop. It was necessary, however, to wait for three years to see if perestroika would survive. In addition, before the will to reform could radicalize and turn into a political movement, the failure of the first of the economic reforms and the discovery of the moronic resistance of the apparatus had to occur.

So the "deviation" started from above, which is to say that instead of being repressed it was promoted by those in power. (This also explains why it had been continually held back by and within the apparatus, which had to undergo a reform coming from its centre while resisting it.) For this reason it had succeeded in its first steps, even if long-term failure was still possible. In any case Gorbachev was a Moses even if he could not see the promised land, even if there was no promised land.

THE REVOLUTION

In order to understand the nature and scope of this revolution, we must relate it to two factors. Firstly, to the totalitarian system set up by the concentrated centralized power of the party. Secondly, to the imperial political axis which tends towards world hegemony in an attempt to escape the internal deficiency of the economic system. The only way to achieve this without actually altering the system was by profiting from developed economies which had been subjugated.

The reforms began slowly in 1986, taking the form of perestroika/glasnost in 1986 to 1988, and become a truly transforming process in 1989–90. In 1989 the revolution began in the USSR and paradoxically this allowed it to commence, develop and spread at an incredible pace over a short period of time, in Hungary, East Germany, Czechoslovakia, and Romania. A weakening at the centre of power in Moscow was all that was needed for everything to collapse on the boundaries.

The revolution that begins in the USSR simultaneously affected the basis of both internal and external politics. As we have pointed out, the two sides are interconnected. The renunciation of hegemony is a key aspect of the revolution. Political strategy becomes directed toward internal reform and away from the domination of the outside world. In 1987 a treaty is signed agreeing to the dismantling of short and medium range missiles. In 1988, a decision is made to cease the war in Afghanistan, and several moderating initiatives are taken on the occasions of international conflicts. Finally, in 1989, a policy of non-intervention prevails as revolutions occur in the people's democracies. It is now clear that the Gorbachev movement leads to the renunciation not only of expansionism but also of the domination of the Eastern bloc. From 1989 onwards, the change in the political course is demonstrable.

The internal revolution begins with the two inseparable joint reforms of glasnost and perestroika. Glasnost, starting off slowly, gradually grows, until in the summer of 1990, it introduces the right to free expression, and the freedom of the press. A person looking at glasnost from a strictly empirical point of view, and unaware that systematic deception is essential for totalitarianism, would think only that just one more censorship had disappeared. But to look at glasnost from the point of view of the totalitarian system reveals that it has the effect of a torpedo which hits the engine room beneath the waterline. Glasnost is not in itself decisive, but it is necessary if a decisive transformation is to take place, since one of the props of the system is the gulagization of information, words and ideas. Glasnost is the simultaneous degulagization of information, images, words and ideas. This results in both a corresponding degulagization of culture, and the re-entry of the intelligentsia into the public arena.

At this point let us remember that from the 19th century onwards the intelligentsia played a major ethical and political role in Russia, especially as political parties had been suppressed in Tsarist Russia, and were later crushed by Lenin and destroyed by Stalin. From Khrushchev's time onwards, especially during the Breshnev era, the intelligentsia fought solidly for respect for facts and for historical truth. The Russian intelligentsia has two great symbolic figures: one, Solzhenitsyn, who focuses on Slavophilism, religion and literature; the other, Sacharov, who focuses on the West, humanism, and science. These men, each opposite to, yet complementing the other, present an unequivocal message of opposition to deception. The entrance of the intelligentsia to the arena, in and through glasnost, plays an enormous role and creates the climate necessary for the awakening life. This is also done under the impulse of the media, in which the intelligentsia has recently been active.

The first instance of this awakening occured in May 1986 at the congress of film-producers, which elected Klimov as its president. Soon afterwards, works previously thrown into the sewers of the system (which detests honour and integrity) re-emerge. At last the great honest novels appear: *The Children Arbat* in 1987, *Doctor Zhivago* in 1988. Thus, glasnost created the conditions for intellectual ferment, which in turn made democratic ferment possible. Here we have the beginning of a key process which will undermine the very foundation of the system: the omnipotence of the apparatus.

Although the anti-totalitarian revolution unfolds in the satellite nations in 1989, at that point only one decisive part of this process had been carried out. Only in 1990, although still incomplete, does it become irreversible. From the end of 1989, the abolition de jure of the legitimacy of the absolute power of the apparatus completes the anti-totalitarian revolution in the people's democracies. This further stimulates and accelerates the process leading to the repeal of the Article which promulgates and assures the divine right of party, Article 6.

The repeal of this Article is not only symbolic, it is also a matter of principle: the principle of public rights and the mythological legitimization of the totalitarianism system; and the principle of popular sovereignty itself. This is why the anti-totalitarian revolution, in all the popular democracies, has laid down quite clearly the abolition of the offensive article by which the apparatus had proclaimed itself absolute sovereign as one of its main objectives and first achievements. According to a circular logic, everything that affects the state truth of Marxism-Leninism affects it as if the veracity of the State and the legitimacy of the party depended on it. So what stands or falls with Article 6 is not only a political monopoly, but also a sacred power, that of the Magi, bearers of truth, incarnated in the beastly heads of the apparatchiks. In Moscow, Article 6 was not removed until February 1990. This achievement not only results in the establishment of a democracy, but is also the single most decisive step in the abolition of totalitarian power.

So the historical whirlwind had left Moscow only to return with a vengeance in 1990. Beginning in the summer of 1989, this whirlwind sets in motion the events in Poland, Hungary, East Germany and Romania. Thanks to Moscow, these countries carried out the anti-totalitarian revolution before Moscow itself did. Everywhere, the monopoly of the party is annulled and the party as an apparatus, based on both democratic centralism and the myth of the possession of truth etc., self-destructs and tries to reconstruct itself in another shape while painfully seeking a social democratic face. In some cases the party splits up, in others it evaporates as happened in Romania (where the party which comprised three quarters of the population disappeared into a black hole in the space of a day). The multi-party system has been established everywhere, and accompanied by a corresponding upsurge of all types of parties. Unions have appeared, the state's autonomy has been restored, and the military wing of the party, directly dependent on the apparatus, has been rationalized and demilitarized. In all these totalitarian systems the party had a military body which was often better equipped than the army (even in the USSR, the KGB had an army, airforce, factories, etc.), as well as its own SS and red Gestapo such as the Stasi and Securitate, which were units dedicated to internal repression. Now the militia is either being removed from the party secretariat and handed over to the government (as in Hungary), or purely and simply destroyed. In the USSR, however, some important bastions of the dismantled totalitarian system still resisted. The huge party was not yet reduced to the condition of an ordinary party, as it retained at least initially its goods, its properties, and its internal and external networks, especially those of the KGB and the army. The party, which was in fact conservative, becomes, in turn, reactionary by making an alliance with all that is anti-democratic and aggressively nationalist in Russia, through which it seeks to restore itself. The KGB can continue to direct things from the shadows without being subject to control by the elected authorities. A process of osmosis occurs between the conservatives of the army which is no longer monolithic and the conservatives of the apparatus. The anti-totalitarian revolution, so quick to erupt in the captive nations, finds it extremely difficult to make headway in an empire which after sixty-nine years bears the deep scars of the most extraordinary system of totalitarianism that history has ever produced.

THE DISINTEGRATION OF TOTALITARIANISM

So what held together at the centre of the totalitarian system now fragments, disperses and disintegrates. The police-militia loses its temporal power which slips away from it along with its spiritual power over sociological and historical truth. It starts to lose its grip on the state and its power over the masses.

The anti-totalitarian revolution, by making the party surrender cultural and economic power, forces it to release its hold on the state which then recovers its relative autonomy. The revolution compels the party to become a normal political one. In the cultural and economic spheres, the party loses its quasi-religious function; it loses its function as a policeman, and its military function, both of which are transferred to the state. In other words, the enormous strength which lay in the heavy concentration of all the party's powers no longer exists. A heavily centralized system collapses along with its centre, as happened to the divine power of the Incas whose empire collapsed once it and its court became captive. In Czechoslovakia, a bunch of arrogant apparatchiks, though armed to the teeth, was not able to withstand the crowd at close quarters. We witnessed on TV the extraordinary phenomenon of Ceausescu's amazement during a mass demonstration which should have gone smoothly, since the dictator had organized it himself, and how instead he fled after jeering broke out.

The beginning of a class struggle accompanies the destruction of the monopolist multifunction power of the party. It is noteworthy that it is in the so-called socialist countries that this struggle regains youthful vitality. This is because there was a gulf, a decisive gap almost without intermediaries, between "them" (the apparatchiks, the privileged nomenclature) and "us" (all who are deprived of rights and privileges, special shops, comfortable homes, private quarters, official dachas, and official vehicles). This class consciousness becomes epidemic with the disclosure of the widespread corruption of the ruling class (it is only Western intellectuals who imagine the apparatchiks to be impartial, incorruptible puritans, inspired by a burning faith, when in reality an extraordinary moral disintegration accompanies the internal disintegration of their faith). So the thaw awakens the class struggle. Nevertheless, the class struggle is diminished and even inhibited by the fact that the revolution in the USSR belongs to the top of the apparatus rather than to the popular base. Also, in the people's democracies, this revolution takes place in a peaceful manner by way of an historic compromise, consciously accepted by both sides to avoid bloodshed. Indeed the revolution takes place by virtue of a gradual passage of change instead of by a decisive confrontation. The change presumes an historic compromise with the rulers and profiteers from the old regime, who are forced to give up their power in exchange for the renunciation of any retribution, revenge or purge. It was such an historic compromise that Juan Carlos negotiated in Spain between Francoists and democrats, when the Francoists let events take their course in exchange for not being purged or judged.

In the USSR, and in the people's democracies, the underlying historic compromise is due to the absence of both bloody purges and judicial proceedings, not only against party officials and bureaucrats, but also against those responsible for massacres, deportations, obscene trials, and assassinations. This revolution is amazingly restrained in comparison to others. Such restraint brings to mind the similar behaviour of Spain, when the Francoists were forced out and replaced by new democratic functionaries. Up to the present (we cannot predict the future) the anti-totalitarian revolution has been taking place peacefully by virtue of the implicit historic compromise between those who formerly had an absolute monopoly on power and the new authorities which include deserters and converts from the previous regime. The advantage of the above compromise obviously lies in the non-violent nature of this revolution.

The non-violent course of the anti-totalitarian revolution undoubtedly relates to the fact that its initial impulse was given by Gorbachev, a figure of compromise and transition who has led political reform from 1987 to 1989 in a way which was slow enough to avoid unleashing a confrontation, but rapid enough to actually cause change. For this reason, the party did not feel the need to act with the power of despair, or to kill to survive. Instead it was offered a face-saving way out, and even given sinecures. Even so, nothing was pre-ordained. Honecker could have fired on the crowd like President Deng did in Tiananmen Square in China and had he done so, the Stalinists in Prague would have followed his example which would have encouraged the Stalinists in Moscow. All these people had been capable in the past and remained capable in 1989 of repeatedly killing to protect their authority. Destiny, which after some hesitation, leaned towards the side of repression in Peking, tilted towards the side of liberalization in Moscow. Why did the despots of

Germany and Czechoslovakia not kill when they still held all the power? Because they knew that this time the Russians would not intervene to suppress the movement. Once it is no longer sustained by the massive power of the USSR, their own strength diminishes as its enormous weakness becomes apparent. So seemingly omnipotent totalitarianism rapidly loses all its substance and effectiveness.

The non-violent nature of the revolution was indispensable for the introduction of democracy. A democracy requires the existence and activity of conflicts, but it is even more important that they do not become extreme and take a violent form, since unleashing violence during a revolutionary period could result in either the victory of a counter-revolution, or a civil war whose outcome if unforeseeable would in any case be non-democratic. All this, whilst still in progress, will continue to pose numerous problems as the absence of a purge means that many elements of the ancient regime remain embedded in the state structures.

Future generations will have to marvel at the extraordinary sequence of events from 1987 to Spring 1990. In the early period progress was slow, up to the emergence of two key themes, glasnost and perestroika, starting was a slow process. Then Gorbachev's pilotage, while at times gaining momentum and at other times slowing, was never neutralized or even checked, nor was it destabilizing though it sometimes reached its limit. This was achieved against the party from within the party, and was facilitated by the Stalinist habit of always agreeing with the General Secretary. He brought about democratic renewal by using the old authoritarian methods. The torrent of events, because of social and national outbreaks, was always headed towards a dismemberment of the extraordinary totalitarian system. From the summer of 1990, though not dispossessed, Gorbachev was forced to work alongside Yeltsin in domestic affairs. This alliance, though fragile, linked the reforming current to the other economic revolution. In any case, the eventual success of Gorbachev's perestroika can only serve to make him lose his authority as chief pilot, and transform him into a federation president.

The anti-totalitarian revolution of itself results in two other revolutions in the USSR whose final outcomes are still unknown:

1. an economic revolution, which could hypothetically transform an ultra-regulated state economy into an economy which is not entirely market-dominated, but in which the market can bring its stimuli and regulations into play is logically unimaginable. For if the transformation were to be carried out violently, the whole society would be destabilized; yet if it were to be carried out gradually it would not work, as the system would suppress any piecemeal reforms one by one. It has been left to life and art, both of which demand ingenuity and improvization, to deal concretely with this problem which neither Western economists (who understand market economies, but not transitions

from totalitarian systems to market economies), nor Eastern ones (who have the opposite problem) can resolve. It is even possible that there will be a period of confusion when a turning away from or even overturning the democratic process could occur;

2. a revolution at the federal level which will transform the empire called the Soviet Union into a confederation of nationalities.

These three revolutions are all interdependent. If the first, the political one, commences before the others (all the more so because the economic reform set in motion in 1986 has been ineffective at the heart of the old political system), it risks experiencing disastrous repercussions during the period of transition when the old system is collapsing before a new one has been born. In this instance, the anti-totalitarian revolution, instead of leading on to a stable democracy, could spill into a nationalist/militarist dictatorship where the born-again conservatives could take their revenge. Similarly, the revolution at the federal level could run aground under the strain of both centrifugal nationalist pressures and economic crises. The three revolutions co-determine and affect each other so they may end up either stimulating or destroying each other.

THE END OF THE SOVIET SYSTEM

The anti-totalitarian revolution does not of itself resolve the problem of nationalities in either the USSR or the former people's democracies, all of which have their own national minorities. It could even be said that the revolution sets free nationalist sentiments and tends to reawaken memories of ethnic, religious and national conflicts which had been put on ice.

In the USSR, the problem is to overturn a de facto empire and transform it into a confederation or a genuine federation. It is a matter of resolving extremely acute national problems, because as these nationalities have been subjugated by conquest they have developed nationalist sentiments whose strength has been augmented by Russian domination which was regarded as a foreign occupation. These nationalist sentiments have different manifestations in the Baltic States (which became part of the USSR by an agreement between Stalin and Hitler) and Armenia, Azerbaidjan, and Georgia. These problems are highly complicated and will require great acumen from both the Kremlin and the national leaders of these countries if they are to unite successfully in a confederation. An event of great significance occurred at the beginning of Summer 1990 when the Russian National Assembly proclaimed the sovereignty of Russia in relation to the Soviet Union. This proclamation had been both preceded and followed by similar ones in practically all of the republics. But it was fundamental to the outcome of these proclamations that the Russian nation itself be dissociated not only from the fiction of a soviet confederation but also from a strictly imperial system. We can scarcely imagine England or

France proclaiming their sovereignty in relation to their own empires at the end of the Second World War. This proclamation of Russian sovereignty is not only an expression of a movement of national regeneration which takes advantage of the anti-totalitarian revolution to free itself. It also establishes a strong link between the reforming party and Russian national sentiment which dissociates itself from the Great-Russian hegemonism inherited from Tsarism and taken over by the Soviet system. Of course, chauvinistic and Great-Russian nationalists who are currently still in a minority would have an historic opportunity if the reformers experience an economic failure. Such a course of events would tragically plunge the Great-Russian people back into the centuries-old historical disaster which the "innocent one" sings about at the end of Boris Godunov:

> Flow, flow, flow bitter tears
> Weep, weep, Christian soul
> Soon the enemy will come and darkness will fall
> A darkness black and impenetrable
> Woe, woe to Russia
> Weep, weep Russian People, hungry people.

It is quite possible that this decolonization will lead to the partial if not total break-up of the empire with a secession of the Islamic nationalities of the South East; and/or the joining together of secessionist Baltic countries into a group of adjoining Nordic coastal states. History is hesitating, it has not yet made a final decisive change of direction. We do not know if the process which has so far only experienced localized short-term crises will remain peaceful or ignite the flames of war. Similarly, we do not know whether the combination of the desovietization of the USSR with the new national problems in the former people's democracies, and with the German re-unification, will provide a widespread Balkanization including both East and West Europe, or a general affirmation of federative treaties.

We are not saying that democracy can in the long run simply establish itself on the ruins of totalitarianism. But in any case the oppressive burden of totalitarianism which looked as though it would continue past the year 2000 appears to have been lifted. This does not exclude the possible appearance of a new totalitarian formula in the next century. Nor does it mean that we will be relieved of similar offensive phenomena once and for all. Such things have existed from time immemorial and will continue to plague our present age in various fanatical religious, racist and nationalist forms. However, unless we witness the birth and world expansion of a new third form of totalitarianism in a future age, these phenomena will have local and temporary manifestations, but not a universal form endowed with the power of unlimited self-reproduction. The DNA code of the system has been ruptured and the totalitarian system which deceitfully called itself socialism is genetically dead. This is the legacy of our fading 20th century. It has shattered the myth of the glorious future, and the comforting message for the next generation is that this myth is dead.

But in this difficult age of ours which has been deprived of this myth, forces of the past have been unleashed, and people are living in the present, without a future. When will we be able to imagine a type of future both fragile and uncertain yet able to give us hope?

Notes

*   The first version of this text was published in the journal *Libération* in February 1990; the present revised and expanded version was included in the book *Un nouveau commencement* by E. Morin, G. Bocchi and M. Ceruti, Editions de Seuil, March 1991. It is reprinted here with the permission of the publishers. Although Morin's reflections are concerned with an early phase of the Eastern European revolution, their relevance to more recent events should not be overlooked. They are, for one, a useful reminder that the anti-totalitarian revolution should not be identified with the transition to democracy; the former has made the latter possible, but by no means certain.

THE LEFT AFTER COMMUNISM

Ferenc Fehér

I

Are we after communism? Strong counterindications seem to warn us against making such a sweeping statement. After all, China, Vietnam, North Korea and Cuba are still existing communist powers, notwithstanding their—already manifest—internal crises varying in form from country to country. And yet, to turn a term of communist jargon against communism, measured "with historical standards", communism is defunct. The major battlefields on which it expired were Eastern Europe and the Soviet Union, in that order. And since the latter had been the birthplace and the crucial testing ground for the communist project, communism's gradual dissolution in the heartland of the gigantic social experiment is a symbolic event.

In Eastern Europe, there is no need for hesitation in discussing the demise of communism. In the centre of the region, in the countries traditionally close to, or forming part of, Europe (Czechoslovakia, Hungary, Poland, East Germany, Croatia and Slovenia), the successor parties of, till recently, ruling communism never polled above 20 percent in the first free elections, and often much lower. In fact, the only surprise that remains to be explained sociologically was that they were not far less successful.[1] (True enough, where an unreconstructed communist group appeared on the political scene, with unchanged rhetorics and aggressiveness, such as the MSZP in Hungary, it could never scrape together the minimal number of votes necessary for getting into the new parliament.) Where the communists wanted to attain any degree of credibility, they had to change the name of their party, also, in great haste, their ideological outlook as well as selecting a new history for themselves.[2] These radical changes were not necessarily mere cosmetic operations. In almost all East-Central European communist parties, a subterranean demi-opposition, or groups of the disaffected, have been present for a long time. The parties were also increasingly exposed to the ideological barrage of the democratic

Thesis Eleven 27
©1990 *Thesis Eleven*

opposition in their respective countries. At least some of them, the likeliest candidate being the Hungarian MSZP, may embark on a genuine transition to social democracy.

In two countries, Romania and Bulgaria, the successors to communism achieved stunning electoral victories. These events, which contradict simplistic expectations, can again be accounted for by a number of scenarios, ranging, as a rule, from an explanation about the weakness of civil society to allegations of electoral fraud. Whatever the truth might be, communism had to pay so heavy a price for being accepted by the electorate in Bulgaria and Romania also, that it would have been inconceivable for them just four or five years ago. The successor parties had to change their names. They had to renounce their ideology publicly and ostentatiously. In Romania, they even had to formally dissolve, and for a few hours of hysteria, legally ban their own party. In both countries they had to abdicate their former role as the party sovereign in state affairs.

Equally important, the defeat of communism was, with the exception of Romania, a fairly peaceful process in which none of the usual communist predictions about a bloodbath staged by the "white terror" came true. (Even in Romania, after the cruel repressions of the regime during the last days of its existence, the execution of the ruling couple ushered in the abolition of capital punishment.) This peaceful overthrow of a long-lasting and extremely violent regime not only put its enemies into a morally superior position, it also demonstrated the—to put it mildly—slender roots of the communist regime, once it was lacking in foreign military support.

In the Soviet Union, whose leadership played the key triggering role in the revolutions of East-Central Europe, the process of dissolution lagged behind the pace of changes in Eastern Europe, for historical and sociological reasons. Numbers have an added social power, and the ten to fifteen million apparatchiks who, regardless of whether or not they were card-carrying members of the party, ran the country seemingly since time immemorial, constitute a medium-sized European country in themselves. They still have the ultimate say in local and central issues, and they can efficiently manipulate elections, as was been shown by the composition of the delegates of the Twenty-Eighth Party Congress. But when they lost constitutional recognition as the ruling party, and were ousted in an increasing number of local and federal elections, and they tolerated, in impotent rage, the rule of the clique of Gorbachev and Co. over them which they, for good reasons, regarded as no better than a conspiracy. Put simply, they no longer had the courage to present their own option to the country without double talk, and in the end futility, as the August 1991 attempted coup indicated.

Two additional factors are perhaps historically even more crucial. First, Soviet communism ceased, even nominally, to be the carrier of a universalist project. Practically, it has not fulfilled this role for decades. The crucial moment of rupture was the break with Chinese communism. In this dramatic hour, it became clear, clearer than it had been at the time of the break with Tito's Yugoslavia, that historic sentimentality about the birthright of Soviet communism would not prevail between communists when the chips were down, that communism had become an easily appropriable power technology catering to nationalist elites. Nevertheless, the Brezhnevites were rightly concerned with a formal abdication from the role of at least a *primus inter pares* in the communist family. Hence their spasmodic, and ultimately failed, efforts to keep together the world movement in the form of spectacular and meaningless conferences, the cliches of which were not regarded as binding even at the very hour when the participants reluctantly agreed to their acceptance.

This is now all over. The Gorbachev leadership became openly hostile to certain Asian communist parties in power (above all, to the North Korean); its relationship to Cuba was, at best, formal and polite, at worst, it became marked by reciprocal accusations. Certain troublesome communist, crypto-communist and potentially communist Middle East and African allies were given short shrift. The Afghan communists, after being supported in their worst excesses, were clearly left to their own devices, except for massive armament support. In Eastern Europe, not only did the Soviet Union not support the communist leaderships, their own appointees, in suppressing the fermenting revolt in the fashion of Tiananmen Square; occasionally, primarily in East Germany and Czechoslovakia, they formally restrained them.[3] Moreover, there was absolutely no overt sign of Soviet willingness to supervise, in the good old bolshevik fashion, their regrouping under the new circumstances. Equally clearly, the last Soviet leaders did not make the slightest effort to halt or slow down the steep decline of communism in Western Europe. In this arena, after the complete volte-face of Italian communism, there are only two genuine communist parties with a following that counts in national politics, although they too are gradually being marginalized: the communist parties of France and Portugal.

It might be of minor importance in pragmatic terms, but for communist self-understanding it is a crucial sign of decline or total defeat that there is not a single theoretically relevant or even debatable communist explanation of their own devastating fiasco. Compare the embarrassed and empty apologies of yesterday's haughty dictators,[4] the smooth metamorphoses of orthodox Stalinists into neo-Thatcherites, the conspiracy theories[5] as the best available account for a world-historic debacle, coupled in the surviving cells of communism with an unrepentant arrogance which denies co-responsibility for some of the most horrendous crimes of recorded history, with the moral and intellectual level of communist self-awakening in the 1920s. In the early 1920s, communism suffered crippling defeats, despite its apparently overwhelming victory in the Russian civil war. The world revolution never came. Communists could hang on to power in Russia only by renouncing some of their major ideological tenets and by introducing the NEP which evidently remained a mystery for the architects of this policy—both for Lenin and Bukharin. They were set back in all major arenas of the European class struggle, above all in Germany and Italy. Their bet on India proved to be misleading, their intervention in China a disaster. Stalin's defiant slogan of "socialism in one country" was more of an admission of defeat than a blueprint for communists outside Russia And yet, at that time communism was still capable of responding to its own critical situation on such a high intellectual and artistic level that although the products of that era can now be relegated from our daily readings to the background of the cultural stage they cannot be disparaged. From Lukacs's and Gramsci's philosophies, both major comments on the defeat, to the sociological serious-ness of the first Trotskyite analyses (which cannot be compared to the paucity of the writings of their heirs and successors), through the novels of Silone or Malraux, communist self-reappraisal was conducted with a kind of earnestness which is always a sign of the existing vitality of a movement. Even on the op-posite pole, amid Stalin's victorious and murderous apparatus, there remained certain elements of theoretical ingeniousness. Ultimately, they, and not pri-marily Mussolini or Hitler, invented the blueprint for totalitarian rule, a power technology which operated for decades as the universal, easily administered wonder drug for all new elites vying for power. This intellectual, if often infer-nal, vitality is now gone. While communists, fallen from power, occasionally ponder one or another of their own misconceived tactical moves, their defeat remains a closed book to themselves. Nor do they seem to understand any longer who they are, what kind of historic needs they satisfy, if indeed they cannot consider themselves to be the anointed agents of a miraculous devel-opment of "the most progressive mode of production" and the repository of "substantive rationality", actors, having a special dispensation from History to act in any way they deem fit.

With a grain of Hegelianism, this increasing lack of self-awareness can be said to constitute a major identity crisis, for there is no self-identity without self-consciousness. (And the desperately preserved self-identity of those com-munists who simply refuse to look the catastrophic fiasco of their cause in the face, is a religious gesture, irrelevant to the solution of a self-identity crisis.) Typical of an *ecclesia militans*, which kept its inquisitors busy, but reduced its major theologians to silence, and which, therefore, was only capable of per-secuting never of assimilating its heretics, communism now has no fall-back ideologies. Even the heretics have left the Church, becoming progressively convinced of the project's ultimate barrenness.

II

What has communism, now historically defunct, left behind? Economi-cally, bankruptcy and chaos of such magnitude that often even old-time critics are flabbergasted. The traditional line of objective criticism of the communist project was a reluctant recognition of the stuntmanship of the omnipotent plan-ners, coupled with the rejection of the price that had to be paid for its dazzling results in terms of liberties and human lives.[6] But when now the whole of what was the Soviet economy is in a shambles, the questions seem to be justified: where is the celebrated stuntmanship now? More important, was the earlier performance of the omnipotent planners largely a matter of window-dressing and doctored statistics?

Four major factors of the present steep economic decline can be listed which in combination prove how futile every single attempt to reform the communist command economy on its own premises had been. First, the *nomenklatura* was incapable of emancipating the surreptitiously growing semi-markets within its system and transforming them into "normal" markets, pri-marily into a functioning market of consumer goods. More precisely, it was too rigid, far too accustomed to its absolute prerogatives, to pay the political price for such a transformation.[7] Second, Stalin's omnipotent planners achieved their stunning victories at a time when the capitalist world-market made its first, as yet uncertain steps, in the direction of a coordinated global econ-omy. When the latter emerged in the post-World War II period, when both the technological preconditions (in the form of the achievements of the in-formation revolution) and the political framework (the Western alliance) were present to facilitate its triumphal march, the *nomenklatura* either had to come up with an alternative option or perish. The fact is that Stalin and his theory of the two world-markets,[8] in other words, the thesis of a total and coercive segregation of communist totalitarianism from the rest of the world and from the global market, has remained the *nomenklatura*'s major theoretical maxim, even when it was politically inclined, or forced, to make very moderate steps toward de-Stalinization. As always, here too, Stalin proved to be the instinc-tive genius of totalitarianism. His blueprint rested on the adamant conviction that his brand of command economy could not compete with capitalism on the same grounds, and therefore segregation was necessary. Furthermore, not even his economically *per se* nonsensical thesis of the maximum satisfaction of all needs was so nonsensical if it is understood within the context of the "dictatorship over needs".[9] It simply meant that all those needs which were authorized by the central authority, should be satisfied, and, conversely, only those needs should be authorized which can be satisfied in a given period. But for this blueprint to succeed, two preconditions had to be met. The "socialist world market" had to be hermetically sealed, not only economically, but also politically and culturally. Stalin would have appreciated Castoriadis's theory of "the imaginary institution of society" in his own way, by recognizing it as a crucial, and for him dangerous, power. Furthermore, all adventures with too big new gains of a reckless conquest had to be avoided, Stalin evidently contended. The first priority was the total absorption of areas which had already been integrated in the Soviet system. The *nomenklatura* made a major tactical mistake, and this is the third factor of its economic collapse, when it eclectically combined Stalin's concept of the "socialist world market" (which it unsuccessfully tried to impose upon the COMECON) with expansionism. The neo-Stalinists were very bad Stalinists in that they never understood Stalin's caution about gaining too much. (Although they could have learned the lesson from the Chinese Sasco that the Soviet centre was too weak to absorb and economically dominate what they had already conquered under the aegis of world communism.) Expansionism meant technological competition with the West, a crucial phase of the Cold War they lost during the Reagan period. It also meant regular contact with the alien world which, and Stalin knew this all too well, would contaminate the Soviet "imaginary institution". Expansionism also involved them in economic transactions on the capitalist world market where their usual panacea, doctoring statistics, fixing prices "politically" and the like, proved ineffectual. Finally, the very moment when the *nomenklatura* began to make frantic efforts, in the form of Gorbachev's campaign for *glasnost*, to convince the populace of their good will and their determination to leave the terror behind, they dug their own grave economically.

During the Gorbachev years, the ultimate secret of Soviet industriousness, the fact that only fear and (for a narrow stratum) the hope of upward mobility made the system run, became unmasked. Once people no longer feared, or feared much less, the punishing iron hand of the state, they simply refused to work. Equally, when ambitious upstarts no longer saw any point in making a career in a system which publicly advertized its decrepitude, not even the system's economic "fixers" were inclined to heed the central instructions. Rather, the trend emerging under Brezhnev continued, and the "red barons" kept amassing private wealth, notwithstanding Gorbachev campaigns against embezzling state funds. The complete, coercively guaranteed, rationality of the system turned into complete anarchy, total planning into chaotic drifting.

Small wonder, then, that the lessons of such a resounding economic fiasco has now been translated into the language of "the triumph of capitalism". But even those who have selected a different vocabulary for themselves, can draw certain conclusions from the present collapse. For the centennial dream of socialism of rectifying the irrationality of the market and redress the social injustices cawed by its mechanism, was not *per se* misconceived. There is, indeed, an inherent lack of rationality in a market economy, first, because it is only clear at the moment of selling whether there is a solvent need for the product and, second, because the seller is only interested in profit, not in the social consequences of profitmaking. As has been pointed out, the only area in which market rationality is invariably confirmed is in technological innovation. Even such an ardent critic of socialism's false claims and pretences as Max

Weber expected improvement from a socialist state bureaucracy, provided that it gave up its dreams of "the substantive rationality" of its blueprints which would authorize it to exclude competition coercively.[10]

But the hypothesis that the socialist corrections of a market economy can have only one legitimate locus, the modern state, was already exaggerated by Weber, and this claim has been pathologically enlarged by the communist bureaucracy. The total merger of state and economy politicized the economic sphere to a degree where it could no longer generate standards of purely economic rationality, its operation became, therefore, entirely and tyrannically arbitrary. It disenfranchised society as far as economic transactions were concerned. It also coercively suppressed several different lifestyles and forms of activity for which there is manifest need in modern society, and which can become niches of certain liberties against the oppressive inclinations of both state and society. The moral of the fable of communism, even for those who have remained critics of the operation of a capitalist market economy rather than its enthusiasts, is thus the following. The critique of market rationality in the name of social justice and the social consensus concerning "the public purpose" of the economy must never assume the form of suppressing or substituting the market economy. A *totally politicized* economy is no longer a political *economy*. The economy, as a sphere, can neither be reduced to a global *oikos*, and thus entirely depoliticized, as, in a surprising harmony, both Castoriadis and Hannah Arendt would have it, nor can it be totally politicized by the state, whatever the ideology of its bureaucracy might be, without grave consequences for both liberties and socio-economic rationality. "The subsystems of modernity", to coin a term commonly used by Habermas and Luhmann, cannot be completely collapsed into one another without a dangerous infraction of the complexity of modernity. The economy can and certainly will be organized according to widely different patterns (of which a collectively owned or partially state-owned socialist model is one of the legitimate competitors); but it should never be completely merged with the state and thus fully politicized. In this sense, a socialist critique of the economy remains a perfectly justified position in a variety of critical voices. But it must no longer claim exclusivity and a privileged position. For there is no metaphysics of the "social question" which would be the exclusive property of a particular political trend, and which would provide an Archimedean point for the appraisal of the present.

Politically, the skies are considerably clearer, if not entirely cloudless, after communism. The Manicheism of the Cold War, whose greatest historical novelist was Le Carré, is over. And while the Western powers, in an understandably triumphant mood, now stress exclusively who is the victor of the Cold War, the world can learn more about its own history by understanding who had been primarily responsible for it. Because, at the very moment that a Soviet leadership appeared for which détente was not a code-name for expansionism via forced concession and agreements extorted under duress, the terrible division of the world was over. More importantly, the totalitarian period has come to a complete stop, at least in the Northern hemisphere. It is in this sense that the 20th century can be called the shortesté one which began with the outbreak of World War I and, in its aftermath, with the emergence of competitive totalitarian regimes, and which ended on the notes of the "glorious" anti-totalitarian revolutions of 1989. Europe, for the first time since the term was politically and culturally coined, now has a chance for a democratic self-integration, even if this will not be the smooth ride as has been predicted. The East-Central European countries have regained their national sovereignty, twice demolished during the last half century, first by Nazi-Germany and later by Soviet-Bolshevik imperialism. They are also en route to social emancipation.

However, as mentioned, the skies are not entirely cloudless. Being after communism also means facing for the first time certain problems which have either been created by communism or have been kept in check by its governments of terror, creating the impression that they had been long solved, whereas they have only become more venomous. The first of these problems is the re-emergence of a type of nationalism which seemed to have been extinct in Europe, and which cannot be appeased by moderation or cultural autonomy. It demands secession, border revisions, new national sovereignties. Admittedly, the problem itself is not a responsibility of communism. A whole ethnic dimension of Europe had been swept under the rug with the creation of the centralized nation state, and it now resurfaces, simultaneously with the disappearance of dictatorships, from Kosovo to the Basque land. Communism only proved totally ineffectual in changing its violent character, perhaps even more so than did liberal democracies. Second, the impending rapprochement and gradual integration of the whole of the Northern hemisphere under the sign of liberal democracy and a market economy which is likely to create the largest zone of internal peace and relative prosperity ever known, and which itself is a salutary change which could be brought about only by overthrowing the communist governments, is likely to usher in a new period of global conflict, one between North and South. Its first swallows have already arrived in the form of the resentment of Latin Americans against the preoccupation of the leading economic powers with Eastern Europe. Finally, there is one after effect of communism which is hard to control even after its demise: the worldwide spreading of the technology of totalitarian rule. The genie is now out of the bottle, and there is a certain similarity between the distribution of nuclear devices and that of totalitarian power technology, since both are matters of know-how. Once this know-how has become publicly available, its spreading cannot be contained.

The demise of communism, so manifest after the revolutions of 1989, has been, understandably, hailed as the ultimate proof of the fiasco of the socialist idea as a whole by the political right. More surprising than the rightist glee is the self-querying mood of so many non-communist socialists who, precisely now, want to find metaphysical or sociological "proofs" and "guarantees" of the survival and longevity of their movement. But there are no such guarantees. Every culture prior to ours harboured influential trends which at some point lost their vitality and creativity and vanished, for various reasons. Our culture is not an exception. It is entirely in the hands of socialists here and now whether that great movement, which has moulded modernity for two centuries, is indeed doomed to extinction or whether, on the contrary, socialism will find the internal energy for rejuvenation.

Viewed in perspective, social democrats and libertarian socialists of all hues and colours would now have ample reason for joy. The scarecrow, whose presence has always triggered the accusation of conspiring to introduce a government of the terror, whenever they proposed social change or reform, is now gone. Yet it seems as though old-time democratic socialists, enemies of communism for reasons of principle, were anxious rather than relieved. This perplexity of (non communist) socialism is a highly revealing feeling, conveying the message that non-communist socialism has never faced seriously the complex issue of the historic achievements and internal limitations of its own theory and politics. The critique of communism seemed to have spared socialism this unpleasant task which can no longer be postponed.

Above all, socialism does not seem to have made an honest inventory of its contribution to the "normal" development of modernity. Even if socialists completely disinherit communism as an intruder into their family, even if, as a result, they accept no responsibility for communism's crimes, the fact still remains that the socialist contribution to normally developed modernity has been so far dangerously curtailed in several areas.

Their major claim to recognition is the legitimization of "the social question", without which the "Roman degeneration" of modernity into Caesarism on the one hand, and the permanent indigence of the industrial proletariat on the other, would have been inescapable. The neglected needs of the working classes, as well as of those who have been forced into idleness, enjoys, for the first time in recorded history, pride of place on the political agenda only as a result of the socialists' stubborn campaigning. This achievement is their remaining glory.

The socialists provided the idea of relative equality and that of social justice with a balanced meaning beyond extremist excesses. They have, furthermore, contributed to the development of parliamentary democracy in the 19th Century, and in Spain and Portugal even in the 20th century, by mobilizing the proletariat (initially an outcast of civil society and almost completely disinterested in politics) to transform itself into an electoral constituency and boost its social and economic power. However, socialism accepted ready-made the idea and the modus operandi of democracy, and it has added virtually nothing to democratic theory and practice. The indifference to, and often the contempt for, liberalism, felt by the majority of socialists, blinded them to the mob-like features and the totalitarian potentials of democracy. Perception of the latter has been traditionally regarded as "aristocratism" among socialists who were also committed democrats.

For the most part, the economic system of modernity developed without the socialists' other than critical participation, which was, admittedly, a crucial function. Even when the socialists did not harbour radical utopias of a marketless society, they have, for good reasons, always considered the market as a necessary evil and, rightly, its logic the principle of a continually reproduced inequality. The only economic strategy they felt affinity with, and whose agents proper they were in government, was the Keynesian. Their traditional, and perfectly legitimate, relationship to the market in the last half century has been cohabitation and a policy of proposing restrictions with a view to social justice (which, in combination, is what "market socialism" is all about). So far, with the exception of Willy Brandt's vague theses on the North-South relationship, socialists were never particularly receptive to the problems arising out of the disproportions of the global economy, although the world economy is now the proper framework (as was the nation-state in Keynes's time) in which recommendations for social justice and (non-market) rationality can be raised and effectively implemented.

Their overwhelmingly urban origins and culture prevented the socialists from adding an iota to the agrarian question. The only redeeming feature in this regard was their zeal in implementing a program during certain agrarian revolutions, land partitioning, which was not their own proposal. Perhaps for that same reason, they also overslept the emergence of the environmentalist issue which has been advocated by non-socialist actors.

As far as nationhood and nationalism is concerned, democratic socialists, or social democrats have an almost entirely unblemished record of being enemies of national, ethnic or race bias of all kinds. (The shameful episode of the Australian Labor Party's "White Australia Policy" remained an incident without further consequences in the annals of socialism.) At the same time, albeit loyal citizens, socialists always felt ill at ease about national identification. They were not internationalists in the communist sense of building a Universal Church of the Grand Inquisitor, but they were certainly cosmopolitan in an age of nationalism. Only one socialist contingent, the Zionist Labor party, became a nation-builder, another, French socialism from Jaurès to Mitterand, has contributed to the greatness of *la nation* with only a single relapse into chauvinism (under Guy Mollet during the Algerian war). The rest of them stood awkwardly on the sideline whenever the nation and its affairs were on the agenda.

Finally, social democrats or democratic socialists have an ambiguous cultural record. For them, communism was tantamount either to state censorship or to intellectual elitism. By contrast, social democrats were betting on a genuine proletarian culture in an age where class culture was already disintegrating. The government of democratic socialists in the welfare state was a benevolent patron of the artists; the socialist movement spread literacy and the light of knowledge where the darkness of ignorance had reigned supreme. We owe the discovery of, and the support for, the best products of working class culture (in Great Britain), as well as some of the best novels (in Scandinavia and post-war Germany) to this welfarist patronage and social democratic spirit. But social democracy, in its aversion to intellectual elitism, has constantly lacked great vision, so necessary for flourishing periods of culture.

The vacuum created by the demise of communism is beneficial for the socialists only if they are capable of making an inventory of their peak performances and serious limitations. For, let us be honest, the existence of communism was not merely an obstacle for democratic socialists. In strange ways, it was also a blessing in disguise. As long as communist governments of the terror or repression existed, it sufficed for democratic socialists or social democrats to point to the communist practices with the remark we shall do it in a different way. This gesture alone guaranteed the votes. But now, with the scarecrow gone, they are alone on the left, and they now indeed have to do the work in a different way or perish. To be capable of performing the new task it is mandatory that they address their own past record.

III

The resounding question in our present reads as follows: "Is radical politics still possible?". It is not as if communism had been so excessively radical in the last forty years. Rather, it had become under Stalin, and continued to be, even more poignantly, under the Brezhnevite gerontocracy, a conservative establishment, with the instinctive fear of change so characteristic of its brand. It was precisely this ossification of official communism that generated the New Left's rebellion in the 1960s as well as the morbid infatuation of parts of it with Mao's cultural revolution. But there has always been a secret symbiosis between communism and radicalism of all hues and colours. Even a totally decrepit communism harboured the *promesse du bonheur* of radicalism by virtue of the potentials of its past as well as the hope of the resurrection of these potentials.[11] The issue is an East-European one par excellence after the revolutions of 1989, primarily because for decades the anti-totalitarian movement has adopted for decades the scenario of "the great republic", mainly, but not exclusively, in Hungary.[12] It has become clear only in retrospect that this typical radical project had already reached its peak with the Hungarian Revolution of 1956, and that it could not be continued. But as a living legacy of the past, the still lingering idea of the great republic calls for a reconsideration of radicalism.

Modern radicalism was a unique blend of three major trends growing out of, and emerging in reaction to, the high Enlightenment, as well as the revolutionary period. In addition, it has remained up until now a phenomenon with a Janus face: leftist and rightist radicalism. Its first feature, shared by both kinds, for example, by Marx and Nietzsche alike, was the drive aiming to overcome the limitations imposed by Christian ontology and anthropology on action and it self confidence. The second was the integration of the Faustian dimension into the project, the belief in the irresistibility of human creativity, unrestrained either by the conventions of the present or by the barriers of (external or internal) nature as constituting an absolute limit. The third factor was a new sense of temporality, for which the "normal time" of the new age, the time of *banausis*, that of philistine preoccupations, was too slow. It had to be, therefore, artificially accelerated.

The renunciation of the conception of "original sin" was indispensable for the rehabilitation of human activity, for restoring its (philosophical and political) self-confidence. The politics of modernity could not simply continue the Christian tradition; it needed a radically new grounding. The new foundation was the recognition of the unique character and value of human action and its unprecedented products in the fields of statecraft and political morality. But the new foundation never proved to be the solid old rock on which Christian politics had been built. "Rehabilitated" political action wildly oscillated between a manifest need for the "anthropological turn' of the actors, without which new politics seemed to be helpless, and periodic relapses into "political theology". This built-in insecurity, both on the right and the left of modern radicalism, was either a source of despair or a trigger for flights into arbitrary myths of self-creation—to the point of a political theology of human deification.

The Faustian dimension, the non-recognition of natural barriers within and without human beings, lent the aura of philosophical superiority to the dirty pragmatics of the 19th century, industrialization, on the left of radicalism. On the right, it increasingly appeared as the great experiment overcoming "nature within", with breeding a new human specimen, exempt from fear and the pangs of conscience. Wagner's central role, as yet unrecognized, in the history of modern radicalism consisted precisely in prophetically shaping and combining both. The inferno of industrial work, remoulding the world and raping nature in *Rheingold*, is the underground foundation of the conflicts in the political heaven of Valhalla. And Siegfried, who knows neither fear nor conscience, the hero of a barbaric Enlightenment who overthrows the traditional reign of gods, is the first revolutionary Superman.[13]

Radical dissatisfaction with the slowness of "ordinary time" appears in its most marked form on the left in its time perception of "permanent revolution". Its background was the merely pragmatic experience of the French revolutionary decades (at least in one of its readings), having grown out of all proportion and elevated to the rank of the Odyssey of modern humankind. "Permanent revolution" as time perception made the pretence of being more than a political experience. It was understood as the dominant temporality of modernity, this "age of revolutions"; also as the lifestyle of the elect few, the vanguard. This is why it implied a strong contempt for the "temporality of those philistines", who were not living in the permanence of revolution. However, Hitler, the epitome of rightist radicalism, his *Blitzkrieg*, his outright contempt for the ordinary life-span of mortals, including his own, can never be understood without taking this radical time perception, common in its rightist and leftist brands alike, into consideration.

Communism, in Eastern Europe as well as in general, has squandered long ago the heritage of its own philosophical radicalism. In it the self-deification of creative human activity has been tamed into blind obedience to a new authority, the Faustian project of industrialism reduced to the level of goulash communism; and the "permanence of revolution" degraded into the permanence of bureaucratic infighting. Moreover, even oppositional—leftist—radicalism has disappeared from Eastern Europe in the last two decades, with "rights language" taking over from the vocabulary of an East European New Left and that of "the great republic".

What kind of balance can be struck among these changes from a leftist point of view? The disappearance of leftist radicalism is undoubtedly an open-ended process. It can lead to the post-modern moderation of certain excessively dynamic trends of modernity as well as to relapses into the grand narratives of neo-conservatism with a penchant for rehabilitating the concept of the sinful, and ultimately futile, nature of human activity. In the first version, the autonomy of modernity will be contrasted to the imperative of its radical transcendence at all costs. For positing modernity as the (potentially) autonomous society and, in the same breath, demanding its absolute transcendence, are contradictory postulates—even if this is not always clarified by the theorist. Autonomy, free self-legislation, presupposes that everyone, the theorist included, participates in the process of self-legislation on an equal footing. But given that transcendence requires a position transcendent to the world judged from this Archimedean point, the postulate of absolute transcendence is, by implication, unequal, authoritarian. The post-modern deconstruction of radicalism is not a *Weltanschauung* of hungover and philistine flight into "inescapable" reality. Put simply, the majority of the new actors in Eastern Europe do not need radicalism of any kind, to the end of a *constitutio libertatis*. They are, as a rule, suspicious of grand narratives. They do not need, unless they fall back on a religious grounding of action, special reminders of the relevance of political action; their own victory, against such overwhelming odds, speaks for itself. They are quite particularly annoyed with the radical perception of time, as they are no longer inclined, to use a wise and philosophically rich metaphor of Agnes Heller, to live in a railway station, waiting for the trains, travelling into the future. The post-modern East European rejection of leftist radicalism is, in brief, the defence of the autonomy of modernity against all types of authoritarian arbitration, honouring its as yet unused reserves and protecting its assumed longevity.

At the other end of the East-European constellation are the manifestos of a religiously coloured, or grounded, disillusionment with human action. The strong anti-utopian drive of a branch of critical literature on Soviet-type societies[14] is problematic not because the authors reject social utopias, but because they implicitly condemn the "audacity" of human projects in rearranging the world of modernity. At the same time, this is why they are symptomatic for the newest mass phenomenon in Eastern Europe: the resurrection of religion and religious politics.

The dangerous phenomenon of the East European situation after communism is the fact that while leftist radicalism is defunct, rightist radicalism is not completely. It would be too early to sound the bells of alarm. Rightist radicalism exists there in a merely embryonic form, often as a lingering memory of an inglorious past (East German neo-Nazism or the Viatra Romanesca as a possible heir to the Iron Guard). So far, it has no theorists and no grand narratives. However, certain trends, which are unambiguous, but temporarily weak or theoretically not yet self-conscious heirs to a highly ambivalent radical populism in the region (in Solidarity, in certain streams of the Hungarian Democratic Forum, in Croatian neo-nationalism) are the first harbingers of a not very promising awakening. In some sense, it is a happy accident that it now exists without its regional counterpart. For the two types of radicalism historically could never balance out each other, rather, they invariably sharpened social conflicts to the explosion point. Whether the dominant post-modern moderation in Eastern Europe can bring right-wing radicalism under control is one of the unresolved mysteries of the new situation.

The world after communism has become decidedly more habitable, although certainly not a paradise. At least one lesson can be learned, when the space evacuated by communism is filled with new projects, and when the problems, which its presence had created and its absence unconcealed, are faced: being after communism is certainly not being at the end of history.

Notes

1. There are various interpretations of the varying electoral success of the communist successor parties in the first free elections. A reasonable explanation of the unexpected 16 to 17 percent Gysi's party polled in East Germany is the assumption of the support of a hypertrophically enlarged state bureaucracy, which has no special affinity with communism, but which does have a very strong sense of job security in the new situation and which finds a shield in the successor party. In Poland, we do not know as yet how, in general terms, the communists will fare, since in the June 1989 elections only the artificially created 35 per cent of the places in the Senate were up for grabs (in the competition for which the communists suffered a

disastrous defeat). A proper, free general election was announced by Prime Minister Mazowieczki just recently. Judging from the first, partial, elections, the communists' general electoral result can be expected to be equally disastrous, and the causes, apart from the overall picture of a staunch Polish anti-communism, which was not lessened by decades of economic mismanagement, need no detailed comment. The successor party of Hungarian communism, which in the middle of 1989 still believed itself able to become the best-polling political force in the elections, gradually out-lived its usefulness for the nation as the horizons of East European emancipation widened. It was also sharply divided internally, and its public showing was, to say the least, lacklustre. The best comment on the causes of the strong showing of Iliescu's National Salvation Front, apart from a general explanation about the weak-ness of civil society, came from Mrs Dvora Avineri, a member of the International Control Commission over the elections, herself Romanian-born, and therefore ca-pable of having conversations with the populace. What emerged clearly from these conversations was that for wide strata of the populace Ceasescu's rule still remained the only standard of comparison, that people did not believe systemic change had taken place, therefore the Front seemed to them as a far more tolerable version of communism which as such deserved support. (Personal communication.)

2. This quick rewriting of party history and swap of ancestors is most evident in the Czech and the Bulgarian case. The Czech communists try to eliminate Gottwald's period as their formative political experience; for their founding father, they return instead to Smeral, whose leadership is as good as forgotten, and who was not party to the Stalinist crimes (while he was, of course, a convinced and manipulative Komintern functionary). For the general characterization of Smeral's leadership see Jacques Rupnik, *Histoire du Parti Communiste Tchecoslovaque* (Paris, 1981) for his role in the Bolshevization of Romanian communism, see Vladimir Tismaneanu, "The Tragicomedy of Rumanian Communism" in F. Fehér and A. Arato (eds), *Crisis and Reform in Eastern Europe* (New Brunwsick, Transaction, 1990), p. 124). The Bulgarians can conjure up a more convincing heritage in the person of Blagoev and the group of the *tesniaki*, this aristocracy of communism, Volsheviks *avant la lettre*, much before Lenin.

3. Ample evidence of the active role of the Gorbachev-group in triggering or, at least shielding the changes brewing in Eastern Europe has been by now gathered. It is common knowledge in East Germany that the commanding officers of the Soviet army had a direct order not to interfere in case turbulences broke out as a result of the foolish obstinacy of the Honecker-leadership. This, fairly loudly announced, order of restraint must have exerted a sobering impact on the Political Bureau which ultimately ousted Honecker. In Czechoslovakia they did more. A resolution of the Soviet Political Bureau (basically the death warrant of the Husak-Jakes-leadership), a document condemning the 1968 Soviet invasion of Czechoslovakia in self-critical terms, had been in existence since early 1989. According to well-informed Czech emigres, the document was shown to Jakes who begged the Soviet leaders to wait with its publication. But since this kind of information never remains, because

it is not intended to remain, a secret, it implied a direct encouragement to the popular movement. The Bulgarian change, the ousting of Zhikov in November 1989, was a palace coup, supported by the Bulgarian army. As such, it simply could not have taken place without the blessing of Gorbachev. Iliescu, as we know from the revelations of Z. Mlynar, was a friend of Gorbachev in the fifties, during their university years in Moscow. Gorbachev must be reopened the channels of communication between the two of them when in office. As such, he can also be seen as the instigator, if not of the popular revolution, certainly of the attempted, and belated, coup against Ceausescu. The least direct role was played by the Gorbachev-leadership in the two countries which have been traditionally the centres of the storm, each having its own distinct, and in its own way, influential, oppositional movement: Poland and Hungary. Nevertheless, there was a historic moment of intervention even in Poland by the Soviet leaders. Rakowski, the last secretary general of the collapsing Polish communist party, made a desperate, and widely publicized, phone call to Gorbachev in June, when the Polish communist leaders first realized that what they had planned as a concession made to Soldarity, was going to be the beginning of a landslide which would demolish them. Gorbachev's answer can be guessed from the historical event that followed.

4. A typical example of this petty rumination of the type Hegel called *die Geschichstschreibung des Kammerdieners*, can be found in the remarks of Günther Schabowski, ex-Politburo member and "reformist" under Honecker, who now speculates in retrospect concerning the chances he and other "reformists" could have had, had they controlled the security apparatus, and the like. "A Wistful Glance Back at When the Wall Fell", *The New York Times* (10 July 1990), p. 8.

5. Shevardnadze described the typical reading of *perestroika* by party hardliners as interpretation via conspiracy theory.

6. See the last book by Raymond Aron which, despite being full of resignation, still insists on the necessity of an "objective understanding" of the Soviet economy. See Aron's polemics against Besançon, in Raymond Aron, *Le Dernieres annees du gede* (Paris, 1984).

7. A very similar interpretation of the collapse of the *nomenklatura*, with a (significant) difference, can be found in Charles Maier, "The German Reunification and the Collapse of Marxism", paper given at the workshop of *Gorbachev and the Germans*, 10–11 May 1990, at the Graduate Faculty of the New School for Social Research, New York.

8. Ferenc Fehér, Agnes Heller and György Markus, *Dictatorship Over Needs* (Oxford, Blackwell, 1981).

9. ibid.

10. Weber's most relevant remarks on the socialist project can be found in *Wirtschaft und Gessellschaft* (Tübingen, J.C.B. Mohr/Paul Siebeck, 1972), pp. 56 and passim.

11. A classic document of this kind of nostalgia for a radicalism which has been lost by, but which may be still inherent in, communism, is Maurice Merleau-Ponty's *Humanisme et terreur* (Paris, Gallimard, 1980).

12. Agnes Heller, "The Great Republic" in A. Heller and F. Fehér, *Eastern Left-Western Left* (Cambridge/Atlantic Heights, Policy Press/Humanities Press, 1987).

13. The best analysis of the presence of capitalism in anger's musical drama stems from Bernard Shaw, "The Perfect Wagnerite", *Major Critical Essays* (Harmondsworth, Penguin, 1986).

14. Leszek Kolakowski is the intellectual master of this strong anti-utopian drive. Its most representative expression in history-writing is Michel Heller and Aleksandr Nekrich, *L'Utopie au pouvoir* (Paris, Calmann-Levy, 1982).

THE WORLD RECONSIDERED: A BRIEF AGGIORNAMENTO FOR LEFTIST INTELLECTUALS

Gunnar Skirbekk

The political events in Eastern Europe in 1989 and the first part of 1990 require some critical re-examination among leftist intellectuals. These events, disturbingly novel as they are, should be analyzed, critically and with self-criticism, against the background of our notions of the modern world and its main characteristics. In this paper I shall make a few sketchy remarks on some of the notions and perspectives which in my view are to be reconsidered, first related mainly to Eastern Europe (Part I), then seen in a broader scale (Part II).

I.

I start with the simple observation that the political and ideological fall of Stalinist socialism in Eastern Europe was experienced with astonishment and euphoria. Nobody had, to my knowledge, predicted that this system would fall apart so quickly and so peacefully. And even though the future is filled with difficulties and uncertainties, it seems plausible to think that this regime and its ideology are discredited beyond the point of possible restoration, at least in this part of the world.

The very unpredictability[1] of the events calls for serious considerations among scholars of different disciplines and political affiliations. For leftist intellectuals there are in addition at least two main points that require a critical reflection,[2] the one being the strength of the *market economy*, the other the strength of *nationalism* in post-communist Eastern Europe.[3] I shall briefly elaborate upon these two points.

(i) It has been quite clear for a long time that the Soviet-type economy does not function well. It has also become clear that the traditional

Yugoslav model, based on decentralization and self-rule on enterprise level, had severe difficulties. I thus assume that most leftist intellectuals tend to support some kind of market economy within political frames which allow for some version of a planned market. These are deep changes among Western leftist intellectuals: the pure market economy remains unattractive, but also the Yugoslav model of economic life has lost its attraction, and the Soviet model has lost its plausibility; what remains is some kind of mixed economy, of a social democratic nature.

In this perspective the apparent sympathy for a market economy among many East European reformers as well as among a large part of the electorate does represent a challenge to leftist intellectuals.[4]

(ii) It has for a long time been well known that there are national and ethnic tensions within what was called the Soviet bloc. But the strength of these nationalistic forces has been a surprise for most Western observers; and for leftist intellectuals, having international solidarity as an ideal and often arguing in favour of an historical "overcoming" of nationalism as a basic force, this emergence of strong nationalism in Eastern Europe calls for a serious re-examination.

There are certainly various explanations for the emergence of Eastern European nationalism. I shall just mention three.

The first one I would call the "out-of-the-ice" explanation: this holds that East European nationalism in its different forms was suppressed by the Soviet system. Nationalist tensions from the pre-Soviet period could not be properly discussed, nor properly "lived through", within the Soviet system. It became frozen, as it were. And once the "glacier" of the Soviet repression "melted" the old nationalist tensions reappeared, like defrosted mammoths coming out of the ice.

The strength of this explanation is its descriptive fit.[5] (It even seems to fit for the case of suppressed national tensions within the federal republic of Yugoslavia, outside the Soviet bloc.) As a sociological explanation, however, it is somewhat weaker. It does not really give a sociological explanation of how nationalism could survive all these forty to seventy years. Its explanatory power, I assume, is rather to be found in its tacit reference to psychological or psychoanalytic explanations of repressed psychic tensions, which tend to survive subconsciously just because they are not verbalized and openly worked out. But in a long-term societal perspective we would like to know why these attitudes and emotions did not change in accordance with other changes in society; or we would like to know which manifest or latent functions they had within this society. If no such function can be demonstrated it seems unsatisfactory, as a sociological explanation, simply to say that they prevailed "under the ice".

Thereby we have already touched upon the second type of explanation for the emergence of East European nationalism, that is, an explanation which claims that nationalism did play a functional role within these societies during the years of Soviet domination, though unrecognized by most observers. To support such a functional explanation one has to go empirically into each case, in order to see whether nationalism of some kind did have such a role and importance within that society. I shall not here try to follow this thread, but merely indicate what I have in mind. One clear case is Poland, another Yugoslavia. For one thing we could investigate the social function of the Catholic Church in Poland and its connection to Polish nationalism, and we could investigate the interconnection between economic difference with Yugoslavia and the call for political and cultural separation in Slovenia and Croatia. In these cases, however, nationalism has for a long time been recognized and this kind of explanation has already been applied. The point is now that similar explanations could be tried out also on cases of nationalism which have hitherto been overlooked in one way or the other — like German nationalism in the former DDR or the strength of Baltic nationalism.

There is still another kind of explanation worth mentioning, namely one which underlines the creative aspect of the emergence of nationalism. It works as follows: the various forms of nationalism were not really there before, frozen under the ice or latently functioning, but once repression withered away they were actively (though often subconsciously) created in order to fill an ideological vacuum that occurred by the withdrawal of Soviet political domination. (This is, by the way, a dominant historical explanation of the emergence of Norwegian nationalism in 1814. I can imagine the same controversy concerning the explanation of the emergence of post-colonial nationalism in the Third World, such as in the movement of négritude.)

The dispute between these three attempts at explaining nationalism has to be settled through empirical research; but the dispute also entails conceptual controversies concerning the proper nature of the agents and the determining factors (be it politically acting individuals, classes or social conditions).

There is a lot more to be said about nationalism and different ways of describing and explaining its emergence in Eastern Europe. The point I would make so far is simply this: nationalism, as a case of particular collective identity, has to be taken seriously, also in modern societies. It has to be taken seriously both as a functional factor within a society and as a factor in human collective identity, limiting a We from a They.

However, the East European experience of nationalism does not occur as something quite unique in our times. It adds to other experiences of nationalism, even in modern societies such as Japan. The latter case is specially interesting since Japan so undoubtedly is a modern society (viz. in technological and economic terms).[6] It therefore contradicts the view that modernity by

necessity leads toward universalism and away from particular collective identities, for example, in the form of nationalism. It indicates that there are different
ways of modernization and different ways of being modern.[7]

The case of Japan might even be made sharper: Japan seems, so far,
to have had less socio-cultural disintegration than Western societies, and the
cohesion of its homogeneous culture might be an explanation for this. Furthermore, the Japanese economy is able to invest in long-term perspectives to
a higher degree than Western societies — a fact which might be analyzed in
the light of the long-term interest embedded in a national culture in contrast
to the rather short-term interest of singular agents on the market. The latter
point is also interesting in an ecological perspective since economic and political agents with a long-term concern are basic requirements in this ecological
perspective.

These brief remarks on possible linkages between particular collective
identities and the economy might also be relevant to the emergence of nationalism and of pro-market sentiments in the Soviet-dominated parts of Europe.
Here I allow myself to start with a rough and speculative model: to the extent
that the Stalinist economy was based on a top-down system of commands with
a threat to those who did not obey and work, we can safely say today that this
system of negative motivation is no longer functioning. It did function at an earlier stage when it was supplemented by a pride of working for the revolution or
for being a Soviet proletarian fighting (or having courageously fought) Fascism.
But this cultural motivation is today severely weakened. It hardly functions any
more. And at the same time market mechanisms, distributing reward and punishment according to market behaviour, have not yet taken over. Thus there is
a strange interregnum during this transition from the old system to something
new within the former State-socialist countries, the Soviet Union included.

This is a question of whether the Stalinist system of top-down command
could ever have overcome the threshold of bureaucratic control. Such control
is easier for quantity than for quality and easier for reproduction of known
products than for the creation of new ones. In this respect it is a question
of whether this system could ever compete with a market system in decisive
fields of modern economy like quality consumer-goods and electronics.

My point, however, is exactly the following: to the extent that the old
Stalinist economy, based on command and threat, is definitely dismissed, there
are two (ideal-type) options for East Europeans when it comes to economic
motivation, either a market economy or a restoration of some cultural motivation. The latter option (some would say, temptation) is one which would
include an interest in nourishing a strengthening of the collective identity; here
nationalism is close at hand. East European nationalism could therefore be
analyzed and investigated in a perspective of such a functional tie to a concern
for economic revitalization (should we say, Japanese style). In this perspective
Russian nationalism could also be investigated as an attempt at the restora-

tion of a functioning economy; it should not merely be interpreted in terms of Russian traditionalism per se.

However, any nationalism of this sort within the Soviet Union could only work counterproductively, that is, against the unity of the existing Union. Such a nationalist (cultural) motivation might perhaps have some importance in order to get Estonians working for the Estonians, or Armenians for Armenians, or Lithuanians for Lithuanians, or Russians for Russians — but hardly all of them for each other. In this perspective a market economy, and a strong presidency, is a safer way to keep the Empire together and afloat, and even hope for economic progress. This was Gorbachev's perspective pitted against the nationalists of various kinds.

At this point I would like to sum up my brief remarks on nationalism and economic motivation in Eastern Europe: intellectuals should take the notion of particular collective identity seriously also in modern societies, both with regard to its function for social cohesion and with regard to its political and economic function. Diversity and particularity should not be overlooked in any of these spheres of modern life. Particular collective identities might even be evaluated as positive,[8] for example, in an ecological perspective. On the other hand, intellectuals should differentiate between legitimate and illegitimate "particular collective identities". In cases of rationally confirmed legitimacy, a rationally founded tolerance is required, whereas in cases of rationally confirmed illegitimacy, criticism and (counteracting) political strategies are required. Such attempts at differentiating between legitimacy and illegitimacy can only take the form of open and enlightened analyses and discussions, the basis of which is exactly the equality of the participants and the universality of the arguments. To this crucial point I shall return in the second part of the paper.

II.

I would now like to mention a few themes that in my view for a long time were disregarded or inadequately treated among leftist intellectuals, though gradually most of these themes are back on the agenda. Since there has been a considerable improvement in reassessing these themes my first point is simply to give a brief reminder of some of the main issues. My second and main point consists in delineating a notion of politics, or of political culture, appropriate to a modern world.

I shall approach the matter by positing three spheres — which for the sake of brevity I call *the sphere of free decision, the sphere of rights* and *the sphere of truth* — and I shall briefly indicate their autonomy as well as their mutual dependence. I shall also briefly indicate some of the levels of autonomy and independence within each sphere. For pedagogical and philosophical reasons I shall proceed in a Hegelian manner in the sense that indicated shortcomings in one position lead over to the next — the power of the negative fuels transcending movements (so to say).

This conceptual triangle is certainly simplistic. The point is to argue in favour of a normative notion of political culture which is multi-dimensional, with an interplay of autonomy and dependence between the various dimensions. I do not say that there are just three (and just these three) "angles". I merely claim that there are at least these three viz. that a normative notion of political culture implies multi-dimensionality (and thereby an emphasis on a "sufficient equilibrium" between the various dimensions).

(A) During the student movement in the late sixties direct democracy was an ideal — for some, the ideal. Direct democracy meant participation, participation both in a process of free speech and open discussion and in a process of decision concerning one's own situation. It meant learning, not only scholarly learning, but learning through participation, through discussion and decision and through the personal experience of conceiving the world in different perspectives dependent on the various contexts within which the various discussions were located.

These, clearly, are all valuable insights. But all along there were, equally clearly, severe shortcomings connected to any model of direct or participatory democracy.

One set of problems is associated with the capacity question: participation takes time, and time is scarce. In an adult world, with professional and family-life duties, lengthy and frequent meetings and teach-ins soon become a problem — and more so if participatory democracy is introduced in all the different spheres of activity in which modern people take part. These are the problems of overburdening.

Another set of problems is connected to the question of how to make decisions. Formally unregulated group-decisions aiming at unanimity can easily lead to the repression of unpopular opinions or neglect of minorities. This point indicates a need for a differentiation between intellectual discussion and voting procedures and it indicates a need for legal protection of free speech and of minority views. In large-scale modern societies, therefore — with many levels, institutions and perspectives — there is not only a capacity need but also a procedural need for transcending participatory democracy in favour of some form of representative democracy. And in accepting representative democracy one also has to accept nomination procedures and elections, parties and interest groups, voting and compromises.

This is the old and well-known discussion of direct democracy (of "the ancient") and representative democracy (of "the modern" — as in Benjamin Constant's criticism of Rousseauean ideals). We need to remind ourselves of the need in modern societies for supplementing participatory democracy (mainly restricted to lower levels) with representative democracy (at high levels).[9]

I shall not elaborate this point further. I shall instead just briefly recall the importance of the corporative system including influential interest groups and of the administrative apparatus and the mass media — institutions characteristic of modern representative democracy. Compared both with the political importance of this institutional sector, and with the amount of empirical research on its various aspects, this sector seems to be insufficiently elaborated intellectually, not least among leftist intellectuals.[10]

Through these intermediary and mixed systems the main political institutions are in mutual connection with the economic system as well as with the sphere of socio-cultural reproduction and creation. At this point our "triangle" could (and should) have been expanded to include the behavioural and decision-making spheres of (i) the market as well as of (ii) tradition (the lifeworld).

Finally I would emphasize the inherent tension between argumentation and voting, or between free and enlightened discussion on the one hand and decision-making by legal procedures leading up to a vote on the other. In politics both are needed, since politics depends on legality and enlightenment — right and truth — at the same time as politics is a domain of power and controversy. An enlightened, law-regulated representative democracy represents a civilized answer to this "war of the gods" (as Max Weber has it).

(B) In embracing representative democracy with its various ingredients a sobering step forward has been taken by leftist intellectuals. Thereby one has also accepted the need for legal regulations, the need for procedures of election, of negotiation and of voting. Legality, law and order are indeed precious ideas, despite the possibility of misuse. Some such misuse is certainly to be expected. But these ideas should not be seen merely in the light of authoritarian repression and as an ideological expression of those in power (be they an overclass, males or parents). Law and order are necessary and basically desirable in any civilized modern society. The need for open criticism is evidently always there. But without these frames of law and legality modern society will most probably deteriorate into an untamed power struggle and repression, nepotism and corruption.

Legal procedures are required for the process of decision-making leading up to voting. But not all issues ought to be open for renewed decision all the time. That would lead to overcharge and to stalemate.[11] Some self-restriction of the power-game of politics is required, a self-restriction through formal procedures which makes the political game more predictable and thus civilized. Along these lines we can talk about the wisdom of political systems that restrict their own freedom of constantly redoing their own decisions. Like Ulysses they rather decide to tie themselves to the mast. The aspect of stability and predictability which follows from this self-restriction is definitely one of high civilizatory value.

Any civilized constitutional system should also pay due attention to human rights — or should we rather say "natural rights" when communities and traditions as well as animal rights and ecological rights are included. Vulgar criticism of the notion of rights has mostly evaporated and this issue is today safely placed on the agenda for leftist intellectuals. The issue to be discussed is not the legitimacy of this notion but the question about the status of various rights or proposed rights and the relation between rights and political decisions — the former question involving a discussion of the foundation of rights and of their mutual interrelations, the latter question involving a discussion of the relation between the domain of what should be decided by reason and remain more or less unchangeable and what should be decided by voting and be more open for changes.[12]

A decisive transition is the one leading from "positive rights" to "natural rights" (to speak in old tongues), that is, from the actually existing legal system to a normative evaluation of this system. Only if this latter possibility, that of a normative evaluation, is granted, can rights in principle be grounded beyond the sphere of power. And this is a point where the discussion among intellectuals, leftist or not, is still to a large extent underdeveloped. I shall therefore briefly elaborate my position on the possibility of a normative foundation which is also related to my previous remarks about discursive rationality and tolerance.

Broadly speaking my position is that of discourse ethics (found in K.-O. Apel, J. Habermas et al.). I shall first refer to a couple of counter-arguments against competing positions (and thus in favour of discourse ethics) and then I shall focus directly on discourse ethics itself.

Scepticism concerning the possibility of a rational foundation of basic norms might have positivistic roots. According to positivism only statements can be true or false norms (that is, basic norms are not — though hypothetical norms are empirically testable — like the claim "you ought to do your homework in order to pass your exam"). It is nowadays well-known that positivism as a position is untenable. A main counter-argument is that of its self-referential inconsistency. Furthermore, it can be shown that there are "institutional facts" inherent in various institutions (such as the idea of "corner" in football), which means that the very distinction between facts and norms is inadequate: within a society there are numerous "institutions", with their inherent norms and values, which can be analyzed and investigated in various ways.

In formulating the criticism of positivism in these terms we are indicating a contextualist (or historicist) position concerning the status of norms: norms are embedded in different contexts. Within each context the context-inherent norms are valid and in this sense mandatory. Different contexts can be overlapping, thus common norms and values can be shared but there is no universal position above the various contexts. Hence, within this position there are no universally valid norms, that is, norms that are obligatory for everybody and that can serve as a basis for a rational criticism of any given context (such as the various "contexts" of religious or national traditions or legal systems within states). In other words, there is no impartiality. (Therefore the attempt at such a rational grounding is frequently interpreted as power in disguise, be it class, race or sex.)

This is a decisive point, and a difficult one. I shall, however, indicate some counterarguments to this contextualism (and relativism):

First of all we have the theoretical problem of describing contextualism without pragmatic inconsistency, that is, without making universal validity-claims in describing a position that implicitly or explicitly denies such a universality. Despite all argument concerning the differences between showing and stating (or claiming) and the like, I cannot really see that contextualism can avoid this inconsistency.[13]

Then we have the practical (political) problem of relativism inherent in this kind of contextualism: according to this position, there is no ground, in universal human rights, for criticism or intervention across political and cultural borders. Thus any claim of a rational foundation of basic rights becomes questionable, and the same goes for any criticism of traditions and states, such as the Third Reich, which violate these rights.

These critical remarks on contextualism point toward a pragmatic notion of discursive rationality which, I claim, gives the best available answer to the question of the foundation of basic norms.

The first argument is one about self-reference: not only are the other positions (positivism and contextualism) shown to be self-referentially inconsistent, but in reflecting on such dilemmas we realize that there is a core of unavoidable while undeniable insights (like the principle of contradiction, which cannot be deductively demonstrated, but which can be shown to be presupposed in any attempt at denying it). This is a peculiar kind of experience, a reflective experience, which requires a pragmatic attitude (in contrast to a semantic or third person attitude).

Through language this insight is intersubjectively accessible, also for criticism. Through language we can argue with each other for and against the different claims that are put forward. In taking part in an argumentation we participate in an activity with constitutive presuppositions upon which we can reflect and which we can thematize and discuss. Within such an argumentative activity we do recognize each other mutually as rational and as fallible — as rational enough to follow the argumentation and as fallible in the sense that each of us needs correction from the others. And in order to take part in an argumentation we have to accept the force of the better argument over against less good arguments, and we have to be interested in improving the given arguments.

What is now said has the status of a claim concerning what is a correct description of a serious discussion, but also of what we undeniably have to presuppose while discussing. The latter claim is (again) one of self-reference. I shall not here tire the reader with a lengthy discussion of the more intricate questions connected to this position. In this paper I shall merely recall a few decisive points:[14]

My interpretation of the notion of "rational consensus", in contrast to "best available real consensus", indicates an unavoidable regulative idea of any argumentative discourse. The operative notion, however, is rather that of meliorism, of improving the best available real position. Here the emphasis is on the elimination of what is not good enough, rather than on the notion of seeking perfection. For this reason I prefer, at this level, a reinterpreted version of the Rawlsian notion of a reflective equilibrium to that of a consensus, viz. to the extent that the term "discursive-reflective equilibrium" indicates that the best available position at any time is (and should be) open to challenges and thus to improvement. New arguments can in principle always emerge and therefore we should seek them out and take them into consideration, in order to try out and possibly improve our given "equilibrium". In saying this I have to add that the reason for talking about consensus is equally decisive, namely the very point that an argument is what can be agreed upon by every rational being who argues under ideal (sufficiently ideal!) conditions. The notion of a valid argument is one that is intersubjectively and universally valid. And for this reason symmetric conditions among the discussants are essential, meaning that liberal virtues (or rights) of equality and free speech can rightly be regarded as presuppositions for rationality — and thus as undeniable norms.

However, in using the term "discursive-reflective equilibrium" in addition to that of consensus (on a somewhat different level) I want to stress the intersubjective aspect of real discourse (in addition to the reflective aspect, which in principle can be taken care of monologically, at least for the time being). This again implies that I regard real discourse, not only the idea of an ideal discourse, as essential, both theoretically and practically. This, by the way, is also a point where one of the basic and valuable ideas of participatory democracy reemerges. Real discourse, in this frame of argumentative rationality, entails that the actual understanding of one's identity, interests and needs is questioned, opening up for a possible change and improvement. This is the deeper meaning of the learning-process inherent in a discursive activity.

In talking about the real discourse and possible changes and improvements one should bear in mind that the "explicit discourse" is just a part of a process within which we have all kinds of after-thoughts on previous discourses and preparations for new ones, connected with various kinds of reading and writing, and often also of travelling (to meet new challenges and perspectives). The latter point indicates three important insights.

(i) There is a gradual transition from discourse to action. This is not merely an empirical claim: even though we have an unavoidable regulative idea of rational consensus, any actual consensus has the status of the, until now, best available equilibrium for the discussants under optimal conditions. And to the extent that an ideal speech situation, or a final consensus, is not available in real discourse, there is no hard core sharply delimited from a soft environment of mere action; there is rather gradual transition (as there is between empirical and transcendental arguments[15]).

(ii) Understanding concepts and principles is immanently connected with use and practice — both are needed (practice *and* principles).[16]

(iii) Finally this indicates that the problem of "transferring" the validity of norms from discourse to society at large is a problem which should not be stated too crudely. To the extent that normative answers are found within the process of discourse their validity for relevant extra-discursive activities is rather like the relation of theoretical validity (found in theoretical discourses) to extra-discursive activities. Furthermore, normative answers within a discourse — though fallible like any discourse-immanent answer, be they theoretical or not — are partly rooted not only in intersubjective consensus but also partly in the adequacy of the concepts involved. Norms never appear naked, as it were, but always within some language, the adequacy of which has also to be decided. Thus the difference between theoretical and normative validity-claims and answers should not be conceived in clear-cut dualistic terms. To the extent that normative answers are tied up with reflectively recognized preconditions for discursive rationality they have the status of norms constitutive for rationality, which is also relevant for everyday life outside the relatively strict activity of argumentation. One can also add to this the Habermasian arguments, both empirical and theoretical, for a universal pragmatics, as well as those concerning the modernization of the life-world.

I shall end these brief remarks on the notion of discursive rationality. My purpose has been to recall how this position allows for a rational grounding of basic rights, thus giving a foundation different from power, interests and partiality.

(C) Non-distorted and enlightened people are required for rational discourse as well as for representative or participatory democracy. The third angle is thus that of enlightenment.

In negative terms this entails an attempt to do away with individual and social distortion. In positive terms it entails the whole system of learning, from the early stages of socialization all through the educational system up to scientific and scholarly research. For one thing, this means that education is a condition for democracy as well as for any rational discourse. But despite this dependence the sphere of research and education (of enlightenment) has its relative autonomy, just like truth it should not be overrun by power (nor by normative rights).

However, when it comes to scientific and scholarly research there is, within large-scale political and economic projects, a rational need to mediate between different disciplines, to bring the insight of the various disciplines into some intelligible whole, which can be discussed publicly and decided politically. This requires for one thing an hermeneutic and reflective competence among the researchers, and it requires legal and practical frames for public discussion.[17]

It is thus worthwhile noticing that *discursive rationality* is a *common denominator* for the highest level at all three spheres of our triangle of *democracy, rights* and *enlightenment*. A lack of understanding of the role and importance of discursive rationality is therefore, in my view, a severe deficit in any notion of political culture. And at this point, it seems to me, there is still some work to be done, in order to bring intellectuals, leftist or not, into an adequate position.

There is then a second conclusion of significant importance for my effort of an ideological reconsideration. Even though my triangular model is fairly simplistic and in need of being supplemented — for one thing economy and culture are left out — it does not only give some hints about dependencies and autonomies and about the need for (and possibility of) a *universalistic (though fallible) discursive rationality* (embracing basic normative themes as well as theoretical ones), but it also indicates the importance of a *balance* between these spheres and levels. Negatively stated we could say that political culture is *essentially multi-dimensional*. It is not one-dimensional in the sense that it makes sense to think of a maximizing of political culture along one dimension alone — be it participatory democracy or moralistic virtue. Any attempt in that direction is doomed to fail, and to lead to disaster, since the very point is that of an *interplay* of *many* factors, not the perfection along one line (". . . radical, more radical, most radical"!).

This is the point where our reflection on a normative notion of political culture reveals its relevance for the issue discussed in the first part of this paper, namely the expansion of market economy and of nationalistic conflicts:

(i) A market economy should find its functional role and realm, relative to these other institutions and spheres in modern society. A market economy should not be allowed to expand in a way that gives relative onesidedness and imbalance.

(ii) National conflicts should be filtered through the various institutions and spheres of a modern society with a differentiated political culture. They should be "laundered" by education and enlightenment, by participatory and representative democracy, by positive and "natural" law, finally seeking legitimacy through a procedural, enlightened and free discussion including everybody concerned.

Politics is not the place for *perfectionism* (as Robespierre and Khomeini thought), but of a pragmatic balance, where the crucial point is not perfection *but sufficiency*. Politics is not a realm for existential exercises or pseudo-religious emotions and aspirations. It is not the realm for utopia and perfection. It is the realm of *a sufficiently good balance and interplay of many factors and concerns*. Through it all though, there is a demand for permanently *improving* discursive rationality.

The important political question is that of what, at any time, is *enough*, what is good enough — or rather, to know, in concrete cases, when the interplay is *not* good enough. And this genuinely political insight cannot be learnt from books or by discussions alone. In addition practical experience is required. Practical experience in this sense is only acquired through a multi-dimensional learning-process, in the "first person" as it were — whereby one learns to see the world from the different perspectives of different activities. This is not the god's eye surveying everything from above, but a pragmatic learning-process of seeing the world from different spheres and levels.

We might say: the time for strong actions and severe interventions is the one when this subtle interplay has got out of balance. In between these moments of crisis, politics should be a realm of un-utopic cool pragmatism, of enlightened pragmatism on behalf of a sufficiently good interplay of factors. However, at least for ecological reasons a state of crisis in terms of long-term imbalance has become a permanent challenge to our political culture, demanding more than short-term and short-sighted pragmatism.

Starting with recent events in Eastern Europe, emphasizing the reemergence of the market economy and of nationalist conflicts, following on with formerly neglected themes among many leftist intellectuals, I have tried to delineate some of the notions and perspectives that in my view have to be reconsidered for any modern society, East European societies included. My main point is that of indicating a fruitful tension, between (i) *discursive rationality* and (ii) *a pragmatic concern for a possible imbalance of the interplay between spheres and levels* — between universal rationality and contextual pragmatism that is constitutive for a *modern world* and for a *political culture*.

This might seem too much, in terms of rationality, and too little, in terms of utopian aspirations. But this, I think, is exactly the lesson to be learnt for modern humans, for leftist intellectuals included.

What then do we have?

Life, I suppose, as long as it still exists, with all its wonder. We have our common rationality and our common world, with a political culture which in a long-term perspective is out of balance, in crisis — be it socio-cultural disintegration or ecological unsustainability.

So there is time for deep and wise interventions, while still keeping the balance that is required.

Politically, what does this mean?

If I am not mistaken these reflections point in a certain direction: not state-socialism, nor Yugoslav socialism, nor free market economy North American style — nor any national-capitalism Japanese style (for its lack of universality).

What remains is some sort of a reasonable social democracy — the term used not for specific political parties, but for a general political approach — social democracy, improved for one thing by a concern for socio-cultural re-production and for urgent ecological questions.

This, I assume, is not the answer desired by all leftist intellectuals. But then, what is the alternative — the political alternative?

Finally, where does this lead us, in geo-political terms? Probably nowhere. But if there should be somewhere to look, rather than somewhere else, it seems reasonable to look at Northwestern Europe, not least Scandinavia — not as an ideal, but only as what is probably less miserable than most other places.

But the basic question is that of moving along, both with a reasonable balance and with a rational and deep concern for a sustainable future on a global scale.

Notes

* This paper was written in Dubrovnik in April 1990 and thereafter distributed to various friends and colleagues, some of whom sent their reactions in return, giving valuable assistance for further elaboration of the paper. To my surprise and without my knowledge or permission a previous version of the paper appeared in *Praxis International* 40, 3/4. Evidently, communication is a fine art, and not only in politics. However, the definitive and genuine version is the one published in this volume.

1. Certainly, various deep problems of the state-socialist system were well known for a long time, inside and outside these countries. But the fast and peaceful disintegration of this system, was to my knowledge unpredicted.

2. A third question is that of the role of nuclear deterrent in the process of changing Soviet politics: Were the Hawks right? i.e. in the sense that the ambitious American plans for further nuclear rearmament (Star Wars included) finally persuaded the Soviet leaders that they could not compete, technologically and economically.

3. The term nationalism is very ambiguous. I shall not even try to define the term, but merely give a first hint: in this paper I use the term primarily for particular collective identity (usually based on a common language and a common specific history) which takes not only conscious but also explicit forms (usually through political manifestations, either to ascertain a cultural domination or to gain cultural recognition and political autonomy). For the discussion of nationalism in Eastern Europe, and thereby of the term itself, see e.g. Miroslav Hroch, "How Much Does Nation Formation Depend on Nationalism?", *East European Politics and Societies*

4, 1 (1990), pp. 101–115. (Contribution in a debate on Roman Szporluk's book, *Communism and Nationalism: Karl Marx versus Friedrich List* (Oxford, Oxford University Press, 1988).

4. This is certainly a complicated question: there is a psychological need to "wash one's hands". There is a strategic desire to "undo" the past by moving in the opposite direction. There is probably a lack of knowledge of political alternatives to the two extremes (marxism and capitalism). And there are probably material reasons for the choice of market institutions, viz. a lack of wealth that could be distributed by a welfare politics. In short, the question is highly complicated, and the final interpretation of the apparent pro-market attitudes in Eastern Europe has to be postponed. In the future, under (hopefully) better conditions, a move toward social democratic solutions could well be expected.

5. This, again, is certainly a complicated question: to what extent are all the former nationalist conflicts "back in the field", and in their former shape? Or are there some former nationalist conflicts and movements that have not reemerged? (What about the former conflict between Czechs and Germans?) Are there today some nationalist conflicts and movements that did not really exist (at least not in the same form) before the communist take-over? (What about the conflict between the Russians and the Azis?) And in the cases where nationalist conflicts and movements do reemerge, in which sense are they really "the same"? (What about the conflict between Serbs and Albanians? To which extent has, for instance, demography added new aspects to this traditional conflict?) These are empirical questions that have to be settled before we can claim that this hypothesis (the "out-of-the-ice" explanation) does give an adequate description.

6. In terms of culture it is certainly another question, where one could argue in somewhat different directions.

7. cf. for example, Johann P. Arnason, "The Modern Constellation and the Japanese Enigma", *Thesis Eleven* 17 (1987), pp. 4–39, and also "Comparing Japan and the West — Prolegomena to a Research Program", mimeo, 31 pp.

8. cf. the French debate on the value of national identity, for example, by the former leftist Régis Debray and the former editor of *Esprit* Jean-Marie Domenach (*Europe: le défi culturel*, Paris, 1990).

9. In parentheses it could be added that intellectuals, and specially young intellectuals with fewer duties, probably have some bias in favour of teach-ins compared with committee work and party politics.

10. Among the exceptions we have Claus Offe who has, as a leftist intellectual, paid special attention to these intermediary levels of modern society. A discussion of (Scandinavian) welfare politics is here of special interest. Professional intellectuals, living their lives in their own setting, tend to be more interested in the bright ideals of political and intellectual freedom than in the dull quarrel of social welfare and social equity.

11. cf. Jon Elster on the political need for tying oneself to the mast, *Ulysses and the*

Sirens: Studies in Rationality and Irrationality (Cambridge, Cambridge University Press, 1979).

12. For instance, should ethical issues, like that of abortion, be politically decided within the legal system (as in the US) or within the parliamentary system (as in most European countries)? And to which extent should such issues, ideally, be taken out of the political sphere all together and be treated purely ethically (as defenders of natural rights argue).

13. cf. my arguments in "Contextual and Universal Pragmatics", *Thesis Eleven* 28 (1991).

14. cf. my comment on these questions in "Pragmatism in Apel and Habermas" in I. Gullvåg and H. Høibraaten (eds), *Essays in Pragmatic Philosophy I* (Oslo, Norwegian University Press, 1985).

15. cf. my remarks in *Truth and Preconditions*, part II (Bergen, 1973).

16. cf. Dietrich Böhler on the interrelation between "principles" and "practice" in "Die deutsche Zerstörung des politisch-ethischen Universalismus" in Wolfgang Kuhlmann (ed.), *Zerstörung des moralischen Selbstbewusstseins: Chance oder Gefährdung? Praktische Philosophie in Deutschland nach dem Nationalsozialismus* (Forum für Philosophie Bad Homburg, Frankfurt, Suhrkamp, 1988), pp. 166–217.

17. cf. my article "Technological Expertise and Global Ethics in a Time of Scientization and Ecological Crisis", written for the journal *Chelaviek* (Moscow) 1 (1990), in English in the *Jahrbuch for the Centre for the Theory of the Sciences and the Humanities* (SVT) (University of Bergen, 1990).

Part Two:
In the Wake of
Postmodernity:
Modernity's
Re-emergence

INTRODUCTION:
THE SYMPTOM OF
POSTMODERNITY

John Rundell

The introduction to Part One of *Between Totalitarianism and Postmodernity* "Between Bolshevism and Democracy" also serves to set the scene for this introduction to Part Two. I want to suggest here that postmodernity is enigmatic; overdrawn and only partially understood. The essays arranged in the second half of this volume are presented as an attempt to extend our understanding of this enigmatic term.

Whilst only some of the essays deal with the question of postmodernity directly, the others can be connected to this line of enquiry. This also enables us to relate the present collection to the debate generated by the more recent work of Jürgen Habermas, who has an almost ghostly presence in this part of the volume. On the one hand, his version of modernity is in stark contrast to the ones sketched, for example, by Zygmunt Bauman and Alain Touraine, whilst on the other, his theory of communicative action, through which he recasts the project of practical reason, becomes a point of critical contact for many of the other contributors.

There is also, though, another direction that this introduction takes apart from the purely contextual. I want to suggest that postmodernity might be a symptom. The question is then, what might it be symptomatic of? This question provides the underlying focus for the following discussion of the papers.

For Agnes Heller and Zygmunt Bauman postmodernity is not only a socio-structural constellation typified by plurality, systemic differentiation and the shift from the idea of a co-ordinated system to one which is disaggregated and thus resists co-ordination. It is also and more positively a "modernity for itself", or a "modernity which has become self-secure which no longer considers itself an *intermundium* between past and future". It is a modernity that has come to terms with those aspects of its past which have been traditionalising and holistic. It is a modernity conscious of itself.

But what is meant by this?

There appears in the postmodern literature to be no agreement (a post-modern irony of postmodernity) about what postmodern means. But in these brief opening remarks two aspects have emerged - on the one hand, post-modernity is indicative of a new social form, and on the other, postmodernity is a new cultural sensibility, a new sensibility of self-recognition. There is a third, the postmodern critique of modernity.

I will, all to briefly, begin with this. The underlying agreement of post-modern critics of modernity revolves around a cultural pessimism inherited from Nietzsche. Nietzsche's cultural pessimism centres on the idea that the standard of freedom can only be measured against a background of distance from normatively affirming contexts whether they be in everyday life or insti-tutional settings. Freedom, thus, is experienced as a celebration of distance, read *difference*, between two types of context, a monolithic and empty modern one, and a playful, pluralised postmodern one.

There are two other aspects of this reconstruction of society in the last quarter of the twentieth century as postmodern. First, there is the collapse of and incredulity towards modernity's two prominent 'cultural fictions'—science and universalism. However, as Axel Honneth points out in "Pluralisation and Recognition: On the Self-misunderstanding of Postmodern Social Theories" "what Lyotard describes as 'the end of metanarratives' is, when dispassionately viewed, nothing other than the accelerated process of narratively constituted traditions". Second, this process of destruction is accompanied by a weakening of not so much the communicative potential of the subject, but his/her com-municative ability in which the capacity to differentiate between reality and fiction or phantasy decreases. A fictionalisation of reality takes place.

This fictionalisation is supposed to account for a presumed emptying of modern contexts which results, as Agnes Heller puts it, in emotional impover-ishment. Yet, as she argues in "Are We Living In A World Of Emotional Impov-erishment?", this claim grew out of a specific context of the German Romantic generation of the late eighteenth and early nineteenth centuries which argued that internal to modernity was a struggle between a tradition that emphasizes the cultivation of emotions, expressed through new literary genres (poetry and the novel), and emotional impoverishment exemplified by a routinised every-day life. But as Heller remarks, it is this constellation of the development of esoteric culture and the feeling of loss that produces the language of "mass culture" and "mass society" developed by those who speak for an esoteric cul-tural milieu. This dialectics of cultivation is projected onto the modern world as a whole, and it is done in a twofold way. On the one hand, aesthetics and aesthetic sensibility become the bearers of oppositional forms, meaning and activity, and on the other, this aesthetic activity develops into literary and artistic forms which transpose the historical-empirical boheme from an artist-musician-poet into a signifying practice or a text with or without contexts, with or without margins.

I do not want to dwell on this aspect of the self-understanding of post-modernity, on what might be termed its totalising critique which emphasises and projects back onto modernity as a whole certain of modernity's colonising features from its own aesthetic standpoint, as this is amply and subtly analysed by both Axel Honneth and Agnes Heller.

Rather, I want to, in the more positive spirit of the opening remarks, open onto the much more central and significant issue of the postmodern image of society—the underlying and unifying focus of the papers collected in this second part of *Between Totalitarianism and Postmodernity*.

In a sociological rather than an aesthetic register, Alain Touraine argues that the idea or image of modernity emerged out of two competing trajectories and sets of experiences. The first concerned the formation of the nation state where modern societies were subsequently analysed according "to a juridical interpretation of social life as a totality of regulated exchange" which emphasised order. Out of this has emerged a critical sociology of power which sees society as an implacable machine that maintains order, privilege and inequality. The second trajectory concerned the formation of industrial society where modern societies were consequently analysed in terms of production, work and change usually linked to the notion of class and progress. A critical sociology of crisis emerges from this current which limits itself to the study of the dysfunctions of the political system, of capitalism, of the personality. If the critical sociology of crisis moves outside the society it emphasises strategic modification of usually a specific institutional field. Here Touraine has in mind thinkers such as Foucault and Bourdieu, especially when they draw on the first current to inform the second.

This dual image of nation state and industry is the double legacy of the sociological concept of society. For Touraine, though, the study of society should be neither about order nor change, but transformation, action and cultural activity. Structurally, for Touraine, this is denoted by a sharper and stronger separation between state and civil society, the acceleration of economic change, the topicalisation of private and everyday life once they both become *noticed* dimensions of social life, and sites for social contestation. There also occurs the internationalization of politics and economy, together with the conflicts that exist between not only the old and new worlds, but also between East and West, North and South, each with its own priorities and models of development. Whilst not unrelated to these developments, although not reducible to them, there is also a shift in the image of conflict from class to social movements. Society, for Touraine, is movement within a discrete cultural field, the collective actors of which attempt to define, portray as well as contest, the cultural models predominant in or relevant to that field. A sociology of social movements, then, is primarily concerned with "the formation of [collective] social actors and the development of their ability to engage in conflicts and negotiations". The differentiation and pluralisation of the sites of social conflict is then accompanied and co-constituted by a pluralisation and differentiation of social movements.

Zygmunt Bauman grasps these motifs of movement and pluralization which also denote a shift from a functionalist to a post-functionalist paradigm of sociological thought, and argues that they become central to the postmodern image of contemporary society. In "A Sociological Theory of Postmodernity", and on a broad canvas, he reconstructs not only the self-understanding of post-modernity, but also along his own lines, its sociological typography. For Bauman, distinctive features of postmodernity are institutional pluralism, variety, contingency and ambivalence. Randomness and disorganisation are its signposts in contradistinction to the signposts of progress and unilinearity, which, for him, typify modernity. Drawing on the work of Touraine and Bourdieu, this randomness and disorganisation is expressed, in Bauman's view, in a shift of focus from the functional image of society to an image which stresses not only a plurality of fields, but also the constitutive activity of the social actors themselves. The notion of power enters with renewed force against the idea of consensual activity to emphasise the permanent and open-ended contestability of resources. However, the particular idea of power also reveals, for Bauman, the postmodern existential condition—inconclusiveness and restlessness. Incessant activity is the marker for the identity of the postmodern subject. This restlessness also means that postmodernity weakens the grasp that the past has on contemporary lives whilst simultaneously preventing this present from colonising any number of possible futures.

Accompanying this change in typography, so Bauman as well as Touraine argue, is a shift in the meaning of modernity's signifying categories, and along with this the forms politics itself take. According to Touraine, the central, forming modern idea of individualism has altered from one concerning utility and juridification, to one concerning not only rights, but also a 'right to be heard'. In other words, the world of non-institutional public political activity expands and differentiates into specific sites and topics of contestation.

Moreover, as Touraine points out, this shift has created two paths. On the one hand, the image and claim to the redemptive paradigm with its image of the totalising and revolutionary transformation of society, has been dismantled and discredited, and not only because of the existence and internal collapse of the Soviet Union and its empire, but also because of a crisis of *faith* in its veracity among Western intellectuals. On the other hand, what might be termed political modernity no longer appears to utilise the grand narrative signposts of equality and distributive justice (the corner stones of social democracy, and its use of the state as the mechanism of redistribution and site of justice). The restlessness and pluralisation of fields manifests itself in both the plurality and visibility of social movements from the women's movement, the ecology movement, consumer movements, and rights movements with the idea of rights being expanded to cover all aspects of life.

Furthermore, this presupposes the existence of a social space in which social movements can be heard, as well as the existence of those social movements whose goal it has historically been to create this space, in other words, to create a political public sphere. To be sure, this is not the invention of the 'new' social movements, but it is the invention of those social movements that historically championed democracy. In this context Lyotard's celebration of the collapse of grand narratives misses the point. For him, the institution which became the bearer of democracy is the French state. But from another heritage, particularly the American as well as the non-corporatist versions of socialism, it is the emergence of *specialised* institutions which reproduced the invention of democratic practices: rational self-determination, universalizable and formal participation in decision making, and non-violent resolution of conflict. The notion of individualism is tied here to a threefold struggle between universalism(tied to the nature of formal democratic practices), particularism (tied to historical, regional and cultural specificity), and the political public sphere. The definition of democracy and its cultural models, as well as its survival, swings between the poles of this interrelated conflict.

Postmodernity is *the experience* of living with the tension of this conflict. What emerges out of this tension is another story concerning modernity apart from the two already mentioned by Touraine—nation state formation and capitalist industrialization—that of democracy. And as Johann P. Arnason points out in his "The Theory Of Modernity And The Problematic Of Democracy", democracy remains *the* undertheorised dimension in both classical-functionalist and marxian reconstructions of modernity. It is for this reason that it has become the point of celebration and confusion in postmodern writings.

Among contemporary thinkers, the most systematic attempt to generate a social theory explicitly from the vantage point of this democratic history, experience and self-understanding of the modern epoch has been undertaken by Jürgen Habermas. In the context of this Introduction the issue is for Habermas, the ability of the life-world to be democratically modernised beyond tradition, that is, to be both the ground and the vehicle for the norms of recognition through which mutual understanding can be reached. Andrew Arato and Jean Cohen in their "Civil Society and Social Theory" follow Habermas' footsteps. They argue that the issue of the juridification of rights should not be seen as a narrative concerning nation state formation, but one aspect of the complex formation of modern democracy in the context of the differentiation between system and life world. Democracy presupposes differentiation and ultimately is grounded in the life-world. The notion of rights has a threefold specificity for them anchored in the life-world. It concerns "cultural reproduction (freedom of thought, press, speech, communication) . . . social integration (freedom of association, assembly) . . . [and] socialisation (protection of privacy, intimacy, inviolability of the person)". In this context, they are sympathetic towards Habermas' insistent attempt to institutionally locate the notion of democracy, and the rights which emerge under its auspices through constitutionality and the juridification of these rights.

At the same time, though, they are critical of his overly constraining commitment to formal legal procedures of democratisation which entails that he views social movements not as instances of creative contestation (Touraine), but rather as principally defensive responses to the systemic invasion of the life-world. However, it can be argued, as they show, that contemporary social movements contain *formally* modern elements as well as substantively traditionalising and modern utopian horizons. It is the tension between these two poles that throws self-determination and autonomy into relief. This may entail that the frontiers which limit individual activity are contested. As Bauman notes, every constraint that appears as an externally imposed limit becomes "a hotly contested frontier". But the state of tension and the pushing back of limits also shows another face of contemporary politics. This manifests itself in tribalism or ethnic rivalry with its own elements of traditionalisation, a politics of desire which wishes to give up the idea of limits altogether, a politics of fear in the face of a wholly contingent world.

It is Arato's and Cohen's contention that the translation of the relevant dimensions of the life-world as 'civil society' is needed to contain the divergent dynamics of the modernising process to make sense of a democracy which is also self-limiting. And as Arato and Cohen, as well as Heller and Honneth, point out, this occurs not so much by identifying in *formal procedural terms* the norms that are in play, but rather in further developing the dual dimensions of symmetrical reciprocity and self-reflection, both of which are internal to the emergence of democracy as a life form. For Honneth postmodernity is not so much symptomatic of living in tension with democracy, but of "a recognition vacuum" in the face of both the erosion of narratively constituted traditions and the pluralisation of individual forms of life. Whilst there has been experimentation in the creation of models of social relationships or forms of life, this experimentation has yet, according to Honneth, to generate a new *Sittlichkeit* or an ethical community. That is, they have yet to develop encompassing patterns of orientation. For him, freedom relies on an intersubjectively constituted and communicatively established world in which even a small number of reciprocally recognised values are shared which allow for mutual self-realisation.

This aim of mutual self-realisation is, in very general terms, the concern and direction of the work of Agnes Heller and Cornelius Castoriadis. To be sure, they have different attitudes to the idea of 'postmodernity', as well as to the postmodern milieu. For Heller, as already indicated, the postmodern world is one of contingency in which all fast, frozen relations have *finally* been dissolved. The reference to Marx here is deliberate, because for her postmoderity "is 'parasitic' on modernity: it lives and feeds on its achievements and its dilemmas"[1] Its achievement has been to have transformed the fate of being born into a stratified, closed world into a contingent world with an open possibility of transforming fate into destiny. In other words, according to Heller, it becomes possible for women and men to think, act and create contexts that are different. The dilemma of modernity is that this openness generates generalised dissatisfaction. As she says, "the fateful and unbridgeable discrepancy between expectation and experience is a source of constant dissatisfaction and discontent".[2] The dissatisfaction is generated out of three decontextualising impulses—industrialisation, capitalisation and democratisation. For Heller, these function primarily as the modern signifiers to which satisfaction itself is oriented, and from which dissatisfaction emerges. One can become satisfied/dissatisfied in the context and pursuit of the goals and aspirations of capitalism, of industrialisation, of democracy. The experience of dissatisfaction, reflected in the postmodern condition, is one of conscious restlessness within, or of jumping between, the three logics or 'signifiers' which compete for allegiance.

Heller's recommendation is in a way very similar to that of Weber's—make a conscious vocational, existential choice and commitment to *one* of the three logics and live this commitment well. For her, this commitment should be to the logic, more specifically, to the way of life of democracy. For Heller, unlike Habermas, modern democracy is not procedural but substantive. It relies on two universalizable values that cannot be irrationalised and which become the signposts to which the rights of recognition and argumentation refer. These values are freedom and life, and according to her can become the points of orientation for the process of reflection about the nature of being dissatisfied. The rationality of the other logics, and their ways of life conduct, can be called into question and irrationalised by one or both of these values. Also, through these the subject can become an object of scrutiny to him or herself. S/he becomes both individually differentiated and consciously self-judging, both to his/her own world and also to his/her self. This occurs for the subject not as a cogito, but as "a person as a whole". This requires the subject to have, what Heller terms, emotional depth. For her, this is inseparable from the capacity of the subject to live and judge well in relation to not only itself, but especially in relation to others.[3]

In contrast to other writers in this volume, for Castoriadis what has been termed postmodernity is really a third phase in the long history of the modern West. The emergence of the third phase after the end of the second World War is signalled for him, by the waning of social, political and ideological conflict, in which the contemporary social movements are seen as partial failures. This is because, in Castoriadis' view there is an atrophy of the political imagination in which the democratic utopia within the modern republic has come to a close through either exhaustion or vacuity. At the end of the twentieth century we are, in Castoriadis' view, in a period of "generalised conformity".[4]

Behind Castoriadis' critique lies his own commitment to what he terms "the project of autonomy" and its elucidation. In an essay that engages, in part, with Habermas' own version of the democratic utopia which is grounded in a double theoretical strategy of language-in-use and evolutionary learning processes, Castoriadis argues that the idea of democracy is inseparable from the interrogation into the nature of rationality itself. This interrogation in turn elucidates an image of the social subject, who is not, in the first nor final instance, rational, but creative. For Castoriadis too, democracy is an historical creation, not a rationalisable learning process.

In order to draw this out, Castoriadis, in his "Individual, Society, Rationality, History", critically encounters Max Weber's historical sociology. Weber's error according to him was, while recognising the specificity of historical forms and civilisations, to impose on this the levelling idea of rationalisation. This also has its corollary in his methodological individualism. Castoriadis further argues that Weber's insistence on a rationalistic connection between causality and understanding, and more abstractly between reason and meaning, each anchored in a egological ontology, conceals a double-sided dynamic. On the one hand, it conceals the embeddedness of the individual in what he terms the 'social-historical', the world of pre-forming orientations that 'fabricate' an individual, and which cannot be reduced to moments or processes of rationality, function, or social location. Rather, for him, the social-historical is made up of imaginary significations, which are the surplus of historically created meaning. If social action and the formation of meaning is irreducible to function and rationality then this, in Castoriadis' view, accounts for the creation of new meanings or significations, institutions and ways of life. These emerge out of an imaginary world which is always creative and inventive, certainly conditional, but never *determined* by the functional imperatives of the social historical.

On the other hand Castoriadis's main task is not simply to thematise and elucidate imaginary significations. Rather, the ontology of the radical or creative imaginary serves to ground the idea of interrogative reflexivity. Philosophical or scientific activity as a particular type of social creation only exists in as much that it "presupposes subjects who have *actually* put into question their belonging to some particular social-historical world. In a sense it is even just that". The idea of interrogation, for Castoriadis, is inseparable from the ideas of the radical imaginary and the project of autonomy, for as he states "this project [has to be posited as a creative imaginary signification] before one can draw out any argumentation". Moreover, this activity of interrogative reflexivity and the project of autonomy also involve the activities of judging and choosing. Through this politics (as a "public activity whose object is the institution of society[5]) both emerges and takes place.

Like Heller, and given his ontology of the creative imagination as the source of interrogative reason, Castoriadis prefers a substantivist form of democracy so that he can capture its essential nature as *activity*. However, it is not just any activity, as Bauman, for example, casts it in the light of postmodern restlessness. Rather, for Castoriadis, it is activity *with* and/or *without* limits. As activity, politics is without limits, for there are no questions which cannot be asked. In Castoriadis' view though, the exercise of this 'right to raise questions' also presupposes specific characteristics of responsibility, courage and shame. These are for him, the corollary of also knowing and confronting the issue of the question of the limits to such questions, and the actions which may arise from such questions. In this sense, for Castoriadis, democracy is neither about celebration or celebrities; it is about risk and the conscious appreciation of this.

This appreciation takes place at the intersecting points between the love and 'practice' of beauty, the love and 'practice' of wisdom, and the care and responsibility of the common good.[6] And yet, the risk and its appreciation creates a tension, for, as Castoriadis also notes, "even when we think, on the best rational grounds, that we have made the right decision, this decision may turn out to be wrong, and catastrophially so. Nothing can guarantee *a priori* the correctness of action—not even reason".[7] This is what makes democracy risky, but never postmodern. (Pericles is not the first postmodern individual). It is the riskiness which also makes it *tragic*. Its existence is never guaranteed. Its first breakthrough in ancient Greece was reversed and forgotten, and if we follow Castoriadis, the modern rediscovery of democracy is threatened with the same fate.

The condition which postmodernity signifies may not yet be as bereft of meaning and possibilities as Castoriadis suggests, but it is certainly a condition of living both with certainty and uncertainty, satisfaction and dissatisfaction. If Heller and Bauman are correct in their reading of the postmodern milieu, then this simultaneity is also consciously perceived. 'Living in simultaneity' also contains another sense, the unresolvability of the tension that this creates. We are living with tension—the grand narrative of dialectical sublation, of the *aufhebung*, is finished. It remains to be seen, though, whether or not this heralds the waning of the historical creation of democracy, or whether, in the face of the "recognition vacuum", a new *Sittlichkeit* will form. It is not so much that modernity is an "unfinished project", but that the democratic moment within its much-longer-than-postmodern history needs to be remade again and again and among its other competing dimensions.

Notes

1. A. Heller and F. Feher, *The Postmodern Political Condition*, Cambridge, Polity Press, 1988, p 11.
2. *ibid.* p 19.

3. cf. A. Heller, *General Ethics*, Oxford, Basil Blackwell, 1988; *Beyond Justice*, Oxford, Basil Blackwell, 1987.

4. C. Castoriadis, "The Era of Generalised Conformity". Preliminary paper delivered at A Conversazione on A Metaphor For Our Times, 19 September 1987, ms; see also "The Retreat From Autonomy", *Thesis Eleven*, No. 31, 1992; "The Crisis of Culture and the State", Centre for Humanistic Studies, University of Minnesota, Occsasional papers, No. 16, 1986.

5. cf. C. Castoriadis, "The Greek Polis and the Creation of Democracy", *Graduate Faculty of Phillsophy Journal*, Vol. 9, No. 2, Fall 1983, p. 94. Reprinted in *Philosophy, Politics, Autonomy*, New York, Oxford University Press, 1991.

6. *ibid.* p. 112.

7. *ibid.* p. 110.

A SOCIOLOGICAL THEORY
OF POSTMODERNITY

Zygmunt Bauman

I propose that:

1. The term *postmodernity* renders accurately the defining traits of the social condition that emerged throughout the affluent countries of Europe and of European descent in the course of the 20th century, and took its present shape in the second half of that century. The term is accurate as it draws attention to continuity and discontinuity as two faces of the intricate relationship between the present social condition and the formation that it preceded and gestated. It brings into relief the intimate, genetic bond that ties the new, postmodern social condition to *modernity*—the social formation that emerged in the same part of the world in the course of the 18th century, and took its final shape, later to be sedimented in the sociological models of modern society (or models of society created by modern sociology), during the 19th; while at the same time indicating the passing of a certain crucial characteristic in whose absence one cannot anymore adequately describe the social condition as modern in the sense given to the concept by the orthodox (modern) social theory.

2. Postmodernity may be interpreted as fully developed modernity; as modernity that acknowledged the effects it was producing throughout its history, yet producing inadvertently, by default rather than design, as *unanticipated consequences*, by-products often perceived as waste; as modernity conscious of its true nature—*modernity for itself*. The most conspicuous features of the post-modern condition: institutionalized pluralism, variety, contingency and ambivalence—have been all turned out by the modern society in ever increasing volumes; yet they were produced, so to speak, "by the way", at a time when the institutions of modernity, faithfully replicated by modern mentality, struggled for *universality, homogeneity, monotony* and *clarity*. The post-modern condition can be therefore described, on the one hand, as modernity emancipated from false consciousness; on the other, as a new type of social condition marked by the overt institutionalization of the characteristics which

modernity—in its designs and managerial practices—set about to eliminate and, failing that, tried to conceal.

3. The twin differences that set the postmodern condition apart from modern society are profound and seminal enough to justify (indeed, to call for) a separate sociological theory of postmodernity that would break decisively with the concepts and metaphors of the models of modernity and lift itself out of the mental frame in which they had been conceived. This need arises from the fact that (their notorious disagreements notwithstanding) the extant models of modernity articulated a shared vision of modern history as a *movement with a direction*—and differed solely in the selection of the ultimate destination or the organizing principle of the process, be it universalization, rationalization, or systemization. None of those principles can be upheld (at least not in the radical form typical of the orthodox social theory) in the light of postmodern experience. Neither can be sustained the very master-metaphor that underlies them: one of the process with a pointer.

4. Postmodernity is not a flawed variant of modernity; neither is it a diseased state of modernity, a temporary ailing yet to be rectified, a case of "modernity in crisis". It is, instead, an essentially viable, pragmatically self-sustainable and logically self-contained social condition defined by *distinctive features of its own*. A theory of postmodernity cannot be therefore a modified theory of modernity, a theory of modernity with a set of negative markers. An adequate theory of postmodernity may only be constructed in a cognitive space organized by a different ensemble of assumptions and needs from its own vocabulary. The degree of emancipation from the concepts and issues spawned by the discourse of modernity will be the measure of its adequacy.

CONDITIONS OF THEORETICAL EMANCIPATION

What the theory of postmodernity must discard in the first place is the assumption of a *systemic character* of the social condition it purports to model: the vision of a system (a) with a degree of cohesiveness, (b) equilibrated or marked by an overwhelming tendency to equilibration, (c) defining its elements in terms of the function they perform in that process of equilibration or the reproduction of the equilibrated state. It must assume instead that the social condition it intends to model is essentially and perpetually *unequilibrated*: composed of elements with a degree of autonomy large enough to justify the view of totality as a kaleidoscopic—momentary and contingent—outcome of interaction. The orderly, structured nature of totality cannot be taken for granted; nor can its pseudo-representational construction be seen as the purpose of theoretical activity. Randomness of the global outcome of unco-ordinated activities cannot be treated as a departure from the pattern which the totality strives to maintain; any pattern that may temporarily emerge out of the random movements of autonomous agents is as haphazard and unmotivated as the one that could emerge in its place or the one bound to replace it, if also for a time only. All order that can be found is a local, emergent and transitory phenomenon; its nature can be best grasped by a metaphor of a whirlpool appearing in the flow of a river, retaining its shape only for a relatively brief period and only at the expense of incessant metabolism and constant renewal of content.

The theory of postmodernity must be free of the last vestiges of the metaphor of progress that informed all competing theories of modern society. With the totality dissipated into a series of randomly emerging, shifting and evanescent islands of order, its temporal record cannot be linearly represented. Perpetual local transformations do not add up so as to prompt (much less to assure) in effect an increased homogeneity, rationality or organic systemness of the whole. The postmodern condition is a site of constant mobility and change, but no clear direction of development. The image of Brownian movement offers an apt metaphor for this aspect of postmodernity: each momentary state is neither a necessary effect of the preceding state nor the sufficient cause of the next one. The postmodern condition is both *undetermined* and *undetermining*. It "unbinds" time; weakens the constraining impact of the past and effectively prevents colonization of the future.

Similarly, the theory of postmodernity would do well if it disposed of concepts like *system* (or, for this matter, *society*), suggestive of a sovereign totality whose welfare or perpetuation all smaller (and, by definition, subordinate) units serve—and thus a totality entitled to define, and capable of defining, the meanings of individual actions and agencies that compose it. A sociology geared to the conditions of postmodernity ought to replace the category of *society* with that of *sociality*; a category that tries to convey the processual modality of social reality, the dialectical play of randomness and pattern (or, from the agent's point of view, of freedom and dependence); and a category that refuses to take the structured character of the process for granted—which treats instead all found structures as emergent accomplishments.

With their field of vision organized around the focal point of system-like, resourceful and meaning-bestowing totality, sociological theories of modernity (which conceived of themselves as sociological theories *tout court*) concentrated on the vehicles of homogenization and conflict-resolution in a relentless search for a solution to the "Hobbesian problem". This cognitive perspective (shared with the one realistic referent of the concept of "society"—the national state, the only totality in history able to seriously entertain the ambition of contrived, artificially sustained and managed monotony and homogeneity) a priori disqualified all "uncertified" agency; unpatterned and unregulated spontaneity of the autonomous agent was pre-defined as a de-stabilizing and, indeed, anti-social factor marked for taming and extinction in the continuous struggle for societal survival. By the same token, prime importance was assigned to the mechanisms and weapons of order-promotion and pattern-maintenance:

the state and the legitimation of its authority, power, socialization, culture, ideology etc.—all selected for the role they played in the promotion of pattern, monotony, predictability and thus also manageability of conduct.

A sociological theory of postmodernity is bound to reverse the structure of the cognitive field. The focus must now be on agency; more correctly, on the *habitat* in which agency operates and which it produces in the course of operation. As it offers the agency the sum-total of resources for all possible action as well as the field inside which the action-orienting and action-oriented relevancies may be plotted, the habitat is the territory inside which both freedom and dependency of the agency are constituted (and, indeed, perceived as such). Unlike system-like totalities of modern social theory, habitat neither determines the conduct of the agents nor defines its meaning; it is no more (but no less either) than the setting in which both action and meaning-assignment are *possible*. Its own identity is as under-determined and motile, as emergent and transitory, as those of the actions and their meanings that form it.

There is one crucial area, though, in which the habitat performs a determining (systematizing, patterning) role: it sets the agenda for the "business of life" through supplying the inventory of ends and the pool of means. The way in which the ends and means are supplied determines as well the meaning of the "business of life": the nature of the tasks all agencies confront and have to take up in one form or another. In as far as the ends are offered as potentially alluring rather than obligatory, and rely for their choice on their own seductiveness rather than the supporting power of coercion, the "business of life" splits into a series of choices. The series is not pre-structured, or is pre-structured only feebly and above all inconclusively. For this reason the choices through which the life of the agents is construed and sustained are best seen (as it tends to be seen by the agents themselves) as adding up to the process of *self-constitution*. To underline the graduated and ultimately inconclusive nature of the process, self-constitution is best viewed as *self-assembly*.

I propose that in the sociological theory of postmodernity sociality, habitat, self-constitution and self-assembly should occupy the central place that the orthodoxy of modern social theory had reserved for the categories of society, normative group (like class or community), socialization and control.

MAIN TENETS OF THE THEORY OF POSTMODERNITY

1. Under the postmodern condition, habitat is a *complex system*. According to contemporary mathematics, complex systems differ from mechanical systems (those assumed by the orthodox, modern theory of society) in two crucial respects. First, they are unpredictable; second, they are not controlled by statistically significant factors (the circumstance demonstrated by the mathematical proof of the famous "butterfly effect"). The consequences of these two

distinctive features of complex systems are truly revolutionary in relation to the received wisdom of sociology. The "systemness" of the postmodern habitat does not lend itself anymore to the organismic metaphor, which means that agencies active within the habitat cannot be assessed in terms of functionality or dysfunctionality. The successive states of the habitat appear to be unmotivated and free from constraints of deterministic logic. And the most formidable research strategy modern sociology had developed—statistical analysis—is of no use in exploring the dynamics of social phenomena and evaluating the probabilities of their future development. Significance and numbers have parted ways. Statistically insignificant phenomena may prove to be decisive, and their decisive role cannot be grasped in advance.

2. The postmodern habitat is a complex (non-mechanical) system for two closely related reasons. First, there is no "goal setting" agency with overall managing and coordinating capacities or ambitions—one whose presence would provide a vantage point from which the aggregate of effective agents appears as a "totality" with a determined structure of relevances; a totality which one can think of as an *organization*. Second—the habitat is populated by a great number of agencies, most of them single-purpose, some of them small, some big, but none large enough to subsume or otherwise determine behaviour of the others. Focusing on a single purpose considerably enhances the effectivity of each agency in the field of its own operation, but prevents each area of the habitat from being controlled from a single source, as the field of operation of any agency never exhausts the whole area the action is affecting. Operating in different fields yet zeroing on shared areas, agencies are *partly* dependent on each other, but the lines of dependence cannot be fixed and thus their actions (and consequences) remain staunchly under-determined, that is autonomous.

3. Autonomy means that agents are only partly, if at all, constrained in their pursuit of whatever they have institutionalized as their purpose. To a large extent, they are free to pursue the purpose to the best of their mastery over resources and managerial capacity. They are free (and tend) to view the rest of the habitat shared with other agents as a collection of opportunities and "problems" to be resolved or removed. Opportunity is what increases the output in the pursuit of purpose; a problem is what threatens the decrease or a halt of production. In ideal circumstances (maximization of opportunities and minimization of problems) each agent would tend to go in the pursuit of purpose as far as the resources allow; the availability of resources is the only reason for action they need and thus the sufficient guarantee of the action's reasonability. The possible impact on other agents' opportunities is not automatically reforged into the limitation of the agent's own output. The many products of purpose-pursuing activities of numerous partly interdependent but relatively autonomous agents must yet find, *ex post facto*, their relevance, utility and demand-securing attractiveness. The products are bound to be created in volumes exceeding the pre-existing demand motivated by already

articulated problems. They are still to seek their place and meaning as well as the problems that they may claim to be able to resolve.

4. For every agency, the habitat in which its action is inscribed appears therefore strikingly different from the confined space of its own automatic, purpose-subordinated pursuits. It appears as a space of chaos and chronic *in-determinacy*, a territory subjected to rival and contradictory meaning-bestowing claims and hence perpetually *ambivalent*. All states the habitat may assume appear equally *contingent* (that is, they have no overwhelming reasons for being what they are, and they could be different if any of the participating agencies behave differently). The heuristics of pragmatically useful "next moves" displaces therefore the search for algorithmic, certain knowledge of deterministic chains. The succession of states assumed by the relevant areas of the habitat no agency can interpret without including its own actions in the explanation; agencies cannot meaningfully scan the situation "objectively", that is in such ways as allow to eliminate, or bracket away, their own activity.

5. The existential modality of the agents is therefore one of insufficient determination, inconclusiveness, motility and rootlessness. The identity of the agent is neither given nor authoritatively confirmed. It has to be construed, yet no design for the construction can be taken as prescribed or foolproof. It lacks a benchmark against which its progress could be measured, and so it cannot be meaningfully described as "progressing". It is now the incessant (and non-linear) activity of *self-constitution* that makes the identity of the agent. In other words, the self-organization of the agents in terms of a "life-project" (a concept that assumes a long-term stability; a lasting identity of the habitat, in its direction transcending, or at least commensurate with, the longevity of human life) is displaced by the process of self-constitution. Unlike the "life-project", self-constitution has no destination point in reference to which it could be evaluated and monitored. It has no visible end; not even a stable direction. It is conducted inside a shifting (and, as we have seen before, unpredictable) constellation of mutually autonomous points of reference, and thus purposes, guiding the self-constitution at any one stage which may soon lose their current authoritatively confirmed validity. Hence the self-assembly of the agency is not a cumulative process; self-constitution entails disassembling alongside the assembling, adoption of new elements as much as shedding of others, learning together with forgetting. The identity of the agency, much as it remains in a state of permanent change, cannot be therefore described as "developing". In the self-constitution of the agencies, the "Brownian movement"-type spatial nature of the habitat is projected onto the time axis.

6. The only visibility of continuity and cumulative effects of the self-constitution efforts is offered by the human body—seen as the only constant factor among the protean and fickle identities. Hence the centrality of *body-cultivation* among the self-assembly concerns, and the acute attention devoted to everything "taken internally" (food, air, drugs, etc.), and everything

coming in touch with the skin—that interface between the agent and the rest of the habitat and the hotly contested frontier of agent's autonomously managed identity. In the postmodern habitat, DIY operations (jogging, dieting, slimming etc.) replace and to a large extent displace the panoptical drill of the modern factory, the school or the barracks; unlike their predecessors, however, they are not perceived as externally imposed, cumbersome and resented necessities, but as manifestoes of the agent's freedom. Their heteronomy, once blatant through coercion, now hides behind seduction.

7. The process of self-constitution is devoid of the advance design and thus generates an acute demand for a substitute: orientation points that may guide successive moves. It is the other agencies (real or imagined) of the habitat who serve as such orientation points. Their impact on the process of self-constitution differs from that exercised by normative groups in that on the whole they neither monitor or knowingly administer the acts of allegiance and the actions that follow it. From the vantage point of self-constituting agents, other agents can be metaphorically visualized as a randomly scattered set of free-standing and unguarded totemic poles which one can approach or abandon without applying for permission to enter or leave. The self-proclaimed allegiance to the selected agent (the act of selection itself) is accomplished through the adoption of *symbolic tokens* of belonging, and the freedom of choice is limitedly solely by the availability and accessibility of such tokens.

8. *Availability* of tokens for potential self-assembly depends on their *visibility*, much as it does on their material presence. Visibility in its turn depends on the perceived *utility* of symbolic tokens for the satisfactory outcome of self-construction; that is, on their ability to reassure the agent that the current results of self-assembly are indeed satisfactory. This reassurance is the substitute for the absent certainty, much as the orientation points with the attached symbolic tokens are collectively a substitute for pre-determined patterns for life-projects. The reassuring capacity of symbolic tokens rests on borrowed (ceded) authority: of *expertise*, or of *mass following*. Symbolic tokens are actively sought and adopted if their relevance is vouched for by the trusted authority of the expert, or by their previous or concurrent appropriation by a great number of other agents. These two variants of authority are in their turn fed by the insatiable thirst of the self-constituting agents for reassurance. Thus *freedom* of choice and *dependence* on external agents reinforce each other, and arise and grow together as products of the same process of self-assembly and of the constant demand for reliable orientation points which it cannot but generate.

9. *Accessibility* of tokens for self-assembly varies from agent to agent, depending mostly on the resources that a given agent commands. Increasingly the most strategic role among the resources is played by knowledge; the growth of individually appropriated knowledge widens the range of assembly patterns which can be realistically chosen. Freedom of the agent, measured by the range of realistic choices, turns under the postmodern condition into

the main dimension of inequality and thus becomes the main stake of the *re-distributional* type of conflict that tends to arise from the dichotomy of privilege and deprivation; by the same token, access to knowledge—being the key to an extended freedom—turns into the major index of social standing. This circumstance lifts the attractiveness of *information* among the symbolic tokens sought after for their reassuring potential. It also further enhances the authority of experts, trusted to be the repositories and sources of valid knowledge. Information becomes a major resource, and experts the crucial brokers of all self-advancement.

POSTMODERN POLITICS

Modern social theory could afford to separate theory from policy. Indeed, it made a virtue out of that historically circumscribed plausibility. Keeping the separation watertight has turned into a most distinctive mark of modern theory of society. A theory of postmodernity cannot follow the pattern. Once the essential contingency and the absence of supra- or pre-agentic foundations of sociality and of the structured forms it sediments have been acknowledged, it becomes clear that the politics of agents lies at the core of the habitat's existence; indeed, it can be said to be its existential modality. All description of the postmodern habitat must include politics from the beginning. Politics cannot be kept outside the basic theoretical model as an epiphenomenon, a super-structural reflection or belatedly formed, intellectually processed derivative.

It could be argued (though the argument cannot be spelled out here) that the separation of theory and policy in modern *theory* could be sustained as long as there was, unchallenged or effectively immunized against challenge, a *practical* division between theoretical and political practice. The latter separation had its foundation in the activity of the modern national state, arguably the only social formation in history with pretensions and ambitions of the administration of a global order, and of a total monopoly, and the procedure of its formulation had to be made separate and independent from the procedure legitimizing an acceptable theory and, more generally, intellectual work modelled after the latter procedure. The gradual, yet relentless erosion of the national state's monopoly (undermined simultaneously from above and from below, by transnational and sub-national agencies, and weakened by the fissures in the historical marriage between nationalism and the state, none needing the other very strongly in their mature form) ended the plausibility of theoretical segregation.

With the state's resourcefulness and ambitions shrinking, responsibility (real or just claimed) for policy shifts away from the state or is actively shed on the state's own initiative. It is not taken over by another agent, though. It dissipates; it splits into a plethora of localized or partial policies pursued by localized or partial (mostly one issue) agencies. With that vanishes the modern state's tendency to precipitate and draw upon itself almost all social protest arising from unsatisfied redistributional demands and expectations—a quality that further enhanced the exclusive role of the state among societal agencies, at the same time rendering it vulnerable and exposed to frequent political crises (as conflicts fast turned into political protests). Under the postmodern condition grievances which in the past would cumulate into a collective political process and address themselves to the state, stay diffuse and translate into self-reflexivity of the agents, stimulating further dissipation of policies and the autonomy of postmodern agencies (if they do cumulate for a time in the form of a one-issue pressure group, they bring together agents too heterogeneous in other respects to prevent the dissolution of the formation once the desired progress in the issue in question has been achieved; and even before that final outcome, the formation is unable to override the diversity of its supporters' interests and thus claim and secure their *total* allegiance and identification). One can speak, allegorically, of the "functionality of dissatisfaction" in a postmodern habitat.

Not all politics in postmodernity is unambiguously postmodern. Throughout the modern era, the politics of *inequality* and hence of *redistribution* was by far the most dominant type of political conflict and conflict-management. With the advent of postmodernity it has lost its dominant role, but remains (and in all probability will remain) a constant feature of the postmodern habitat. Even such an eminently modern type of politics acquires in many cases a postmodern tinge, though. Redistributional vindications of our time are aimed more often than not at the winning of *human rights* (a code name for the agent's autonomy, for that freedom of choice that constitutes the agency in the postmodern habitat) by categories of population heretofore denied them (this is the case of the emancipatory movements of oppressed ethnic minorities, of the black movement, of one important aspect of the feminist movement), rather than at the express re-distribution of wealth, income and other consumable values by the society at large.

Alongside the survivals of the modern form of politics, however, specifically postmodern forms appear and gradually colonize the centrefield of the postmodern political process. Some of them are new; some others owe their new, distinctly postmodern quality to their recent expansion and greatly increased impact. The following are the most prominent among them (the named forms are not necessarily mutually exclusive; and some act at cross-purposes):

1. *Tribal politics.* This is a generic name for practices aimed at collectivization (supra-agentic conformation) of the agents' self-constructing efforts. Tribal politics entails the creation of tribes as *imagined communities.* Unlike the pre-modern communities the modern powers set about to uproot, postmodern tribes exist in no other form but the symbolically manifested commitment of their members. They can rely on neither executive powers able

to coerce their constituency into submission to the tribal rules (seldom do they have clearly codified rules to which the submission could be demanded), nor on the strength of neighbourly bonds or intensity of reciprocal exchange (most tribes are de-territorialized, and communication between their members is hardly at any time more intense than the intercourse between members and non-members of the tribe). Postmodern tribes are, therefore, constantly in *statu nascendi* rather then *essendi*, brought over again into being by repetitive symbolic rituals of the members but persisting no longer than these rituals' power of attraction (in which sense they are akin to Kant's *aesthetic communities* or Schmalenbach's *communions*). Allegiance is composed of the ritually manifested support for positive tribal tokens or equally symbolically demonstrated animosity to negative (anti-tribal) tokens. As the persistence of tribes relies solely on the deployment of the affective allegiance, one would expect an unprecedented condensation and intensity of emotive behaviour and a tendency to render the rituals as spectacular as possible—mainly through inflating their shocking power. Tribal rituals, as it were, compete for the scarce resource of public attention as the major (perhaps sole) resource of survival.

2. *Politics of desire.* This entails actions aimed at establishing the relevance of certain types of conduct (tribal tokens) for the self-constitution of the agents. If the relevance is established, the promoted conduct grows in attractiveness, its declared purposes acquire *seductive* power, and the probability of their choice and active pursuit increases: promoted purposes turn into agents' needs. In the field of the politics of desire, agencies vie with each other for the scarce resource of individual and collective dreams of the good life. The overall effect of the politics of desire is heteronomy of choice supported by, and in its turn sustaining, the autonomy of the choosing agents.

3. *Politics of fear.* This is, in a sense, a supplement (simultaneously a complement and a counterweight) of the politics of desire, aimed at drawing boundaries to heteronomy and staving off its potentially harmful effects. If the typical modern fears were related to the threat of totalitarianism perpetually ensconced in the project of rationalized and state-managed society (Orwell's "boot eternally trampling a human face", Weber's "cog in the machine" and "iron cage" etc.), postmodern fears arise from uncertainty as to the soundness and reliability of advice offered through the politics of desire. More often than not, diffuse fears crystallize in the form of a suspicion that the agencies promoting desire are (for the sake of self-interest) oblivious or negligent of the damaging effects of their proposals. In view of the centrality of body-cultivation in the activity of self-constitution, the damage most feared is one that can result in poisoning or maiming the body through penetration or contact with the skin (the most massive panics have focused recently on incidents like mad cow's disease, listeria in eggs, shrimps fed on poisonous algae, dumping of toxic waste—with the intensity of fear correlated to the importance of the body among the self-constituting concerns, rather than to the statistical signifi-

cance of the event and extent of the damage). The politics of fear strengthens the position of experts in the processes of self-constitution, while ostensibly questioning their competence. Each successive instance of the suspension of trust articulates a new area of the habitat as problematic and thus leads to a call for more experts and more expertise.

4. *Politics of certainty*. This entails the vehement search for social confirmation of choice, in the face of the irredeemable pluralism of the patterns on offer and acute awareness that each formula of self-constitution, however carefully selected and tightly embraced, is ultimately one of the many, and always "until further notice". Production and distribution of certainty is the defining function and the source of power of the experts. As the pronouncements of the experts can seldom be put to the test by the recipients of their services, for most agents the certainty about the soundness of their choices can be plausibly entertained only in the form of *trust*. The politics of certainty consists therefore mainly in the production and manipulation of trust; conversely, "lying", "letting down", betrayal of trust, abuse of privileged information emerge as the major threat to the already precarious and vulnerable self-identity of postmodern agents. Trustworthiness, credibility and perceived sincerity become major criteria by which merchants of certainty—experts, politicians, sellers of self-assembly identity kits—are judged, approved or rejected.

POSTMODERN ETHICS

Similarly to politics, ethics is an indispensable part of a sociological theory of postmodernity pretending to any degree of completeness. Description of modern society could leave ethical problems aside or ascribe to them but a marginal place, in view of the fact that moral regulation of conduct was to a large extent subsumed under legislative and law-enforcing activity of global societal institutions, while whatever remained unregulated in such a way was "privatized" or perceived (and treated) as residual and marked for extinction in the course of full modernization. This condition does not hold anymore, ethical discourse is not institutionally preempted and hence its conduct and resolution (or irresolution) must be an organic part of any theoretical model of postmodernity.

Again, not all ethical issues found in a postmodern habitat are new. Most importantly, the possibly extemporal issues of the orthodox ethics—the rules binding short-distance, face-to-face intercourse between moral agents under conditions of physical and moral proximity—remain presently as much alive and poignant as ever before. In no way are they postmodern; as a matter of fact, they are not modern either. (On the whole, modernity contributed little, if anything, to the enrichment of moral problematics. Its role boiled down to the substitution of legal for moral regulation and the exemption of a wide and growing sectors of human actions from moral evaluation.)

The distinctly postmodern ethical problematics arises primarily from two crucial features of the postmodern condition: the *pluralism* of authority, and the centrality of *choice* in the self-constitution of postmodern agents.

1. Pluralism of authority, or rather the absence of an authority with glob-alizing ambitions, has a twofold effect. First, it rules out the setting of binding norms each agency must (or could be reasonably expected to) obey. Agencies may be guided by their own purposes, paying in principle as little attention to other factors (also to the interests of other agencies) as they can afford, given their resources and degree of independence. "Non-contractual bases of contract", devoid of institutional power support, are thereby considerably weakened. If unmotivated by the limits of the agency's own resources, any constraint upon the agency's action has to be negotiated afresh. Rules emerge mostly as reactions to strife and consequences of ensuing negotiations; still, the already negotiated rules remain by and large precarious and under-determined, while the needs of new rules—to regulate previously unanticipated contentious issues—keep proliferating. This is why the *problem* of rules stays in the focus of public agenda and is unlikely to be conclusively resolved. In the absence of "principle coordination" the negotiating of rules assumes a distinctly *ethical* character: at stake are the principles of non-utilitarian self-constraint of au-tonomous agencies—and both non-utility and autonomy define *moral* action as distinct from either self-interested or legally prescribed conduct. Second, the pluralism of authorities is conducive to the resumption by the agents of moral responsibility that tended to be neutralized, rescinded or ceded away as long as the agencies remained subordinated to a unified, quasi-monopolistic legislating authority. On the one hand, the agents face now point-blank the consequences of their actions. On the other, they face the evident ambigu-ity and controversiality of the purposes to which actions were to serve, and thus the need to justify argumentatively the values that inform their activity. Purposes can be no more substantiated *monologically*; having become per-force subjects of a *dialogue*, they must now refer to principles wide enough to command authority of the sort that belongs solely to ethical values.

2. The enhanced autonomy of the agent has similarly a twofold ethical consequence. First—in as far as the centre of gravity shifts decisively from het-eronomous control to self-determination, and autonomy turns into the defining trait of postmodern agents—self-monitoring, self-reflection and self-evaluation become principal activities of the agents, indeed the mechanisms synony-mous with their self-constitution. In the absence of a universal model for self-improvement, or of a clear-cut hierarchy of models, the most excruciating choices agents face are between life-purposes and values, not between the means serving the already set, uncontroversial ends. Supra-individual criteria of propriety in the form of technical precepts of instrumental rationality do not suffice. This circumstance, again, is potentially propitious to the sharpening up

of moral self-awareness: only ethical principles may offer such criteria of value-assessment and value-choice as are at the same time supra-individual (carry on authority admittedly superior to that of individual self-preservation), and fit to be used without surrendering the agent's autonomy. Hence the typically postmodern heightened interest in ethical debate and increased attractiveness of the agencies claiming expertise in moral values (e.g. the revival of religious and quasi-religious movements). Second, with the autonomy of all and any agents accepted as a principle and institutionalized in the life-process composed of an unending series of choices, the limits of the agent whose autonomy is to be observed and preserved turn into a most closely guarded and hotly contested frontier. Along this borderline new issues arise which can be settled only through an ethical debate. Is the flow and the outcome of self-constitution to be tested before the agent's right to autonomy is confirmed? If so, what are the standards by which success or failure are to be judged (what about the autonomy of young and still younger children, of the indigent, of parents raising their children in unusual ways, of people choosing bizarre life-styles, of people indulging in abnormal means of intoxication, people engaging in idiosyncratic sexual activities, individuals pronounced mentally handicapped)? And—how far the autonomous powers of the agent extend and at which point their limit is to be drawn (remember the notoriously inconclusive context between "life" and "choice" principles in the abortion debate).

All in all, in the postmodern context agents are constantly faced with moral issues and obliged to choose between equally well founded (or equally unfounded) ethical precepts. The choice always means the assumption of responsibility, and for this reason bears the character of a moral act. Under the postmodern condition, the agent is perforce not just an actor and decision-maker, but a *moral subject*. The performance of life-functions demands also that the agent be a morally *competent* subject.

SOCIOLOGY IN THE POSTMODERN CONTEXT

Strategies of any systematic study are bound to be resonant with the conception of its object. The orthodox sociology was resonant with the theoretical model of the modern society. It was for that reason that the proper accounting for the self-reflexive propensities of human actors proved to be so spectacularly difficult. Deliberately or against its declared wishes, sociology tended to marginalize or explain away self-reflexivity as rule-following, function-performing or at best sedimentation of institutionalized learning; in each case, as epiphenomenon of social totality, understood ultimately as "legitimate authority" capable of "principally coordinating" social space. As long as the self-reflexivity of actors remained reduced to the subjective perception of obedience to impersonal rules, it did not need to be treated seriously; it rarely came under scrutiny as an independent variable, much less as a principal condition of all sociality and its institutionalized sedimentations.

Never flawless, this strategy becomes singularly inadequate under the postmodern condition. The postmodern habitat is indeed an incessant flow of reflexivity; sociality responsible for all its structured yet fugitive forms, their interaction and their succession, is a discursive activity, an activity of interpretation and re-interpretation, of interpretation fed back into the interpreted condition only to trigger off further interpretative efforts. To be effectively and consequentially present in a postmodern habitat sociology must conceive of itself as a participant (perhaps better informed, more systematic, more rule-conscious, yet nevertheless a participant) of this never ending, self-reflexive process of reinterpretation—and devise its strategy accordingly. In practice, this will mean in all probability replacing the ambitions of the judge of "common beliefs", healer of prejudices and umpire of truth with those of a clarifier of interpretative rules and facilitator of communication; this will amount to the replacement of the dream of the legislator with the practice of an interpreter.

Notes

The ideas sketched in this article have been inspired or stimulated by readings and debates far too numerous for all the intellectual debts to be listed. And yet some, the most generous (even when unknowing) creditors must be named. They are: Benedict Anderson, Mikhail Bakhtin, Pierre Bourdieu, Anthony Giddens, Agnes Heller, Michel Maffesoli, Stefan Moravski, Alain Touraine. And, of course, Georg Simmel, who started it all.

PLURALIZATION AND RECOGNITION: ON THE SELF-MISUNDERSTANDING OF POSTMODERN SOCIAL THEORISTS

Axel Honneth

Even the decision to take the category of the "postmodern" seriously within social philosophy today requires a certain justification: the object area of all theories with this title is unclear, their conceptual framework for an analysis of processes of social change is surely too narrow, and, besides, their individual bearing too self-satisfied, indeed unsympathetic. Every fresh concern with the fashionable concept makes all the more dramatically clear those inadequacies which were inherent in it right from the beginning: whether "postmodernity" should characterize only a changed constellation in the cultural realm or a new type of social integration, whether empirical rather than normative explanatory claims are connected with the concept, and to what extent reality, however changed, should enforce a total renewal of our understanding of theory—all these are questions that have so far remained entirely unclarified. Having first emerged in the easily graspable field of architectural history, though robbed of all conceptual clarity on its further journey, the category nonetheless retains its widely effective and interdisciplinary suggestiveness: at least vaguely, it seems to be able to indicate socio-cultural processes of change and help articulate a diffuse state of consciousness. In this situation, the following form of debate with theories of the "postmodern" may be meaningful and helpful: to take seriously as far as possible their content in respect of a diagnosis of the times in order then to confront it critically with the normative reference system within which they describe and evaluate new processes of development. Whoever proceeds in this manner, namely on the basis of a critique of ideology, separates the descriptive core of a theory from its interpretive framework in order to be able to present the reality grasped by this theory in a different, materially more appropriate light. In what follows, I shall attempt this, first by briefly outlining the diagnosis of the times contained in the "postmodern" conception (I), then by inquiring into its theoretical framework of interpretation, which I suspect to be a Nietzschean tinged concept of aesthetic freedom (II), in order to at least sketch, in a final step, a communication-theoretic alternative interpretation (III). The guiding viewpoint of these theses is that the developmental tendencies correctly observed by postmodern theories can only be appropriately interpreted if, instead of regarding them from the poststructuralist viewpoint of an increase in aesthetic plurality and freedom, they are regarded from the perspective of a crisis in the social relations of recognition.

I.

In the social-theoretic concepts of postmodernity, experiential processes are dealt with, which first became evident in the cultural upheavals in the 1980s, though they have their roots in the economic and social changes of post-war capitalism. These experiences reflect developmental tendencies which amount to a disintegration of the social lifeworld and indicate a new, dangerous threshold in the individualization of society's members. The formula proffered by postmodern social theories for the tendencies outlined is that of the "end" or "dissolution" of the social; I see primarily three relevant complexes of experience which are thus grasped. Briefly:

(a) The technological innovations of the last half-century—and not least because of pressure from the internationalization of capital—have led to the emergence of a media and advertising industry which now envelops almost the entire world with a network of electronically produced information channels; this system of media-steered communication. Its most pointed forms of expressions today are the computer and television, and it increasingly appropriates the cultural achievements of the aesthetic avant-garde whilst profitably incorporates them into the reproduction mechanisms. However, by culture thus becoming, to a growing extent, both the bearer and the ideology of capitalist growth processes, it definitively loses its social buttress in the everyday lifeworld: cultural activities, whether rock concerts, football or works of art, are extracted from the direct communicative context of participating laypersons and concomitantly presented to solitary subjects as objects of merely passive observation. Therefore, a *tendency to dissolve the aesthetic mediating medium of the social lifeworld* accompanies this increasing incorporation of culture into the economic utilization process. Cultural activities lose their character as a communication-generating *praxis* within the societal world of interaction and assume the character of a merely secondary, electronically reproduced outer world—in short, culture becomes a technological environment for humans robbed of their aesthetic potential (cf. as an overview, Jameson, 1986).

(b) Today, the danger of a dissolution of the aesthetic-cultural mediating medium of the lifeworld is accompanied by an erosion process of its normative binding force. What Lyotard describes as the "end of meta-narratives" is, when dispassionately viewed, nothing other than the accelerated process of a destruction of those narratively constituted traditions, in which the members of a community could communicatively reach an understanding in the present about a common past and a correspondingly projected future (Lyotard, 1986; Honneth, 1984). Cultural traditions of this kind, that is, narratively constituted, context-spanning presentations of societal development, seem, on the one hand, to lose their philosophico-historical basis of legitimization with the definitive shattering of metaphysical background certainties. On the other hand, however, there is still no equivalent of a post-metaphysical character for the identity-securing and communicating-generating functions of the disintegrating meta-narratives. For this reason, there is a danger that, together with the erosion of cultural-normative traditions—as were provided, for instance, by the philosophico-historical constructions of the socialist or religious traditions—the cultural-normative interaction medium of the lifeworld will dry out. Because the one, narratively generated "history" disintegrates into many particular "histories", subjects can no longer reach an understanding beyond the borders of their respective reference group.

(c) Finally, the dissolution of the aesthetic and normative substance of the social lifeworld is also accompanied by a weakening of the subjects' ability to communicate. On the one hand, the loss of cultural binding forces through which social groups had expressively and normatively reproduced themselves, tends to cause subjects to become atomized individuals for each other. Furthermore, with the dwindling biographical significance of industrial labour, that traditional form of individual self-realization is also lost in which individuals learned, in the course of their occupational involvement, to perceive and value themselves as productive, cooperative partners in a societally useful field of activity. Taken together, both tendencies lead to a state of increasing disorientation, indeed fragmentation of the individual subject. Because it is severed from the communicative bonds of life styles supported by tradition, Jean Baudrillard sees the solitary, internally flattened subject so exposed to the influence of the electronically fabricated media reality today that it is gradually beginning to lose the cognitive ability to distinguish between reality and fiction. A *process of fictionalization* of reality within the social lifeworld takes place through which the atomized individual becomes an imitator of styles of existence prefabricated by media. On a wider scale this leads to an artificial pluralization of aesthetically shaped lifeworlds. Because the individual has lost the communicative buttress of a commonly shared cultural and narrative *praxis*, s/he is overcome by the superior force of that secondary stream of images which incessantly urges him or her to simulate unfamiliar styles of life. The place of internally motivated ways of self-realization is being increasingly taken by the pattern of a mediagenerated, aesthetically organized biography (cf. as a general presentation, Baudrillard, 1983; for a critique, Kellner, 1989: ch. 3).

As these three complexes of experience show, it is primarily changes within the communicative infrastructure of the social lifeworld to which post-modern social theories with a sensitiveness for the times react. Neglecting, to a large extent, political and economic factors, they register a dissolution of those direct interaction media of culture and narrative tradition within every-day life, by means of which subjects could previously relate to one another communicatively. The effect of the accelerated disintegration of social binding forces is a tendency to empty subjectivity motivationally so that the electronic media world can then compensatively encroach on this emptied subjectivity with its offers of simulation. Summarized in this manner, the concept of the "postmodern" represents hardly anything more than a current perpetuation of the pessimistic diagnosis expounded by Adorno and Horkheimer in the chap-ter on the "culture industry" in their *Dialectic of Enlightenment*. The peculiar character of the new concept, however, reveals itself only when one precisely examines the theoretical frame of reference within which the stated develop-ment processes are interpreted and evaluated: in contrast to the *Dialectic of Enlightenment*, postmodern social theories give the diagnosed concatenation of cultural erosion and individual loss of authenticity a positive, indeed often, an affirmative interpretation.[1] The conceptual means that make possible such a calculated *dedramatization* of the observed dissolution processes are the result of the application of an aesthetic concept of individual freedom. As I would like to explain briefly in the second part of this paper, this concept makes it possible to see, in the disintegration of interaction-generating binding forces, the chance for a playful unfolding of individual peculiarities, of "difference".

II.

Like all social theories oriented toward a diagnosis of the times, be they Durkheim's or Weber's, Adorno's or Gehlen's, the concept of the "postmodern" is also based on an ultimately philosophical motif. As we know, the *Dialectic of Enlightenment* is theoretically dependent on a concept of the subject which stands partially in the philosophy of life tradition and in romanticism, and par-tially in psychoanalysis—a concept of the subject, from whose perspective the emergence of the modern culture industry discloses itself as a further step in the self-reification of man. In postmodern social theories in an apparent counter-move a completely different concept of the subject is applied, one which will make it permissible to see, in the destruction of humankind's social bonds, the chance for an expansion of its freedom. The change in perspective which comes about in the transition from the *Dialectic of Enlightenment* to the theory of the "postmodern" is roughly comparable to the one Georg Simmel observed in the development from Schopenhauer to Nietzsche. Whereas Schopenhauer remained oriented toward the idea of an objective purposiveness of human life, he was propelled into the pessimism of his metaphysics of the will in view of its definitive impossibility, freed himself of such negativism by uncoupling the human life process from every connection to an all encompassing, posited purpose, and constituted the meaning of human life as a mere intensification of its possibilities. The idea of "self-realization", which of course always presupposed theoretical reference to some life goal, is here replaced by the notion of experimental self-creation on the part of human beings:

> Nietzsche's attempt is to remove the meaning-giving goal of life from its illusory position outside of life and to put that goal back into life itself. There was no more radical way to do this than through a vision of life in which self-directed augmentation is but the realization of what life provides as potential, including means and values. Every stage of human existence now finds its meaning not in something absolute and definitive, but in something higher that succeeds it in which everything antecedent, having been only potential and germinal, wakes up to greater efficiency and expansion. Life as such has become fuller and richer: there is an increase in life. Nietzsche's "overman" is nothing but a level of development which is one step higher than the level reached at a specific time by a specific mankind. He is not a fixed goal which gives meaning to evolution, but only expresses the fact that there is no need for such a goal, that life in itself, in the process of replacing one level with a fuller and more developed one, has its own value. (Simmel, 1991, pp. 6–7)

Such an aesthetic model of human freedom is what underlies, in one way or another, all versions of a theory of the "postmodern". Apart from not insignificant differences in specifics, they share the fundamental orientation toward an idea of individual self-creation influenced by Nietzsche: here, human subjects are presented as beings whose possibilities for freedom are best realized when, independent of all normative expectations and bonds, they are able to creatively produce new self-images all the time. The standard for freedom, which the individual can reach in experimental self-creation, is therefore measured according to the distance he can establish between himself and the cultural value sphere of his time (cf. Rorty, 1989: 96ff; Menke, 1990).

However, because this formulation evokes the impression that, with the postmodern concept of freedom, it is a matter of an aesthetic interpretation of negative freedom, it is important to keep apart the two moments brought together in accordance with the idea: "negative freedom" in the sense of an inner independence from all tradition and community means for the individual subject at the same time gaining a new, as it were, "positive" freedom of experimentally testing all possible forms of life. It is only this attitude of free experiment with oneself—an attitude acquired through distance—that gives negative freedom the positive sense intended by the idea of self-creation since Nietzsche.

Even this brief description shows in all clarity how the connection between the central philosophical motif and the diagnosis of the times is constituted in postmodern social theory: if the individual's freedom increases only to the extent that s/he can leave the normative and cultural expectations of his or her time behind him while engaging in the innovative creation of possibilities for life, then the social lifeworld must be regarded primarily as a shackle for the individualizing force of aesthetic self-invention. The affirmative picture of the present-day situation—a picture where the various concepts of the postmodern meet—is therefore the result of the presupposition of an idea of aesthetic freedom. The socio-cultural tendencies of our time must certainly be described as an indication of a disintegration of the social lifeworld, however, the increased chance for a liberating of the subject to the possibility of socially unconstrained self-creation can also be assumed here—the "loss of the social" carries with it, not only the destruction of the communicative infrastructure of the lifeworld, but also the possibility of creating new free space for the playful unfolding of individual differences. The term "difference" thus means here that the biographical peculiarities of every individual subject, its specific manner of self-creation, can better unfold the fewer the normatively encompassing bonds and contexts it is involved in.

This affirmative interpretation of our socio-cultural situation must become doubtful when the validity of that aesthetic model is questioned. As soon as the idea that subjects can solipsistically achieve self-realization independent of normative bonds is contested, it is also invalidated which makes it permissible to see in the dissolution of the social a chance for the unfolding of individual peculiarities. Since Hegel, the concept of recognition has been responsible for the critique of such solipsistic models of self-realization. Hegel's own concept implies that human subjects are constitutively dependent on the normative approval of others in forming their identity, because they can ascertain their practical claims and goals only on the basis of the positive reaction of a counterpart.

Of course, this intersubjectivity-theoretic concept can only compete with Nietzsche's doctrine of freedom in that it posits the experience of recognition not only as a constitutive presupposition of identity formation, but at the same time as a condition for the practical realization of freedom. Subjects are really only capable of realizing the possibilities of freedom when they can, without constraint, positively identify, from the perspective of assenting others, with their own objectives. The realization of freedom presupposes the experience of recognition because I can be in true and complete accord with my action goals only to the extent that I can be sure of the normative agreement of a communication community which, if not a concrete one, is at least an idealized one. In this intersubjectivity-theoretic sense, Hegel constantly distinguished at all stages of his theory formation between the same three degrees in the realization of freedom; it is important to keep them apart here because it is only in this way that the contrast to Nietzsche can be appropriately located. For Hegel, the freedom of expressing needs is measured firstly according to the experience of recognition in love, just as it is realized, first, in the relationship between parents and children, later in the sexual relationship between men and women, or in friendship (natural freedom). For Hegel, secondly, the freedom of individual self-determination arises from the experience of legal recognition, just as it is established in modern law by the institutional anchoring of equal rights of freedom (social freedom). Finally, the freedom of personal self-realization arises, for him, from the experience of an ethical [*sittlich*] recognition, just as it is guaranteed by social communities in that they allow the individual's aims in life to be interpreted in the light of commonly shared values as a contribution to, or an enrichment of, the collective good (freedom of self-realization). It is this last dimension of personal self-realization that allows us to comprehend Hegel's conception as a systematic critique of Nietzsche's aesthetic doctrine of freedom.

Thus, on this interpretation, the freedom of self-realization is not measured according to the distance the individual can establish between himself and the cultural lifeworld, but according to the degree of recognition he can find in his social environment for his freely chosen goals. Instead of being defined by the scale of distance from all normative bonds, the increase in personal individuality is determined here by the degree to which individual differences are communicatively granted, indeed encouraged (cf. Honneth, 1990). Here I cannot discuss, even briefly, such an intersubjective concept of ethical life where, in the tradition of Hegel and Mead, self-realization is coupled to the social precondition of successful forms of reciprocal recognition. However, in conclusion, I shall roughly sketch the consequences arising for the interpretation of the abovementioned developmental tendencies when the Nietzschean concept of freedom is replaced by the one coming from the theory of recognition tradition. It should become apparent that what is perceived from the perspective of postmodern conceptions as an indication of aesthetic pluralization must first of all be interpreted as a sign of a serious crisis in the structure of recognition in highly developed societies.

III.

If the diagnosis of the times presented by sociological theories is decisively co-determined by premises at the level of the basic philosophical motifs, then it must be possible to draw negative conclusions for the "postmodern" interpretive approach from the intimated critique of Nietzsche's conception of freedom. The affirmative picture it produces for the present cannot simply continue to endure as soon as it is theoretically contested that the increase in personal freedom can be determined as a process of the individual production of new self-images. The critical counter-thesis, according to which the realization of freedom is dependent on corresponding forms of social recognition, allows, characteristically enough, the starting point of postmodern social theories to appear in a different light: that the socio-cultural world, from which current developmental processes seem to distance us at present, may not be merely regarded as a hindrance to individual freedom. Rather, it must also be viewed as a specific organizational form of the individual freedom of self-realization. The time of the "great narratives", which Lyotard speaks about when he wants to characterize the cultural disposition of social modernity, can, according to everything we know today, best be determined as a constellation of the form of industrial ethical life [*Sittlichkeit*]: through which not only the values coupled to professional life had become such a general—though subculturally often undefined—medium of recognition, but also at least the male members of society could attain social esteem for the way of life associated with labour.

The decrease in the significance of industrial labour, to which Baudrillard's postmodern diagnosis of the times directly refers, brings about the decline of industrialism's ethical life in developed societies today. Primarily two processes have begun to deflate the social value of industrial labour to such an extent that its entire milieu of values is in danger of dissolving along with it:

(a) The continuous growth of the service sector—a growth equally prevalent in the international comparison of capitalist societies—dislodged the classical forms of industrial labour as the standard role model for occupational activity long ago. When one speaks of gainful employment today, the paradigmatic image is no longer provided by the industrial sector's forms of labour, which are subject to technical performance assessment. Rather, it is provided by the "reflexive" activities in the service sector.

> In both private and public enterprises, activities such as teaching, curing, planning, organizing, negotiating, controlling, administering, and counselling—that is, the activities of preventing, absorbing and processing risks and deviations from normality—are overwhelmingly wage-dependent, just as is the case with the industrial production of commodities. These service activities are, however, different in two respects. First, because of the heterogeneity of the 'cases' that are processes in service work, and due to the high levels of uncertainty concerning where and when they occur, a technical production that relates inputs to outputs can often not be fixed and utilized as a control criterion of adequate work performance. Second, service work differs from productive work in the lack of a clear and uncontroversial 'criterion of economic efficiency', from which could be strategically derived the type and amount, the place and timing of 'worthwhile' work" (Offe, 1985: 138).

This empirical hypothesis can be summarized as follows: all in all, with the expansion of the service sector, the sphere of labour loses the traditional criteria of success, to which the social esteem for industrial labour had hitherto been experientially attached.

(b) The second causal chain which is at the root of the decline in the significance of industrial labour is not of an economic, but of a cultural nature. Evidently, the degree to which employment determines individuals biographically and shapes them in a way characteristic for the particular labour situation is decreasing dramatically in the developed societies of the West. This decentralization of the labour sphere vis-à-vis other spheres of life, its marginalization in the individual's biography, is a phenomenon diagnosed by many theorists, though evaluated in extremely different manners (from Bell's conservatism, through Dahrendorf's liberalism, to Offe's "left-wing" social theory). Nonetheless, because the ethicization of labour can only function under conditions which, in the first place, permit that the labourers be able to find self-confirmation, approval and recognition as morally acting persons, as bearers of duties, the decline in the biographical significance of labour also points to a dissolution of the ethical medium of recognition constituted by industrial labour.

Thus, both tendencies can be summarized as follows: traditional patterns of self-realization lose their cultural support in the lifeworld's well-proven forms of recognition. Just as the theorists of the "postmodern" correctly view it—and of course they are not alone—the decline of the industry-related value milieu is accompanied by the chance of a pluralization of individual life-forms. However, what these theorists cannot appropriately take into account, because of their specific conception of freedom, is the fact that the experimental testing of new ways of life has so far lacked all social support in a newly emerging form of ethical life. Cultural everyday praxis is freed step by step from its received value commitments and traditions without them having already been replaced by encompassing orientation patterns, within which the individual subjects' attempts at self-realization could find intersubjective recognition.[2] Pointedly worded, it is this recognition vacuum which first brings about the growing willingness to accept life styles prefabricated by the culture industry as aesthetic substitutes for socially depleting biographies.

If the above-sketched description is not totally erroneous, theories of the postmodern present an incorrect interpretation for correctly described developmental processes. Because they take a Nietzschean concept of freedom as their point of departure, they are unable to reflect upon the appropriate cultural preconditions for the propagated pluralization of individual life styles. These preconditions would lie in the development of a post-industrial form of ethical life, a concept of which is totally lacking in postmodern social theories.

Translated by John Farrell

Notes

1. Here I deviate from Gerd Irrlitz's interpretation; he distinguishes between an affirmative and a critical concept of the "postmodern" (Irrlitz, 1990). I think all concepts of the "postmodern" have at least one affirmative feature in common, viz. to see in the process of the "dissolution of the social" the chance for an expansion of aesthetic freedoms for individuals.

2. A similar approach for grasping the socio-cultural situation in highly developed societies is proposed by Heinrich Popitz, who distinguishes between five "recognition needs" which appear in an historical sequence (Popitz, 1987).

References

Baudrillard, Jean, *Die Agonie des Realen* (Berlin, Merve, 1983).

Honneth, Axel, "An Aversion Against the Universal: A Commentary on Lyotard's Postmodern Condition", *Theory, Culture and Society* 2, 3 (1985), pp. 147–157.

Honneth, Axel, "Integrität und Mißachtung: Grundmotive einer Moral der Anerkennung", *Merkur* 501 (1990), pp. 1043–1954.

Irrlitz, Gerd, "Subjekt ohne Objekt: Philosophie postmodernen Bewußtseins", *Sinn und Form* 1 (1990), pp. 87–115.

Jameson, Fredric, "Postmodernism, or the Cultural Logic of Late Capitalism", *New Left Review* 146 (July–August 1984), pp. 53–92.

Kellner, Douglas, *Jean Baudrillard: From Marxism to Postmodernism and Beyond* (Cambridge, Polity Press, 1989).

Lyotard, Jean-François, *The Postmodern Condition* (Minneapolis, University of Minneapolis Press, 1984).

Menke, Christoph, "Distanz und Experiment: Zu Nietzsches Theorie ästhetischer Freiheit" (ms., Frankfurt am Main, 1990).

Offe, Claus, "Work: The Key Sociological Category?" in *Disorganized Capitalism: Contemporary Transformations of Work and Politics* (Cambridge, Polity Press, 1985), pp. 129–150.

Popitz, Henrich, "Autoritätsbedürfnisse: Der Wandel der sozialen Subjektivität", *Kölner Zeitschrift für Soziologie und Sozialpsychologie* 39 (1987), pp. 633–647.

Rorty, Richard, *Contingency, Irony, and Solidarity* (Cambridge, Cambridge University Press, 1989).

Simmel, Georg, *Schopenhauer and Nietzsche* (Chicago, University of Illinois Press, 1991).

IS SOCIOLOGY STILL THE STUDY OF SOCIETY?

Alain Touraine

THE STUDY OF CHANGE

Interpretations of social life are transformed together with the realities which they try to grasp. The search for laws of history now belong to the past of the social sciences and is no longer compatible with strictly scientific projects. In more general terms the evolution of the social sciences has led them to abandon speculation about the essence of the social, the perfect society or the conditions of universal peace, and to concentrate instead on the analysis of the mechanisms through which humans transform their situation, create their history and try to master the changes which this action sets into motion.

During its 150-year long official history, sociology was above all a reflection of three kinds of social change. Firstly, the rapid take-off of production and living standards in one part of the world. For a long time people used the concepts of modernity or modernization, and later those of growth or development, to refer to this profound transformation; it is reflected in the contrast between traditional and modern structures as well as between developed and underdeveloped (or central and peripheral) countries. Sociology thus studies societies characterized by rapid change, whereas anthropology studies societies with a weak will or capacity to change, and history, in between the two other disciplines, is concerned with totalities—civilizations, political regimes, or modes of production—which undergo changes while retaining some permanent characteristics. The acceleration of economic change is due to the recent but massive impact of science and its technological applications on the process of production. This fact has from the outset served to keep alive the dream of a scientific society.

The second type of change is the expansion of public life at the expense of private life. If past historians were often exclusively interested in kings, invasions or the great works of art and thought, that was primarily because the everyday life of slaves, peasants and tradesmen left few documents behind and seemed to be outside history. Today the social sciences have to take note of rapid transformations in all spheres of personal and collective life. Demographic change is one of the most important cases in point. Some countries double their population and others reduce it substantially in a few decades. Private life becomes an integral part of the field of history and the social sciences. These transformations are partly due to the effects of economic development, industrialization, urbanization and rising living standards, but also to the impact of science, particularly biology, which has developed more rapidly during the last fifty years than during its previous history, and is only now becoming capable of explaining and manipulating the mechanisms of heredity.

The third level is partly the result of the first: the internalization of change and of the analysis of change. This has yet to be universally accepted. We still insist on calling those who study social change in Africa "Africanists" and reserve the label "sociologists" for those who study it in Europe or North America. And we still talk about "Orientalism", whereas there is no corresponding notion of "Occidentalism". Entrenched prejudices still lead us to assume that Latin American sociologists can only talk about their own region, whereas those of the more central countries are contributing to general sociology even when they are only concerned with their own country. But despite such obstacles, the interdependence of West and East, North and South is much more generally recognized than it was in the recent past. It is no longer possible to develop a sociology of industrial organization or of the state on the basis of exclusively European data.

These three developments—the acceleration of economic change, the penetration of social change into everyday and private life, and the internationalization of social and economic facts—constitute the background to the most recent transformations of the social sciences. The latter define themselves more and more as approaches to the analysis of social change.

FROM ORDER TO MOVEMENT

The acceleration and expansion of change has modified our image of social life. The latter is dominated by the level of action through which human societies create and transform themselves. The analysis of modern societies, which is the specific field of sociology, was at first identified with the study of political and juridical institutions, because the most important things in these societies were the movement of commodities and capital, the security of roads, the respect of contracts and the standardization of weights and measures; this gave rise to a juridical interpretation of social life as a totality of regulated exchanges. By contrast, industrial society gave priority to production over exchange and work over transport. While the central categories of social analysis in the first phase were those of the market and the city, money and law, the guardians and the law-breakers, industrial society shifted the emphasis to the machine and the factory, social relations of production, wages and profits, strikes and managerial power, the latter often supported by public authority. Before the industrial revolution, the analysis of change was separated from that of order, because the causes of change were mainly external: the availability of new raw materials or the discovery of new markets, conquests or the replacement of one dynasty by another. But sociology—as the offspring of industrial society—naturally inclined to define society in terms of change. This is the underlying significance of the distinction between community (*Gemeinschaft*) and society (*Gesellschaft*), first formulated by Tönnies and later developed by Durkheim in terms of forms of integration and division of labour. For Weber, Durkheim and Parsons, modern society is above all characterized by a movement towards modernity, i.e. the process of rationalization and secularization. This image of a society in permanent movement is linked to the philosophy of the Enlightenment, but it was not sufficient for the purposes of sociological analysis. From the sociological point of view, modernization was as destructive as it was creative: it uprooted individuals from their original environment, destroyed local solidarities, proletarized the workers and created dangerous and unhealthy cities. Moreover, it proved impossible to conceptualize the whole of social life as change, because industrialization only affected the means of production and did not directly modify needs, ideas and languages. Sociology could take a reformist or a neo-conservative turn, but in either case, it was always trying to re-establish order within change and integration against a background of fragmentation. Hence the peculiar ambiguity of this discipline: it was oriented towards progress and modernity, but also engaged in the search for a principle of order which would be for modern societies what religion, political institutions and education had been for traditional ones. The ambiguity is built into the very idea of society, a basic but by no means simple concept of classical sociology; an unstable mixture of social modernity and political order, it reflects the historical reality of the nation-state. In fact, the analysis of change or development is always concerned with concrete totalities, nations dominated by states whose task is to maintain or construct the unity of the nation in the context of ongoing transformations. Classical sociology thus tends to identify the study of social change with that of political and institutional order, and this spontaneous identification is today reproduced by sociologists of the emerging nations, particularly in Latin America and the Arab world. The convergence of social and political categories in the central concept of *institution* is thus characteristic of classical sociology and corresponds to a limited scope of social change. This helps to pinpoint one of the most far-reaching changes in experience and thought during the last century: when people lived within a national (or even infra-national) space, the nation was synonymous with society, but the obvious dissociation of these two realities in our era of economic and cultural internationalization (accompanied by a reactive search for more immediate identities and communities) undermines the received image of society.

There is another image, still in the process of formation, which reflects more adequately our increased ability to transform our own existence. During the last fifty years, we have discovered that we can not only organize the exchange of material goods and produce them more efficiently on the basis of the division and mechanization of labour; we can also produce symbolic goods, languages and informations and modify our relationship to ourselves, most obviously through the progress of biology and medicine. Social life is no longer perceived as a restricted space for liberty in a universe of necessity but as an indefinite and perhaps infinite space, so that we must abandon not only the conception of the human world as a microcosm within a macrocosm, but also the idea that social life takes place within essential limits which in practice coincide with those of the nation-state and its juridical institutions or educational programs.

This is why such concepts as decision, strategy and change have become so important for contemporary sociology. The *sociology of organizations*, as it is usually labelled within the profession, centers on the notion of a *limited rationality*, introduced by H. A. Simon. On this view, actors are not guided— more or less effectively—by an absolute principle of rationality, as the ratio- nalist philosophers and the rationalizers of industry tended to assume; they defend their interests in complex situations which they can only to a limited extent know and control, and they try—as M. Crozier puts it—to control the "zones of uncertainty". This reversal of perspectives is translated into economic practice: the American pattern of *rationalistic* management, based on general principles such as the separation of functions and a far-reaching formalization of decision-making processes, is replaced by the Japanese model of *strategic* management which is more concerned with the goals to be achieved and the road to them than with the general principles of organization. The pressures of international competition have certainly helped to bring about this change. In the sphere of education, the work of S. Papert reflects the same kind of trans- formation. Papert was influenced by Piaget's ideas and accepts the distinction between developmental levels of logical thinking, but tries to understand the learning process as a movement of the whole person towards the desired goal, rather than as a submission to the laws of rational thinking. A similar mixture of impersonal calculation with personal desire and imagination is characteristic of the most modern organizations, such as the electronic enterprises in Silicon Valley that have become as representative of a new model of economic life as the automobile factories were half a century earlier. The social sciences have also borrowed from the natural sciences the idea that the most com- plex systems are not governed by absolute rules but must rather be capable of changing their goals, absorbing new information and retaining a margin of indeterminacy; they must, in other words, be oriented towards change, adaptation and invention, no less than towards the reproduction of given forms of organization and stable patterns of behaviour.

But there are other approaches to the sociology of change. The analyses of Simon and Crozier go beyond the organizational level of change and suggest an interpretation of social life as a *political* process, i.e. as a complex of initiatives and negotiations. The concept of the institution thus acquires a new meaning. Where earlier theorists saw a primacy of instituting rules over the instituted, we are more inclined to see a political process of the formation of norms; this is exemplified by the institutionalization of labour conflict and collective negotiations. At a higher level, the sociology of change explains social organization as the result of conflicts between actors that strive to control and implement the means of action by society upon itself—the field of historicity, as I prefer to call it. This involves above all the techniques of production, information, communication and administration in the broadest sense.

As we shall see, this also changes our understanding of social actors and social conflicts. In this context—the most global perspective on social change—the contrast with classical and pre-classical sociology is particularly pronounced. The social philosophers—e.g. Locke and Montesquieu—were interested in the preconditions of social order; sociology, born of the industrial revolution, was concerned with ways and means of reimposing order on the "great transformation" (K. Polanyi). Today we can no longer rely on principles of order or images of the just society; we can only think in terms of action, change and social relations, and theorize in terms of strategies, politics, or—as I prefer—the conflictual self-production of society.

It is true that the sixties and seventies saw the emergence of another image of social life, diametrically opposed to the one sketched above. Some French philosophers adopted the ideas of Marcuse, who had stressed the increasing capacity of modern societies to control and contain themselves. In different ways, Althusser, Foucault and Bourdieu developed and diffused the image of society as an implacable machine which serves to maintain inequality, power and privilege. This idea of sociology as a critique of order has been popular among the intellectuals and the social groups most directly influenced by them (particularly teachers and social workers); it will always have an important role to play in social thought, because every "open" complex of social and political relations tends to transform itself into a "closed" system of integration and exclusion, reproduction of privileges, and justification of the established order. In a similar way, a sociology of crises must be added to the sociology of action and order. The classics were already interested in anomie and the effects of proletarization, and the current emphasis on action and change makes us more sensitive to the obstacles which still prevent the formation of new social actors, especially in the case of social, ethnic and cultural minorities.

But we risk losing sight of this complementarity of different subdivisions of sociology if we do not recognize that—at least in our societies—the analysis of social relations and the management of change is the most central component. It is just as untenable to see in social life only crisis and decomposition as it is to reduce everything to control, order and reproduction. We must therefore separate the legitimate fields of sociological research from the ideologies which are symptoms of a cultural crisis rather than results of concrete analyses. The critical sociology of order reflects the disappointment of those who had believed in the existence of revolutionary subjects in industrial society and then saw them transformed into instruments of a totalitarian order. This explains how it became the dominant ideology of the universities: after May 1968, an obsolete discourse retreated into academia to escape the confrontation with reality, whereas new practices proliferated in social life but went largely unnoticed by intellectuals (with the exception of the feminists).

By contrast, a sociology of action and change casts doubt on all interpretations which describe social life in terms of a system of an organism capable of self-regulation and striving for equilibrium. Not only do the roles of institution and socialization lose much of their importance; more fundamentally, the very idea of *society* should be eliminated. In an earlier phase, sociology was the study of society; it should now be defined as the study of social relations and—increasingly—social change. The idea of society, which was—as noted above—inseparable from the triumph of the nation-state, was an image of order. As if change could only be understood with reference to an order, as if the various aspects of social life were the organs of a body regulated by a central mechanism; as if outside the social order there was only chaos, private interest and violence.

SOCIETY AND NATURE

The increasing capacity of our societies to modify and transform their environment can lead to growing imbalances between social life and the equilibrium of nature. Expensive machines call for shift work, which is dangerous for biological rhythms; new techniques allow us to synthesize images and sounds in a way that is as far removed from natural patterns as most products of chemical industry. This hyperindustrialism therefore encounters obstacles and resistances, not only in the context of cultural practices but also on the level of social thought. According to Serge Moscovici, the "question of nature" is becoming as important to our world as the "social question" was during the industrial era. The latter was the internal symptom of a type of social and economic organization, whereas the question of nature arises from the collision between social action and the natural world in which it intervenes in such a way that some fundamental patterns are upset. The end of the era of sustained growth coincided with the emergence of a counter-culture which preferred equilibrium to growth and saw the quest for identity as more important than productivity. This current includes both intellectual and emotional expressions of a broad movement which appeared simultaneously in various parts of the world as a rejection of externally imposed development and as a defense of threatened communities and their cultural foundations. It seems that after two centuries of triumphant enlightenment and progress, we are now witnessing the counter-offensive of particularism against achievement, to use the terminology of R. Linton, and a return from society to community (Tönnies). The interdependence of the species and of all the elements in the eco-system is invoked as an argument against the Cartesian vision of a conquest of nature by human reason. On a more theoretical level, this reaction led to the triumph of structuralism. In psychoanalysis, Lacan rejected the approaches which centred on the formation of the ego and reintroduced the unconscious, now regarded as structurally similar to language, as a dominant theme. Lévi-Strauss transformed anthropology by going beyond functionalism, not towards an analysis of historicity (i.e. the self-transformation of society through work innovations and conflicts), but in the other direction—by showing how the human mind as a fundamental component of human nature is at work in social and cultural structures. The progress of cognitive science now allows at least partial reproduction of the functioning brain. Simon sees this as a further step towards the overcoming of subject-centred modes of thought, along the line which led from Galileo to Freud. The epic image of industrialization, associated with railways and aviation, mines and metallurgy, gives way to a more scientific knowledge of the laws of nature; a more effective adaptation of man to his own nature and to his place in the universe thus becomes possible. This movement derives some of its strength from the horrified reactions to excesses committed in the name of reason and the domination of nature. The second half of the 20th century has thus been characterized by an anti-voluntarist trend which seeks protection against totalitarianism and against the exterminist consequences of the logic of domination. Europe is now seen less as the homeland of philosophers than as that of the Nazi and Soviet concentration camps. The anti-interventionistic current which draws its inspiration from these experiences is often transformed into a critique of industrialism, but it finds some support in the most advanced sciences.

More in tune with the reality of modern societies are the reflections of Edgar Morin, who tries to bring the social sciences closer to the natural sciences and to use some innovations of the latter, particularly the ideas of complexity and organization, for this purpose. Complex systems do not confine themselves to the reproduction of an order (in that case, change would only come about by chance, as the classic analysis of Jacques Monod shows); they are capable of modifying their goals and their rules of functioning, of increasing their complexity and managing change. Paradoxically the natural sciences are now taking the first steps towards a new theory of change, whereas the social sciences are still far too attached to a model of order which—as Morin shows—does not correspond to the human world, but rather to the non-organic level of the organization of nature. A debate on these issues might help the social sciences to get rid of mechanicist and organicist survivals, but may not go far enough to equip them with the concepts they now need. Physicists and biologists are not dealing with systems capable of transforming their environment into history by changing the patterns of their own activity. But the human sciences need both contact with a general scientific model and a clearer definition of their own specific tasks. It is thus as necessary for sociology to draw inspiration from the ideas of such scientists as Ilya Prigogine and Henri Atlan, as it is to develop concepts appropriate to the study of human phenomena in social situations, characterized by the accelerated production of technical, social and cultural changes.

The merit of systemic analysis was that it broke with subjectivism and voluntarism and thus with the dominant ideological orientations of an era obsessed with development. It reminds us that modern societies are neither transparent implementations of an autonomous project, nor expressions of a unilaterally imposed logic of domination; they are, rather, complex totalities, capable of learning and therefore characterized by a certain degree of indeterminacy with regard to their internal functioning. As a result of the crisis of modernistic voluntarism, it is no longer plausible to oppose spirit to matter, the soul to the body, or man to nature; human action is recognized as the highest level of complexity and self-productive capacity in a pyramid of systems without which it could not exist, most obviously because of the dependence of the spirit on the body and the brain. Similarly, our morality no longer tells us to get rid of passions and desires, but rather to elevate them to the level of an explicit relationship to ourselves and to integrate drives and images into the construction of the personality. Instead of opposing the conscious to the unconscious or defining the unconscious in such a way as to put it outside the reach of the self, we are inclined to define the subject in terms of desire rather than work and in terms of individuality rather than participation in a collective project. Our rejection of the brutality associated with policies of industrialization and development may at first lead us to dream of a return to nature and its supposed equilibrium; but it can also—and more importantly—lead us towards an alliance of subjectivity and nature, capable of resisting the power which was born from the triumphs of scientific and technical reason.

THE UNITY OF SOCIETY

The abovementioned transformations of social thought raise a fundamental question: Is everything change? Is there no principle of integration and equilibrium in social life? Social thought was concerned with the unity of society before it developed into an analysis of social change. Different cultures have generated different myths in order to account for their foundations—beginning with totemism, which was an interpretation of the social systems of exchange, rather than a general search for symbolic correspondences. Our societies have mostly retained memories of their origins, and sometimes translated them into models of social contact. For a long time, we used to identify society with the nation and to define the latter—as Renan did—in terms of a will to live together. With regard to institutions rather than culture, we still define society in terms of the legitimacy of the power and the laws that rule within a certain territory. But is not our lived experience becoming increasingly incompatible with these interpretations? Our life is less and less lived within a national framework, partly because of the growing internationalization of economy and culture and partly because of the growing divisions within our countries: we now distinguish the highly productive sectors and regions, integrated into the international economy, from the less productive or marginalized ones, characterized by lower incomes and more limited exchanges. In other parts of the world, the internal contrasts are even more visible: is it still possible to talk about Korean or Japanese society, when a rapid industrialization has—in the first case—turned a Confucian society upside down, and the traditional culture as well as the social hierarchy has—in the second case—been destroyed by economic and social mobilization, after having served the purposes of the latter for some time? The classical idea of society was inseparable from national movements, and the idea of a collective consciousness was above all the consciousness of belonging to a national state. Today, individuals are increasingly determined by their movements rather than by their belonging, by the relations of competition, cooperation and conflict in which they are involved rather than by membership in collectivities that could be identified on the basis of values or a distinctive history.

This does not mean that all consciousness of belonging to a concrete social totality disappears, but it undergoes a major transformation. The internal identification with the nation through images and beliefs tends to give way to an external one, based on the awareness of international relations of competition and domination. In France and its neighbouring countries this has strengthened the idea of the West and, to a lesser extent, that of Europe. The West is defined less in terms of its values than in terms of its identification with one nuclear superpower and its opposition to the other. Europe will become more than a common market or a region of free trade as it develops a positive or negative identity on the political and military level: either by developing its own strategic capacities, or by creating a de-nuclearized or even de-militarized zone. In many cases, the rejection of colonial or imperialist domination has given rise to new nations without any pre-existent integral unity. In more general terms, the identification with the state as a political and military actor on the international scene is separated from a national, cultural and social consciousness which is thereby weakened and often decomposed.

The limited separation of state and civil society, which goes back to the 18th century, is now being accentuated to such an extent that it destroys the very idea of society. The most extreme version of the division separates a complex and changing field of social relations from a state which is above all charged with international responsibilities. This leads to the decomposition of the political field itself. Patriotism, based on the identification of nation and society, disappears; the very idea of the republic is undermined both in the state-centred French version and in the American one, which lay greater stress on the law and the elected instances. Politics was at the heart of modern societies and for a long time, it seemed clear that particular social problems must be integrated into more general political options. Even during the heyday of the workers' movement both Social Democrats and Communists regarded political action as a higher form of the collective action of organized workers. The party was supposed to play a more important role than the trade union. Today the dissociation of social actors from the state has reached such extremes that there is no longer any internal principle of social unity and integration. All that is left are the economic or military threats from outside, and the acceptance of "rules of the game" that guarantee that mutual consideration of individuals and groups, rather than social integration. In the sphere of education the idea that the school should produce citizens is less and less acceptable; it was at first replaced by the demand for equal opportunity, but now the dominant theme is the development of the personality and individual creativity of every child.

If the idea of unity and integration of society is invoked at all, it tends to be formulated in a defensive mode and associated with the rejection of deviant, marginal or criminal minorities by the majority. Our industrialized societies no longer have the pyramidal distribution of incomes, where the most numerous categories are also the poorest, instead the middle strata have gained in strength, and this lead to anti-elitist orientation as well as to the exclusion of groups regarded as marginal or dangerous. This would seem to be the most widespread vision of social life—a mass of consumers, associated with each other through markets, more or less dominated by public or private monopolies and oligopolies, separated both from the rulers who are absorbed in international relations and from the marginals who are both supported by and excluded from society.

But if this image reflects a pronounced trend in contemporary social life, it is also true that it corresponds more clearly to the interests of those who reduce social life to consumption rather than to the whole field of observable experience. We cannot give up all ideas of the internal unity of society and thus reduce it to a market protected by boundaries.

The fundamental fact of the growing separation of society and the state can also be interpreted as the progressive constitution of civil society. Where the concept of the latter appeared in the 18th century, it was associated with the idea of social classes and their conflicts, centring on the control and use of the results of economic production. Today it is even more true that society is the totality of stakes of social conflicts. Because industrial societies have increased their ability to intervene in their own structures—in other words: their capacity of self-production—the field of conflicts has been broadened and at the same time separated more clearly from political struggles in the strict sense, i.e. those that have to do with the conquest of state power. The real centre of social life is the general and permanent debate about the utilization of new technologies, new instruments for the transformation of personal and collective life. If we look back at the long century of industrialization, our first impression is that the workers' movement played a central role for which there is no successor. But a closer examination shows that the contemporary debate has become much more multi-faceted, ramified and comprehensive than the social question then was. From nuclear industry to genetic engineering, from the media to the universities—in all those domains we see the development of discussion and of currents of opinion which all relate to the same central question: under what conditions can our technological potential be used to enhance the liberty and security of every individual, instead of subordinating individuals and groups to a technocratic power? This question is not only important in itself; it also shows us the limits of the image of social life as pure change. We should not think of ourselves as simply consumers or, at best, strategists, defending our interests within complex organizations and controlled markets. Change is not simply the sum total of modifications of the environment; it is also a sign of cultural creativity and of a power which has expanded beyond the spheres of economy and politics into the production and diffusion of informations and—in a more general sense—symbolic goods, i.e. culture. In this sense, contemporary sociology can take the guidelines of classical sociology to their most extreme consequences. Even more than before, it is concerned with the study of modernity, the self-transforming capacity of society; and it sees the struggle for social control over this capacity as the structuring principle of social life.

SOCIAL RELATIONS AND SOCIAL MOVEMENTS

We are now witnessing the decomposition of previously central analytical categories. When we talked about social classes, we were at least implicitly alluding to the idea of the *estate* (in the sense of a "third estate"), i.e. to the combination of economic conditions of life and hereditary privileges (or exclusion from privileges). Even today, the word "bourgeois" suggests the rentier rather than the industrialist. But such inequalities, reinforced by symbols and institutional mechanisms are less and less relevant to our societies. The notion of class therefore tends to disappear and it is most frequently replaced by the abovementioned image of society which separates a central mass from a privileged minority at the top and the more numerous marginals at the bottom. The sociologists who try to defend the image of a highly stratified and hierarchical society have to rely on an ideological construction to make themselves heard; they compare real societies with an ideal society that would be characterized by perfect mobility. But this model bears no semblance to reality: who would want to live in a society where children would be separated from their parents at birth, in order to prevent the consolidation of inequality during the first years of their life? This kind of abstract egalitarianism is sometimes invoked to show how far the democratic societies have departed from their principles. But concrete experience has another story to tell: social barriers are constantly lowered, even if it is true that some luxury goods become common among the rich before they are diffused more slowly among the rest of the population. A shared mass culture has become the predominant pattern in the countries where the majority of households owns television sets, radios, refrigerators, washing machines and cars; where schooling has been extended by several years; where the signs of social hierarchies (especially with regard to clothing) are disappearing; and where economic growth has led to a geographical and social mobility which is often underestimated. These obvious facts do not add up to the picture of an egalitarian society, not even in the sense of equal opportunities, but they show the inadequacy of concepts which have more to do with a society of reproduction than with a society of growth, change and mass consumption.

But if we go beyond these initial observations, we must raise the question of the nature of social actors and hence also conflicts and negotiations in societies that are characterized by change rather than by order. And here we arrive at one of the most important shifts in social thought. For a long time, it was taken for granted that an objective situation determines collective and individual behaviour and that the conditions of peasants, tradesmen and workers, defined in economic and political terms, would give rise to peasant, popular or worker's movements. In the Hegelian-Marxist tradition, theorists talked about the transition from a "class-in-itself" to a "class-for-itself", thus assuming that a class can be defined without reference to a class consciousness, and that specific actors, such as political parties or groups of intellectuals, have the ability to "give" consciousness to the social strata which do not develop it in a natural fashion. This idea has been substantiated by historical research; it was very often a crisis of the state accentuated by the rebellion of privileged groups, such as the French aristocracy at the end of the 18th century, that created an opening for the expression of popular discontent, and the resultant movement was radicalized as the social and political order disintegrated. But in contemporary industrial societies, situations do not determine actions, it is, rather, action that brings to light relations of domination and subordination which lack a visible juridical or political expression. The concept of class must therefore be replaced, as a central category of sociological analysis, by the concept of the *social movement*. The main reason for this is that the actions of those who hold power now tend to effect the whole of social life, because they produce models which determine the patterns of a mass society. Consequently, at the receiving and potentially resisting end, we no longer find clearly delimited groups, such as the wage-labourers in a factory but rather a *public*—the public which watches television or receives medical treatment. The action which it can undertake is not objectively pre-determined; on the contrary, an actor is only constituted by the detachment from the situation of the consumer who oscillates between the attitudes of dependent conformism and global rejection. Let us take the example of medical services: images of our body, our health, and even of our life and death, are above all formed by scientific medicine; but the very success of the latter leads to a dissociation of the patient from the ailments, which in turn motivates doubts about scientific medicine and interest in other methods that are often neither well-established nor easily understandable. This may seem an irrational reaction, but it is at least a response to the alienation of the patient from his illness and it can develop into a demand for more individualization of medical care; it can even lead to new developments in medicine that would—as already in genetics—result in a better understanding of individual differences. It is easy to see that behind the struggle between two kinds of medicine, ridiculous as it often is, there is a defence of the sick individual, directed not against science as such, but against the de-personalization of the apparatuses of medical care. Within the latter, administrative bureaucracy and medical technocracy act as rivals and as allies at the same time.

Should we say that the patients are protesting against medical domination similar to the economic domination that was resisted by industrial workers? Such metaphors would be dangerous, because the situation of the worker was determined directly by the organization of work and the management of the enterprise, whereas that of the patient derives its meaning from his claim to the right to control one's own existence and, in particular, own body. Analogously, the opponents of nuclear power cannot be identified with a particular social category (although it is true that people with tertiary education are over-represented among the anti-nuclear activists), and their action can have very different meanings, ranging from the most conservative and defensive communitarianism to an anti-industrial counterculture, to the contestation of technocratic power, or to a hyper-modernistic project of transition from a society based on energy to a society based on information. Only the movement in action, if it reaches the appropriate level of contestation, can bring such differences out into the open and allow the corresponding currents to organize themselves—perhaps even to transform themselves into veritable social groups.

To sum up: in a society dominated less by the transmission of privileges than by the power to model collective experience, the existence of social actors no longer precedes their action—it is produced by it. The idea of a "class-in-itself", defined without reference to its consciousness of itself, is therefore unacceptable. Slaves and serfs lived in social conditions defined by the law, and the constraints to which they were subjected made collective action difficult and prevented the development of a conflictual class consciousness. The workers' movement was, by contrast, resisting a power that was more economic than political and defined in general rather than personal terms; it therefore emphasized possible action more than imposed domination. The new social movements have moved further in this direction. They are more concerned with active intervention, rather than simply with breaking the links of dependence; and above all, the social actor who resists domination now appeals more and more directly to the values of creation and change, which in the past seemed to be monopolized by the ruling groups, whereas the dominated ones were more inclined to envisage a return to the past and to condemn historical evolution as a fall from a golden to an iron age.

Classical sociology hesitated between the study of social integration and the construction of a meaning of history. Society was seen as existing in history and as moved by it from tradition to modernity; its main task was to defend its cohesion while completing the mutation. Today the idea of evolution has disappeared and been replaced by the more neutral concept of change. On the other hand, actors are now recognized as more than simply the components of society or the limbs of a social body; they are real actors who transform the increased ability of society to act upon itself into actions, conflicts and negotiations which give rise to forms of social and cultural organization.

Contemporary sociology is therefore divided into two major schools of thought. One of them gives first priority to decisions, strategies and the organization of change; its attention is focused on ruling elites, more specifically the groups which play a leading role in social change. The other is primarily interested in social movements, the formation of social actors and the development of their ability to engage in conflicts and negotiations. Is there perhaps a continuity between the central themes of classical sociology—order and evolution—and those of contemporary social thought: social change and social movements? It would be risky to construct a direct affiliation; but it is true that the sociology of change, and more particularly the sociology of organizations, presents itself the successor to the sociology of the social system, which it both continues and transforms, as we can see from Simon's references to Parsons. On the other hand, there is a less direct but nevertheless profound affinity between those who tried to understand the human subject through a teleological model of evolution and those who—even if they reject evolutionism—are now trying to rediscover the actor behind the mechanisms of self-regulating systems.

SOCIETY AND POLITICS

The most direct expression of the transformations of social thought we have analyzed is that social actors, long considered as the masses or the people in whose name the politicians spoke and acted, now appear as the bearers of their own meaning, creators of their own actions who are no longer willing to be the *basis* of a political party. If we add to this the sharper separation of the state and civil society discussed above, then the political system appears both as a weak zone of social life and as a highly autonomous mediation between social actors and the state. The idea of representative democracy affirmed the priority of the represented over representation, but it also transferred the centre of gravity of action from the first to the second, as if the essential dimension of making oneself heard was to be well represented, which explains why so many lawyers became politicians. By contrast, when social movements seek to directly confront their opponents and to act independently on public opinion, the political system loses in part its representative role; the parties become coalitions of interests, ideas and groups, especially when the constitution reinforces the power of a head of state elected by universal suffrage. In France we observe a sharp decline of class parties after the decline of parties of local elites. On the left the Communist Party has had to gradually abandon references to the proletariat and to the working class in order to appeal to all workers and even the French people. The Socialist Party, despite retaining for some time a working class language, has become much more diversified than its ideology indicates.

This weakening of political parties has reached an extreme level in Japan, where on the one hand the state and on the other social actors or at least enterprises are very strong. The American situation is characterized by the strengthening both of the state and of extremely diverse social actors and by a certain weakening of political parties, especially as an effect of the primaries. These examples illustrate an important transformation of contemporary social thought. For a century, above all in France, the opposition of right and left incorporated at the same time opposed representations of society and very different conceptions of the role of the state. Hence the role of intellectuals who, since the Dreyfus affair, lined up either on the right or the left and gave the opposition of the political camps a more general dimension. Students fought for political causes just as they had earlier fought over literary themes. The social sciences as a whole fought against this *primacy of politics*. First of all historiography, whose renewal displaced political history in favour either of economic or cultural history; in economics, certainly despite the growing role of public intervention in economic life, since it is more aware of the general problems of the international economic system, of the effects of science and technology on the one hand and of micro-economic decisions on the other; and even more sociology, as it constantly foregrounds cultural innovations, social actors and the effects of inequality or power, thereby limiting from all sides the realm of political actors.

This retreat of the political effects above all the central French notion of *revolution*. It was justified to speak of an age of revolutions, opened by the American and especially the French revolution, prolonged and extended by the Bolshevik revolution and in a different fashion by the Mexican, and reaching all parts of the world with the Chinese revolution and the anti-colonial revolutions of the Third World. The essence of revolution is to identify a social movement with a political action, social claims with the seizure of state power and popular liberty with the meaning of history—another means of bringing together the social and the political. Today, by contrast, we separate these two orders and even tend to consider their logics as opposed, and the power born of revolution as destructive of the social movements which gave rise to it. This was the reason, on the bicentenary of 1789, for a critical reflexion on the French Revolution which greatly diverges from the highly political and unifying conception disseminated by Mathiez and his pupils. We are now sceptical of the continuity and unity of the revolutionary period. More recent experiences, in the Soviet Union, in China, Algeria, Ghana, or even closer to us in Portugal, have taught us the distance between the struggle for and the seizure of power. In the course of the last decades we have seen popular libertarian movements, directed against the state and in particular against its external actions, rather than socio-political movements, directed above all to a seizure of power identified with the transformation of society, as was still the case at the time of the Popular Front.

This weakening of political action, however, also has more positive consequences for the revolution in social thought. The autonomy of political mechanisms reinforces the importance of politics as an object of the social sciences. For a long time their natural approach, after a period of extreme interest in institutions, was to explain political facts by social facts and to incorporate political science into sociology. Today we observe a contrary movement, not a return to fairly limited studies of the functioning of institutions but a more philosophical reflexion on justice, respect for individual rights, and the relations between the law and the state. We no longer expect that political forces represent social interests; we rather expect of political institutions that they permit the formation of social action, protect minorities and individuals, facilitate negotiations, avoid violence. Hence we encounter a renaissance of reflexion on the law which had lost much of its force in France—even if it was always maintained in certain countries such as the United States. This reflexion has been stimulated by the critical analysis of totalitarian regimes and of dictatorships which have replaced national liberation movements in many countries of the Third World. The main outcome of these reflexions has been to separate representative institutions from the state and, in turn, both from the people as the sovereign social and political actor. The idea of popular sovereignty was the foundation of modern democracies which delegitimized kings and oligarchies. Today, now that the danger of an aristocratic reaction is excluded and the excesses committed by the authoritarian identification with a people prevented from expressing itself freely are well known, democracy is defined less by the sovereignty of the people than by the disappearance of any sovereign. Democracy tends to be defined by respect for minorities and above all individual rights, and thus as an ensemble of rules which prevent the formation of absolute power.

The separation of social movements and political forces leads also to the increase in importance of *public opinion* as the sphere of expression and influence of organized social actions, whether social movements or interest groups are involved. The power of the false idea that the media can mould and transform opinions and attitudes has held back awareness of the extraordinary importance of the media as the arena of public opinion. After the creation of a limited public sphere (Habermas) by the European bourgeoisie in the 17th and 18th centuries and its progressive extension through political parties and trade unions, we observe today an expansion of public opinion far beyond the frontiers of the political system, to such a point that the population of western countries, who rightly complain about the often mediocre quality of many radio and television programmes and the contents of most newspapers and magazines, are so attached to the news, the debates, the cultural messages which they receive from the mass media that they would not put up with their absence in authoritarian regimes, which take great pains to transmit "high" culture. The social sciences have been slow to study public opinion, which can be explained in part by the fear that the intellectuals have of being threatened in their role as shapers of opinion.

Social thought long sought to define the good society and to see civilization as the social integration of individuals, where desocialization was identified with crime, madness or suicide. The rights of man were not separated from those of citizen. French public schools saw their principal task as tearing children away from their particular backgrounds and making them members of the Republic, and thereby of the world of the true and the beautiful. In many countries schools had the clear role of national integration, even of creating a civic spirit and in certain cases a nationalist spirit. The current debates about the school indicate that this conception is no longer so easily accepted, not only because the integrating and universalistic school does not assure the equality of all and perhaps even reinforces social inequalities, but above all because many think that the main role of the school is to form neither citizens nor producers but individuals, persons capable of making choices, of taking initiatives and of respecting the difference of others, thanks to their knowledge and the formation of personality. This conception originally had aristocratic connotations, at Summerhill for example, but it was been reinforced and transformed by the simple observation that the universality of truth needs to be combined with diversity of teaching approaches and that unequal chances can be diminished by taking account of the personal and collective characteristics of the pupils. This presupposes that the teacher is no longer the intermediary between the children and general truths or society as a whole, but is defined by his/her relations to those taught, relations both individual and collective and which demand the association of the particular and the universal. Thus it is not surprising that when racist prejudices and discriminations re-emerge the most effective opposition comes not from abstract egalitarianism but from the idea that all are different, and that one must recognize the diversity of individuals beyond national, ethnic or supposedly racial categories which are always too global and superficial. "Do not interfere with my world" is an effective anti-racist protest because it draws on this new consciousness of individuality.

How do we explain the rise of this theme which was long marginalized, indeed even frequently associated in a negative fashion with the bourgeois spirit? First of all by the decline of collectivist ideologies, but we need to go further. The representation of the subject, i.e. individual creation, was "exteriorized", situated outside of the social realm since the latter was largely concerned with the rules of the reproduction of social and cultural organization. This transcendence of the subject diminished as the capacity for the self-production and self-transformation of society increased. It gradually ceased to have a religious form, called itself reason or history, became social but still gave society a certain transcendence. In our century, where the collective capacity for self-production and also for self-destruction seems to be without limit, the representation of the subject could no longer base itself on transcendence, on a meta-social guarantee. Two paths opened up. On the one side, the renunciation of transcendence and of the idea itself of the subject, which leads to the triumph of utilitarianism, which can take the simple form of the natural pursuit of interest or the more refined form of aesthetic hedonism. Individualism triumphs here over values and norms and is open to the development of the destructive tendencies of an individual defined solely by pleasure. On the other side, the recognition of the individual, not in submission to the forces of interest or pleasure but in the very particularity, which constitutes difference, and which can only be experienced in relation to others, recognized in their individuality and difference. The decisive movement in this direction has been achieved by the women's movement which first of all rejected all images of *the* woman. We do not speak of man—except to name the human species—but of men; women then demanded that we speak in the same manner of them. We should no longer accept that woman is defined in relation to a collectivity, a lineage or even a nuclear family, or to a man or children, but neither should we seek to replace a masculine image of the subject, religious or warlike, by any feminine image whatever; let us place at the centre of our ethics the study of the relations between a man and a woman, defined both by their sexual difference and their individuality. In France A. Fouque has shown better than anyone the path which has led radical women via homosexual action to the creation of a new heterosexual relation based on equality and difference. The subject is thus freed from all transcendence and all teleological or eschatological visions; he/she experiences him/herself in communication. It is insufficient to define contemporary individualism as the product of the crisis of ideologies or of collective action, as if this were nothing but a narcissistic return to the self. It may well be that this aspect is present, but the appeal to the individual has shown itself just as capable as previous representations of the subject of creating a collective mobilization. Thus the success of Amnesty International, the defence of human rights, and campaigns such as the rescue of the boat people.

This individualism is not self-absorbed since it fights against the degradation of transcendence into absolute power, the rule of the state and of social power in all its forms. Only recently this appeal to the social, to the collective, appeared liberating. Society still lived largely from the idea that the public realm liberated and the private enslaved, because the public realm is constructed on reason and the social contract, whereas the private realm transmitted inequality, privilege, irrationality. Gradually this ideology has been reversed; we admire the *zek* who preserves his individuality and his strength of refusal in the Gulag, the resister hunted by the police. Beyond that, we respect all freedom of conscience, we demand a clause of conscience protect journalists, whose newspapers change orientation with changes of ownership. We think that in a rapidly changing society schools should give the individual the ability to orient him/herself, to take initiatives, to make choices, to work and communicate with others. Sometimes these ideas are given negative expression, as if it were necessary to learn nothing in order to communicate better or as if the school should abandon all guidance. Such caricatures, however, are only drawn by those who resist the transformation of school, for whom it is above all an agent of order and of the transmission of inequality as well as of knowledge. If it is true that one must fight against community schools which would recreate ghettos, it is still more necessary to distrust the models imposed from above, which, having sought to spread aristocratic behaviour now attempt to generalize a middle class model, of which the teachers themselves are the best representatives. The principal role of the school is to transform general knowledge into an instrument of personal formation and not to rob individuals of their particularity.

Thus technology and individualism, instead of being in opposition, are associated. In societies which changed less rapidly social norms dominated and knowledge included both knowledge and modes of expression or work, regulated by a functional and hierarchized conception of the social order. The decline of knowledge of the national language in school has often been denounced; it is also necessary, however, to understand this decline of a highly constructed discourse as the crisis of traditional society and the rise of a culture in which individualism is associated with the use of techniques separated from any social code.

These transformations have led to the disappearance of all reflexions on the essence of society and, by the same token, on the individual, whose nature and needs would be defined outside of social roles. Individuals and society are not separable, which does not mean that the individual is defined only by the norms which apply to the social status occupied, whether wage earner or employer, father or daughter, citizen etc., but that behaviour must always be explained by the social relations in which a person is embedded. Thus the old quarrel between objectivists and subjectivists disappears. Sociology identifies itself with a *rational explanation* of social behaviour. Deviance in particular was explained either by objective factors, poverty, uprooting, absence of education or by factors of personal pathology. Today there is a strong tendency not to study the marginalized or delinquents but the social ensembles of which they form part, and to analyse their behaviour as symptomatic of the lack of or the search for influence on their environment. A more sociological conception of the social actor does not lead to privileging determinism, opposed by the champions of liberty, but to overcoming such an opposition in order better to understand the actor in the network of social relations, and also as a complex agent of the transformation of the environment.

ECONOMIC DEVELOPMENT AND CULTURAL SPECIFICITY

The discovery of the central role of individualism in our type of society helps us to understand an even more striking phenomenon which appears to both parallel and oppose it: the defence of cultural specificity in countries on the path to development. Evolutionism, which placed western nations at the head of the caravan of history and invited less modern countries to imitate their experience, served more often to legitimize colonial domination than to accelerate the modernization of dependent countries. The very idea of the convergence of East and West in a common modernity looks like an illusion a generation after Khrushchev. In fact these conceptions have been abandoned almost everywhere; the inverse appeal to national or regional cultural specificity has reached a deafening level. If the 19th century was dominated by the utilitarian and materialist universalism of capitalist civilization, the 20th century has been dominated by the role of states mobilizing projects and resources in order to modernize their countries by force or to defend an identity menaced by the penetration of the foreigner and economic rationality. At the end of our century the most active historical force is not the modernizing rationalism of the French or the Bolshevik Revolutions, it is Islamism. Everywhere in the world we observe the defence of identity and community, from the renewal of Indian movements in Central and South America to the awakening of nationalities on the periphery of western Europe or the resistance shown by Polish and Irish catholicism. In the most industrialized countries themselves we observe the creation of communities and neighbourhoods in search of a certain cultural homogeneity. After hippie culture we not only have the culture of homosexuals, but also of ethnic minorities or pensioners working for their own space and control of territory. This has reached the point that contemporary social problems are often defined as the struggle of minorities, and in place of a declining class struggle there are wars of religion and offensive or defensive crusades, especially in the Middle East.

Social thought is confronted by a burning problem: should it defend the universalism of reason and progress or does this mean identifying with the interests of the dominant countries? Or alternatively, should it justify the defence of cultural specificities; but does that not lead to support for authoritarian regimes, even theocracies which only appeal to belief in order to better maintain power based on regressive and corrupt terror?

This dilemma has only been posed in these terms since the decline of the spirit of Bandung. There was a period, after the war and the great wave of decolonization it engendered, when the newly independent countries rejected imperialism at the same time as the industrialized countries discovered that their interest lay in developing research and the home market rather than holding on to captive markets for low quality products. The colonizing and the previously colonized countries found for a time parallel solutions for combining modernization with cultural specificity by getting rid of the destructive or paralysing forms of political and financial hegemony. It was also during this period that intellectuals of the left triumphed in the West and above all in France, affirming the unity of the struggles for democratic freedoms in the West, the workers, revolutions in the East and the movements of national liberation in the Third World.

This parallelism of West, East and South has given way to their divergence. If one part of the Third World joins the First by becoming the *new industrial countries*, where despite relapses democracy is gradually strengthened or introduced, as for instance in Brazil or South Korea, another part resists modernization led from above and from outside, and the liberation movements which emerge, for instance in Iran, are quickly overtaken by neo-communitarian movements, of which Islamism is the most important. Social thought cannot be indulgent to intellectual nationalism, even less to state terrorism which forbids research and the expression of opinions; but it is directly interested in the general problem of the relations between cultural specificity and general factors of rationalization and development.

Conceptual progress here consists in breaking with an ideological representation of western modernization. To say that the West has overthrown barriers and caused the light of reason to rise over the modern world corresponds more to the opinions of the party of managing elites than to the historical truth. In particular, studies of the Middle Ages have overturned the old perspectives of the opposition of traditional and modern society, in which the French Revolution marked the turning point. Now feudalism appears to us as a form of the separation of civil society and the state as opposed to Turkish or Chinese patrimonialism, and Christianity, which renders to Caesar what is due to Caesar and to God what is due to God, appears more favourable to modernization than Islam's merging of temporal and spiritual power. Moreover, western development seems to be tied to the disquiet and sense of guilt which comes from the Judeo-Christian tradition. Western development is thus due less to the triumph of interest and reason than to the force of religion and the capacity to save. It thus has a specificity as strong as that of the countries of the Third World today. We do not have on the one side a universalistic West and on the other a Third World appealing to its specificity. In the whole world cultural specificity and general factors of modernization are related. The largest field of research for the social sciences is opened up by the comparative study of the paths of development, each defined by its mode of relation between reason and cultural specificity—and also by the forms of rupture between them.

All this serves to show that the social sciences can only progress by placing themselves on a global level, although they remain too often socio-centric, privileging a single type of historical experience. This ought to lead to the perception of a truly European cultural and intellectual milieu, since there are general features of European modernization which should be compared with those of Latin America, the Arab world or India. This also makes the case of Japan extremely important, as this country has combined modernization and even westernization with the maintenance of national culture and the defence of national independence since the Meiji revolution. More than any other country Japan helps us to understand that the modern does not replace the traditional as day replaces night but that tradition is also the source of its own transformation or at least can be reinterpreted. This is not meant to lead to the populist utopia for which the return to the past will permit the construction of a future avoiding all the ruptures of capitalist or socialist industrialization. Between abstract western rationalism and all the forms of populism or cultural nationalism we need a body of analysis which studies the traits common to all the processes of development and the differences, especially cultural and political, which distinguish them.

This study of the paths of development must not be confused with the study of the internal problems of industrial or modern societies. It has become harder to confuse social structure and mode of historical development—the classic sociological definition of modernity—but we have not yet drawn all the consequences of their separation. We still call capitalism both the social relations of production particular to industrial society and a mode of industrialization in which the owners of private capital play the role of the managing elite. We must separate these, however. The workers' movement opposes the managers and many studies have shown that their demands are the same in socialist as in capitalist countries. On the other hand, political mechanisms and struggles differ according to whether industrialization is directed by a national or foreign bourgeoisie or by a national or foreign state. Similarly, we must distinguish between socialism as the ideology of the workers movement and socialism as state industrialization. It is true that the two axes of analysis are never completely independent of each other. More importantly, however, they must never be confused with each other. A sociology which reduces everything to change tends to assert that structural problems no longer exist; a sociology too attached to models of the past gives exclusive importance to the functional problems of the socio-economic system. The central problem of sociological explanation today is to study the determinants of the relations between the synchronic and the diachronic axes of analysis, between problems of structure and problems of development. The need for comparative analyses is clear here.

THE CHANCES OF DEMOCRACY

What international comparisons show most clearly is the opposition between the politics of development and democratic mechanisms. The western model rested on the idea that modern society produced its own modernization and that the field of social freedom expanded the more economic development accelerated. We now know that this indigenous development has only occurred in a few countries, almost only in the new countries of European colonization with great natural and spatial resources at their disposal and in need of attracting labour. And even here in this American type development was directed by the barons of finance and industry, whose conquering power imposed limits to democracy. Wherever modernization comes up against major internal or external obstacles, development mobilized around a voluntarist state is alien and often hostile to democracy, since the main problem is to transform society, to break its traditions and forms of organization in order to force the penetration of modernization. The more voluntaristic development is, the more democracy is threatened. The 20th century has been the century of development and of voluntarist modernizing and authoritarian states, to the point that democracy was often rejected as the expression of global domination exerted by the countries of indigenous modernization. Even in the West democracies coped badly with the great crisis of the 30s, from which they only emerged with the war and the state intervention it entailed. After a long period dominated after 1945 by authoritarian and "developmental" regimes, where the strongest global tendency was the alliance of post-colonial nationalisms and communist regimes, i.e. the two main types of voluntarist regimes, the question now is: do international competition, demographic pressure and the demands of a new scientific and technical revolution, i.e. the acceleration and generalization of change, mean that the world as a whole must move towards the replacement of democracy by the authoritarian politics of development? We are all aware of a growing pressure for each country to mobilize, which requires internal consensus, strong decision-making capacities and considerable pressure to direct the efforts of all to the future, whereas democracy rests on the idea that society is confronted by choices which involve negotiable conflicts, leading to solutions which respect different interests and submitting rulers to the control of the ruled.

The impression has spread that democracy only belongs to those nations which were once dominant and are now living in a still agreeable decadence before their decline accelerates and they are forced to adopt authoritarian regimes in response to the menacing crisis. This perception has dominated the greater part of our century. It challenges so directly our conception of social life that it necessarily takes central place in the reflexions of the social sciences. Do they not risk appearing superfluous if they do not tie themselves to objective practices? Everything which has been said so far indicates that the social sciences of change are above all sciences of action, of decision, debate and conflict. They thus cannot avoid confronting practical questions; they must reflect on the conditions under which a world in change, development and crisis can manage its functioning and its future while yet remaining democratic. Sociology in the 19th century sought above all knowledge of progress; sociology at the end of the 20th century must be above all the scientific analysis of the chances, forms and limits of democracy, first of all on the global level, and then within our own mode of development and organization.

On the global level contemporary social thought is dominated by the exhaustion of the authoritarian modes of development. The Soviet Union, a formidable military and political power, is also a society economically, socially and culturally paralysed. Nobody denies any more the failure of the Great Leap Forward of the Chinese Cultural Revolution. The great voluntarist projects of development in Africa have in general failed; the military regimes of Latin America, identified with economic miracles, have nearly all collapsed under an exceptionally serious economic crisis.

Given these failures, two paths of development seem to encounter a greater success: on the one hand, the stressing of the indigenous factors of change and the creation of a society of innovation, which presupposes an extension of political and cultural freedoms; on the other, the combination already referred to of instrumental objectives of production and of specific cultural and social motivations. These two forms of the combination of universalism and specificity are very different, but they are both opposed to the equally reductive solutions of either state colonialism or the subjection of all social life to economic rationality. The search to combine cultural specificity and technical and scientific modernization in the Third World involves above all not the opposition of external modernization and communitarian development but the management of their inevitably tense relationship. What is the situation in western industrialized countries confronted by the need for a leap forward? A mobilization Japanese-style or Korean-style would come up against strong resistance. On the contrary, solutions are being sought in a growing separation of the state and civil society. The main obstacle to development is the confusion of the state and social actors. This is the case for Europe and for most of the Latin American countries. Hence the success of France or Italy, countries of relatively weak industrialization after World War II: they set up ruling state elites capable of mobilizing important resources for long term investment in the name of national interest, and undertook at the same time the difficult and incomplete task of breaking the factors of cultural and political immobility and rigidity. Similarly, the United States created after 1945 a capacity for state initiative, at the same time as American society became more complex and mobile. This representation of the factors of progress, on the one side a greater state capacity for investment and decision and on the other a greater complexity and mobility of social life, which presupposes strong, independent actors and ever growing public freedoms, is opposed to conventional ideas. Some speak of mobilizing a necessary consensus, others seek in interest and in the market the key to development. Some have a political and military conception of social life, others reduce it to the economy. Both sides deny the existence of social actor, defined both by their orienting values and the social relations in which they are embedded. Hence the present crisis of social thought. It is often reduced to a reformism which irritates some because it impedes the search for profit and others because it imprisons actors in the apparatus of the neo-corporatist state. Social thought can only be renewed by a clear awareness of the need to strengthen the international mission of the state and to extend and diversify public space. Now that we have the growth of a mass culture which is not only passive, the spread of new techniques and the appearance of social actors and negotiations in areas long subject to administrative authority or economic power, it is no longer acceptable for social thought to remain imprisoned in the idea that society is subject to an implacable logic.

The social sciences have accompanied industrial society, its triumphs and cries and then its cultural and economic decline. They then turned in on themselves for some years and became discourses on knowledge, just as for a while the cinema or the novel became their own objects of analysis, due to the loss of the capacity to apprehend the new reality and behaviour. This period of doubt and doctrinaire attitudes is over. The world is moving too fast for it still to be possible to explain why it cannot move. The social sciences are undergoing a profound mutation; they are becoming sciences of action and change and no longer sciences of history or human nature. The modernizing capacity of our societies depends to a large extent on their capacity to provide themselves with instruments of analysis which correspond to their functioning and their mode of change, as they are modified by the progress of the sciences, cultural transformations and the opening up of international relations.

Translated by Johann Arnason and David Roberts

Notes

1. * This essay is published with the kind permission of Hachette, Paris.

CIVIL SOCIETY AND SOCIAL THEORY

Andrew Arato and Jean Cohen

REDISCOVERING CIVIL SOCIETY

The aim of this essay is to vindicate a set of concepts which have been revived by contemporary social movements to articulate their projects of democratization, but which are open to the charge of being used merely ideologically, in order to promote certain forms of mobilization. In particular, we want to argue that the concept of civil society is more than a mere slogan. Indeed, if properly reconstructed, the concept can resolve several theoretical and practical problems confronted by contemporary analysis and social actors. We intend to show, moreover, that a reconstructed concept of civil society can clarify the possibilities and limits of projects for further democratizing formally democratic societies.

Social movements in the East and the West, the North and the South have come to rely on various interesting, albeit eclectic syntheses inherited from the history of the concept of civil society.[1] They presuppose (in different combinations) something like the Gramscian tripartite framework of civil society, state and economy, while preserving key aspects of the Marxian critique of bourgeois society. But they have also integrated liberal claims on behalf of individual rights, the stress of Hegel, Tocqueville and others on societal plurality, the emphasis of Durkheim on the component of social solidarity, and the defense of the public sphere and political participation stressed by Habermas and Arendt.[2]

We intend to demonstrate the plausibility of a *modern* concept of civil society in light of these developments, despite what many analysts from Schmitt and Luhmann to Arendt and Koselleck have rightly shown to be the difficulties of applying any of the inherited versions of the concept to contemporary institutions and forms of action.[3] Moreover, we shall show that our reconstruction can yield an immanent, self-limiting utopia of democratization, without which the projects of social movements cannot avoid a self-destructing fundamentalism at best.

THE RECONSTRUCTION OF CIVIL SOCIETY

Anyone who wants to utilize the concept of civil society faces a double task. First, one must demonstrate the continued normative and empirical relevance of the concept to modern social conditions. Second, one must account for the negative dimensions of contemporary civil societies while showing that these are only part of the story, not the whole. We think that the recent work of Jürgen Habermas makes a major contribution in both respects.[4] We shall therefore reconstruct the concept of civil society on the basis of Habermas's development of a dualistic social theory that differentiates the logics of system and life-world.

Habermas himself does not offer a theory of civil society.[5] But his analytical distinction between the logics of system and life-world allows us to situate civil society within a general theoretical framework which permits the most comprehensive analysis of the various dynamics of contemporary western societies. On the one hand, the framework allows one to articulate the positive side of the achievements of modern civil society without closing off the possibility of an immanent critique of its specific institutional configurations. On the other hand, the dualistic framework can account for the negative side of modernity analysed by so many critics. Indeed, the distinction between system and life-world shows that the totalization of either the positive or the negative perspectives involves one-sided and ideological formulations. Finally, the dualistic framework allows for the articulation of a "self-limiting utopia" of society that avoids fundamentalist interpretations. It thus vindicates the normative promise associated with the concept of civil society ever since Aristotle, that has been revived today, Foucault and Luhmann notwithstanding, by contemporary collective actors.[6]

Habermas's thesis that there are two subsystems differentiated out from the life-world implies a model that corresponds to a tri-partite framework of the Gramscian type. One can, without much difficulty, identify the state and the economy with the two media-steered subsystems. The concept of system integration is a good first approximation of the mechanisms by which the capitalist economy and the modern bureaucratic administration coordinate action. Moreover, the concept of the social integration of a life-world through the interpretive understanding of a normatively secured, communicatively reproduced consensus outlines at least the space in which a hermeneutically derived concept of civil society can be located. Yet it is not self-evident that the concept of the life-world can be translated into that of civil society. On the contrary, these concepts seem to operate on two very different categorical levels.

Nevertheless, Habermas's concept of the life-world has two distinct dimensions which, if adequately differentiated and clarified, allow us to pinpoint the exact place of civil society within the overall framework.[7] On the one hand, the life-world refers to the reservoir of implicitly known traditions and taken-for-granted background assumptions which are embedded in language and culture, and drawn upon by individuals in their everyday lives. On the other hand, the life-world, according to Habermas, has three distinct structural components: "culture", "society" and "personality". To the degree to which actors mutually understand and agree on their situation, they share a cultural tradition. Insofar as they coordinate their action through inter-subjectively recognized norms, they act as members of a solidary social group. As individuals grow up within a cultural tradition and participate in group life, they internalize value orientations, acquire generalized action competencies, and develop individual and social identities. The reproduction of both dimensions for the life-world involves communicative processes of cultural transmission, social integration, and socialization. But—this is the main point for us—the structural differentiation of the life-world (an aspect of the modernization process) occurs through the emergence of institutions specialized in the reproduction of traditions, solidarities and identities. It is this institutional dimension of the life-world that best corresponds to our concept of civil society.

Of course, *every* society develops institutions which assure the transmission of culture, integration and socialization. *Civil* societies, whatever their form, presuppose a juridical structure, a constitution, that articulates the principles underlying their internal organization. Within the context of a *modernized* life-world (see below), however, civil society exist only where there is a juridical guarantee of the reproduction of the various spheres in the form of *sets of rights*. Why? The differentiation of the modern state and the capitalist economy is not only a complementary condition of the structures of a modernized life-world. The power and expansion of these spheres or subsystems also make the structures of this modern life-world singularly unstable and precarious. While the uncoupling of state and economy from the life-world is the pre-condition of that unburdening from constraints of time without which communicative action coordination is impossible, their logic can penetrate and distort the reproduction of cultural, social and socializing institutions. These institutions can be stabilized only on the basis of new forms of juridification, i.e., *rights*, which constitute the terrain of civil society, when accompanied by an appropriately modern form of political culture that valorizes societal self-organisation and publicity. In this context, we can isolate three complexes of rights: those concerning cultural reproduction (freedoms of thought, press, speech, communication); those insuring social integration (freedom of association, assembly); and those securing socialization (protection of privacy, intimacy, inviolability of the person). For the moment, we are not concerned with the relationship of these complexes with other rights which mediate between civil society and either the capitalist economy (rights of property, contract, labour) or the modern bureaucratic state (political rights of citizens, welfare rights of clients).

To be sure, the discourse of rights has been accused of being purely ideological and, even worse, the carrier of statist penetration and control of populations. The classical Marxian objection is that formal rights are merely the ideological reflex of capitalist property and exchange relations. And yet, clearly only some rights have an individualist structure and not all of them can be reduced to property rights. The typically anarchist objection (raised by Foucault) is that rights are simply the product of the will of the sovereign state, articulated through the medium of positive law and facilitating the surveillance of all aspects of society. No one can bind the state to respect its own legality; whenever it does so, its own interests must require it. But, while the state is the agency of the legalization of rights, it is neither their source nor the basis of their validity. Rights begin as claims asserted by groups and individuals in the public spaces of an emerging civil society. They can be guaranteed by positive law but are not equivalent to law nor derivable from it; in the domain of rights, law secures and stabilizes what has been achieved autonomously by social actors in society. Universal rights, then, must be seen as the organizing principle of a modern civil society whose most dynamic institution is its public sphere.

Here we can only summarize the theoretical gains from reconstructing the concept of civil society through the use of the concept of a life-world differentiated from the economic and state systems. We shall do so in four short points.

1. Beyond Traditional Civil Society

If Habermas's concept of the life-world allows for a conceptualization of civil society, that is not equal to the global framework of the civil system. Civil society is a dimension of the life-world, institutionally secured by rights and, of course, distinct from, but presupposing, the differentiated spheres of economy and state. Moreover, the thesis of the modernization of the life-world points beyond those interpretations that either make unacceptable concessions to the traditional version of civil society (Hegel, Parsons) or reduce it to a purely individualistic, privatized and/or class version of capitalist or bourgeois society (liberalism, Marx).[8] A modernized life-world involves the communicative opening up of the sacred core of traditions, norms and authority to processes of questioning and discursive adjudication. It entails the replacement of a conventionally-based normative consensus by one that is reflexive, post-conventional, and grounded in open processes of communication. Thus, when linked to the concept of the life-world, the paradigm of communication does not construe modernization as equivalent to the dissolution of all tradition, only of a *traditionalistic relationship to tradition*. In uncovering the communicative infrastructure and rationality potential of the life-world, Habermas moreover, provides the theoretical tools for showing that the dissolution of traditional forms of solidarity or authority need not result automatically in the emergence of a one-dimensional society pervaded only by strategically acting individuals devoid of resources for autonomous solidarity or meaning. On the contrary, the modernization of the life world and of civil society constitutes the cultural and institutional precondition for the emergence of rational and solidary collective identities and autonomous actors who develop the capacity to, and responsibility for interpreting and lending significance.

The dualistic social theory of Habermas thus provides an answer to both Parsons and Luhmann. The communicative rationalization of the life-world implies that a *gemeinschaftliche* coordination of social action (normative action based on unquestioned standards—Parsons) can have modern substitutes. This insight allows Habermas to turn the Parsonian concept of "societal community" (or civil society) away from its strategic pole of interpretation (based on the notion of influence as the steering mechanism), while putting its traditionalist pole into the context of the possible modernization of tradition itself.[9] A new, reflexive relation to tradition becomes conceivable. Equally important, the differentiation of the components of the life-world implies the end of a unified corporate organization of society and the dissolution of an all encompassing ethos or *Sittlichkeit*, without destroying the possibility or need for social integration (Luhmann).[10]

Such reflexive and critical relations to tradition presuppose cultural modernization: the differentiation of the cultural spheres into sets of institutions specialized around cognitive-instrumental, aesthetic-expressive and moral-practical values (Weber). Cultural modernization in this sense makes possible the development of post-traditional, post-conventional egalitarian and democratic forms of association, publicity, solidarity and identity. In civil societies situated in a modernized world, a plurality of actors can rely on a horizon of mutually presupposed meanings and norms and participate, if need be, in their redefinition or renegotiation. Only on such a cultural basis is the replacement of a traditional by a post-traditional civil society conceivable.

2. The Negativity of Modern Civil Society

It goes without saying that Habermas by no means maintains that these potentials of cultural modernity, or civil society, have anywhere been adequately realized. Modernization in the West has proceeded according to a *selective pattern* that distorted the potentials of civil society.[11] Indeed, the contrast he draws between a potentially nonselective and actually selective pattern of modernization allows him to combine the diametrically opposed assessments of contemporary civil society (e.g. the positions of Parsons and Foucault) as alternatives *within* modernity. In more concrete terms, Habermas maintains that the rationalization of the life-world with respect to the realization of cultural potentials in the aesthetic and moral/practical domains has been blocked to a significant extent. The rationalization of the economic and administrative subsystems and the preponderant weight given to their reproductive imperatives has proceeded at the *expense* of the rationalization of civil society. The resulting gap between the expert cultures involved in the differentiated value spheres of scientific knowledge, art and morality, and the general public leads to the cultural impoverishment of a life-world whose traditional substance has been eroded. However, contrary to the all-too-popular Weberian thesis,[12] *it is not cultural modernity, per se, but its selective institutionalization and resulting cultural impoverishment that is problematic.*

The one-sided institutionalization of the cognitive-instrumental potential of cultural rationalization (initially in scientific communities, and later in the two subsystems) further prepares the ground for the penetration of the media of money and power into action areas of civil society which require integration through communicative processes. Acting subjects become subordinated to the imperatives of apparatuses which have become autonomous and substitutes for communicative interaction. But the distinction between system and life-world, between state, economy and civil society, allows Habermas to show that it is not the emergence of differentiated political and economic systems and their internal coordination through system integration that produces the loss of freedom, but, rather, the penetration of an already modernized life-world by their logic and selective pattern of institutionalization. Habermas calls this penetration the "reification" or "colonization" of the life-world.

The discussion of the negative dimension of a selectively rationalized, partly colonized and insufficiently modern civil society implies that the existing version of civil society is only *one* logically possible path of institutionalizing the potentials of cultural modernity.[13] At issue is not merely the fact of differentiation, but the relation between the terms of the system/life-world model. Societal modernization always involves the replacement of some aspects of social integration by system integration.[14] But Habermas distinguishes between the effects of the differentiation of the subsystems out of a *traditionally structured* life-world, and those resulting from the penetration of steering mechanisms into a life world that has *begun to modernize.*

In the first case, the cost of capitalist and/or statist forms of modernization is the destruction of traditional forms of life and the development of economic and political institutions pervaded by domination.

But the gain, in addition to relative economic and administrative efficiency, is the opening of the life-world to modernization and the creation of a post-conventional culture of civil society. As indicated earlier, modernization involves not only the emergence of the economic and administrative subsystems, but also developments within the cultural and societal levels of the life-world. Indeed, the two processes presuppose each other. The life-world could not be modernized without the strategic unburdening of communicative action-coordination by the development of the two subsystems. In turn, they require institutional anchoring in a life-world that remains symbolically structured, communicatively coordinated, at least partly modernized, and socially integrated (*pace* Luhmann). On the simplest level, the subject of private and public law is needed by an economy coordinated through money exchanges and a state administration organized through bureaucratically structured power relations. This "subject" can emerge only if the requisite cognitive and moral competencies and institutional structures are available in the life-world.[15] Without these developments, a "fully modern", post-traditional—universalist, egalitarian and democratic—coordination of civil society would be impossible.

This development is evident in the relationship between the public and private spheres of a modernizing civil society, and the economy and state. Habermas maintains that the life-world reacts in a "characteristic way" to the emergence of the two subsystems out of its societal component. "In *civil society*, socially integrated spheres of action become formed into a public and private sphere, in opposition to the system-integrated action spheres of economy and state, which are related to each other in a complementary manner".[16] The nuclear family, specialized in socialization, is the institutional core of the private sphere. These institutions facilitate the emergence of a public composed of private individuals able to enjoy culture and to develop public opinion necessary for their participation as associated individuals in social integration and, as citizens, in political life. Thus, to a certain extent, the internal differentiation of the institutions of civil society matches the differentiation of the two subsystems of economy and state.

In the case of the colonization of the life-world, the cost is the undermining of the communicative practice of an already (partly) modernized life-world and the blocking of the (further) modernization of civil society. It is a real question whether one can continue to consider unambiguous the gains (such as state-guaranteed security) in such a context. For institutions specialized in socialization, social integration and cultural transmission are increasingly functionalized to serve the imperatives of the uncontrolled and expanding subsystems. As the communicative coordination of action is replaced by the media of money and power, there will be more and more pathological consequences.[17]

The advantage of this framework over dichotomous models is that it allows for clarification of the structural interrelations among the key terms by severing the ideological one-to-one correlation of civil society with the private sphere (understood as the economy) and the state with the public. Instead, the three-part model yields *two* sets of public and private dichotomies: one at the level of the subsystems (state/economy), one at the level of civil society (public opinion formation/family).[18]

The four dimensions of the system/life-world distinction are related through a series of "exchanges" made possible by the institutionalization of the media of money and power. This framework thus enables one to clearly distinguish between, for example, the institutions of one private sphere that are coordinated communicatively (family or friendship relations) and those of a different one that are coordinated primarily through steering mechanisms (the economy).[19] The same holds true for the two analytically distinct "public" spheres. Accordingly, one can begin to conceptualize processes of deprivatization that do not *ipso facto* involve statization. One can also find an answer here to the fusion argument (Schmitt), by showing that state intervention in the economy does not necessarily entail the absorption or abolition of an autonomous civil society.

Finally, on the basis of this tripartite framework, Foucault's version of modernization can be put into its proper perspective. The colonization thesis, in short, provides a cogent *theoretical* account of the "negativity" of modern civil society *described* so penetratingly by Foucault, without confusing the negative side for the whole. For example, if, as is the case in late-capitalist welfare state systems, the subsystems penetrate the private sphere of the family and subordinate it to their imperatives, the role of the dependent *consumer* (with respect to economic requirement) comes to predominate over the roles of *worker* and autonomous *family member* or actor in civil society. If (with respect to administrative requirements of loyalty) system imperatives penetrate the public sphere, then the *citizen* role becomes fragmented and neutralized, with the result that the burden of depoliticization must be borne by an overinflated *client* role rooted in the private sphere. (The explosion of entitlements claims and the "ungovernability thesis" have their locus here.) These structural transformations in the public and private sphere of civil society account for the pathological and reifying versions of individuality, privacy and citizenship in a selectively institutionalized, colonized modernity.

Habermas concretizes his analysis of the negativity of contemporary developments in his discussion of welfare state social policy, which is seen to involve the administrative penetration (through juridification) of areas of civil society previously exempt from such interference.[20] The monetization and bureaucratization of social relations in civil society is a highly ambivalent process; while it creates a set of social rights and securities, it does this at the cost of (a) creating a new range of dependencies and (b) destroying existing solidarities and capacities for self-help and the communicative resolution of problems by actors themselves. For example, the administrative handling of care for the aged, of inter-familial relation, and of conflict around schooling involves processes of *bureaucratization* and *individualization* that define the client solely a a strategic actor with specific private interests that can be dealt with on a one-to-one basis. But this involves a violent and painful abstraction of individual from an existing social situation, damage to their self-esteem and to interpersonal relations. *Monetization* of these areas of life also has negative consequence. Retirement payments cannot compensate for the sense of purpose in life and self-esteem of an elderly individual who has been forced out of a job because of age. Finally, the *therapeutization* of everyday life fostered by the social services of welfare agencies contradicts the very goal of therapy—to achieve the autonomy and empowerment of the patient. As soon as administratively-based professionals claim expertise and exercise the legal power to enforce their claims, a cycle of dependency is created between the patient-client and the apparatus.

The dilemma in each case consists in the fact that welfare state intervention in the name of serving the needs of civil society fosters its disintegration and blocks its further rationalization. Foucault's description of the techniques of surveillance, individualization, discipline and control is thus explicitly accommodated in Habermas's analysis. Nevertheless, despite appearances, Habermas does not rejoin the Foucauldian (or, for that matter, the neo-conservative) critique of the welfare state. For him, legality, normativity, publicity, legitimacy, rights are not only the carriers or veils of disciplinary mechanisms. The colonization thesis accounts *only* for the negativity of modern civil society. From the standpoint of the system/life-world distinction, Habermas is able to point to the *two-sided character* of institutional developments in contemporary civil society, thereby revealing his framework to be the wider one. Indeed, with respect to the institutional analysis provided in *Theory of Communicative Action*, we want to argue that Habermas has ten a major step forward compared with his earlier formulations by providing room for an analysis of the dualistic character of some, although not all, of the core components of civil society.[21] And yet we will show that the institutional description is incomplete, and that the theoretical framework, in one key respect, is flawed.

3. The Institutional Doubleness and Alternatives of Civil Society

Despite the potentials for colonization in the contemporary situation, the whole of civil society cannot be reduced to its negativity. The institutions of a modernized life-world have resources of their own. So civilization in modern civil society leaves greater scope for the formation of post-conventional personality types. Modernized cultural forms set in motion discursive practices and expectations that cannot be kept away entirely from everyday life through selective institutionalization. As associations are transformed into bureaucratic organizations, new egalitarian and democratic associational forms tend to emerge. Moreover, blockages in the modernization of the life-world due to colonization are counterproductive also for the modern state and economy (loss of legitimacy, reduction of the work ethic, etc.). To be sure, the net result of these trends has not been the reversal of reification. Instead, what reemerges is a *dualistic structure* of the institutions of civil society that yields a series of alternative potentials of further development.

Habermas assesses the doubleness of the institutions of contemporary civil society in the domains of legality, political and cultural publicity, and the family. First, in the domain of legalization, there is the alternative of law functioning solely as a *medium*, as a vehicle for the penetration of the life-world by money and power, or as an *institution* that secures and formalizes the normative accomplishments of the life-world. The development of legality up to the contemporary democratic welfare state involves both the modernization of civil society, its protection through rights, *and* its penetration by administrative agencies. It is in this double nature of law that one must locate the ambiguous character of the contemporary juridification of society. As a "medium", law functions as an organizational means, together with money and power, of constituting the structures of economy and administration such that they can be coordinated independently of direct communication. As an institution, on the other hand, law is "a social component of the life-world itself. . . on a continuum with ethical norms and communicatively formed spheres of action".[22] Juridification in this sense plays a regulative rather than a constitutive role, serving to expand and give a binding form to communicatively coordinated spheres of action. This empowering dimension of legal regulation conflicts with the authoritarian dimension of bureaucratic intervention carried by legalization itself. In this regard, Foucault's error is to have focused exclusively on the role of law, and even rights, as a medium, while dismissing its freedom-securing, empowering institutional moment as mere show. Contrary to Foucault, to reinforce the legalization of civil society in the second sense would involve stressing the regulative role of law and securing an autonomous, self-regulating, yet universalistic civil society, without increasing administrative penetration.

The institutional developments in the political and cultural public spheres and in the modern family are similarly dualistic. The principles of democratic legitimacy and representation imply the free discussion of all interests within the institutionalised public sphere (parliament) and the primacy of the life-world with respect to the two subsystems. But the uncoupling of the centralized public sphere from genuine participation leads to the exclusion of a wide range of interests and issues from general discussion. On the other hand, as the ambiguous welfare state policies reveal, the pressures of the life-world cannot simply be ignored by representative systems even in their present highly selective form of functioning. Here the positive option (which Habermas himself does not focus on) would be the further democratization of formal democracy.[23]

In the domain of what used to be the literary public sphere, one cannot simply construe the development of the mass media as a purely negative sign of the commodification or administrative distortion of communication. To be sure, the possibility of social control increases with the top-to-bottom, centre-to-periphery model of mass communications. Yet, generalized forms of communication deprovincialize, expand and create new publics. Moreover, the technical development of the electronic media does not necessarily lead to centralization—as is now evident, it can involve, horizontal, creative and autonomous forms of media pluralism. Here, then, the alternatives are between the manipulative logic of the culture industry and the emergence of counter-publics and counter-cultures able to make use of the new media of communication in non-hierarchical ways.

Last, but hardly least, Habermas challenges the old Frankfurt school thesis (which he used to share) that the assumption of socialization by the schools and the mass media and the erosion of the property-based, middle class, patri-archal family destroys both the father's authority and the ego-autonomy of the children. From the standpoint of the system/life-world distinction, the picture looks rather different. The freeing of the family from certain economic func-tions and the diversification of socialization agencies create the potential for egalitarian, inter-familial relations and liberalized socialization processes. The potential for communicative interaction in this sphere is thereby released. Of course, new sorts of conflict and even pathologies do appear when these po-tentials are blocked. If the demands of the formally organized subsystems, in which adults must participate, conflict with the capacities and expectations of those who have experienced the emancipatory socialization processes, severe strains occur. The institutional alternatives immanent in the family thus involve either its further replacement by other, functionalized socialization instances, or its retraditionalization, or the substitution of egalitarian for patriarchal inter-familiar relations, complemented by liberalized socialization processes.

We would like to add to Habermas's own list of alternatives within civil society the dual possibilities inherent in modern associational life: on the one side, the reduction of associational life to formal, bureaucratic and closed or-ganizations (corporatist systems), on the other, the revitalization of voluntary associations through internally democratic, open and public forms of group life.[24] In our view, indeed, the resolution of all the alternatives in question in a democratic direction depends primarily on the outcome of this last alternative.

4. The Utopia of Civil Society

In an age when totalizing revolutionary utopias have been discredited, the dualistic model of civil society we have reconstructed avoids "soulless" re-formism by allowing us to thematize an immanent, *self-limiting*, self-reflexive utopia of civil society. We can thereby link the project of self-limiting, radical democracy to some key institutional premises of modernity. The slogan "so-ciety against the state" has often been understood in a fundamentalist way to mean the generalization of participatory democratic decision-making, as the coordinating principle, to all spheres of social life, including the state and the economy. Indeed, the ideal of free voluntary association, democratically struc-tured and communicatively coordinated has always informed the utopia of civil society, from Aristotle to Marx. But such a totalizing "democratic" utopia threatens the very basis of modernity (differentiation, efficiency). Moreover, it is not even desirable on a normative level, because it would involve such an overburdening of the democratic process, thereby discrediting it and opening it to subversion by covert, unregulated strategic action.

As opposed to this, the self-limiting utopia of radical democracy based on the dualistic model of civil society would open up "...the utopian horizon of a civil society, in which the formally organized spheres of action of the bourgeois (economy and state apparatus) constitute the foundations for the post-traditional life-world of *l'homme* (private sphere) and *citoyen* (public sphere)".[25] The institutional anchoring of this utopian conception is based on the consolidation of the modern state and modern market economy, to which the life-world reacts in a "characteristic way".[26] As indicated earlier, the carving out of a non-state public sphere and a non-economic private sphere expresses both this reaction and the need of the subsystem to secure institutional grounding in a modern life-world.

To be sure, the attempt to entirely functionalize public and private spheres to serve the needs of state and economy began almost simultaneously with their emergence. Nevertheless, it is never fully successful; the normative utopian claims of civil society are never dissolved fully. The *utopian horizon of civil society* consists in the preservation of the boundaries between the different subsystems and the life-world, along with the influence of normative considerations, based on the reproductive imperatives of the life-world, over the formally organized spheres of action. Life-world contexts, freed from system imperatives, could then be opened up to allow for the replacement, when relevant, of traditionally secured norms by communicatively achieved ones. Traditional forms of social integration and solidarity (corporate communities) could be replaced by associational forms open in principle to communicative (and democratic) coordination. Expressed in terms of the potentials of cultural modernity, the utopian model of a post-traditional, modern civil society would entail the full rationalization of all the institutions involved in the reproduction of culture (art, morality, science), their autonomy from one another, and the enrichment of the communicative practices of everyday life by these achievements. The *self-limiting* aspect of this utopia refers to the restriction of the communicative coordination of action to the institutional core of civil society itself and, thus, to an *indirect* influence on other spheres, instead of attempting to totalise this communicative organising principle to all of society's steering mechanisms.

THE POLITICS OF CIVIL SOCIETY

What is the potential for the dynamic realization of the positive alternatives of civil society? It must be noted that Habermas's analysis of new social movements in *Theory of Communicative Action* does not link them to the positive side of contemporary civil society. He focusses only on the defensive reactions to the negative side of its institutions. Habermas thus interprets the new movements as a particularistic and defensive reaction to the penetration of the social life by the economy and state. He does not see them playing any role in furthering the rationalization of the life-world, which in any case would also imply an offensive strategy. We believe that it is the absence of a key category of civil society, that of association, which leads Habermas to an implicit acceptance of a breakdown model of the rise of social movements and their resulting defensive strategy. Without a (revised) concept of voluntary association, both within the institutional analysis of civil society and with respect to the dynamics of social movement mobilization, collective action can only appear as reactions to normative disintegration or other types of dislocation accompanying modernization. The bases of non-traditional solidarities both within and across groups cannot be adequately understood, while the utopia of civil society loses its immanence.

Only in his most recent political writings has Habermas begun to revise this assessment and to link movements to the positive potentials of the institutions of contemporary civil society. In a series of articles and essays written between 1981–85, Habermas has recognized the offensive side of social movements:[27] their contestation of the negative aspects and their role in the *fulfillment* of the positive potential of civil society. Accordingly, the revival of the emancipatory promise of the early modern public sphere is depicted in terms of a plurality of associations oriented to the reconstruction of democratic public life on all societal levels. Movements are construed as the dynamic factor in the creation and expansion of public spaces in civil society. Finally, Habermas (several years after the most advanced East-central European formulations) formulates a programme of self-limiting, radical democracy. His greatest difficulty, however, is in constructing a position that would involve some kind of control over the functionally differentiated subsystems (state and economy) even by democratized societal associations and publics. It is not at all clear, on the basis of the system/life-world distinction, how movements can accomplish anything more than the further development of political culture or new identities.

These difficulties bring us to the heart of our project of reconstructing, theoretically and practically, civil society. It is our contention that the translation of the relevant dimensions of the life-world as "civil society" is needed to make sense of the double political task of self-limiting, radical democracy: the acquisition of influence by publics on the state and economy, and the institutionalization of the gains of movements within the life-world. Three antinomies express the difficulty faced by Habermas and all those who would use his abstract theory for such a project. First, there is an antinomy *within* new social movements between "fundamentalisms of the great refusal" and "innovative combinations of power and intelligent self-limitation".[28] The second antinomy is *between* grass-roots associations in the life-world and organizations capable of influencing state and economic systems, but only at the cost of bureaucratization (i.e. penetration by the medium of power). The third antinomy exists between the social and the political, and between the institutions of the life-world and those of the state and the economy.

Our distinctive political position is best presented in terms of an attempt to provide a preliminary resolution of these antinomies. We have already amply documented our own view of the antinomy in the self-understanding and projects of contemporary movements.[29] We have also argued that a higher level of self-reflection, rooted in a dialogue between theory and its movement addressees, has the potential of reinforcing identities and strategies based on self-limiting radical democracy. In the case of an abstract theory such as that of Habermas, the dialogue requires a series of bridging concepts like those offered by our theory of civil society.

A more serious issue is presented by the next two antinomies. How can movements resist the Michelsian iron law of oligarchy? Would they not themselves reproduce the organizational structures determined by power and money the moment they attempted to influence the subsystems of state and economy? Can the movements' form survive the step over the boundaries of the life-world and influence structures coordinated through means other than normative or communicative interaction, without succumbing to the pressure for self-instrumentalization? In short, can they move forward without giving up the life-world/system distinction that seems to abandon the ultimately most powerful spheres to system rationality?

Here we can only address these questions briefly. If one focusses on any given association or movement grouping, the Michelsian dilemma seems unavoidable. Contemporary theories of social movements reflect this; they seem to be divided between the stress on either organization and strategy or on identity. Nevertheless, we think that the uncovering of civil society as the deepest basis of the radical democratic challenge helps resolve at last part of this difficulty. Accordingly, we conceive of the "victory" of movements not the complete achievement of their substantive goals or their self-perpetuation as movements but, rather, as the democratization of the *values, norms, institutions, social identities* rooted ultimately in a political culture. In this context, the category of "rights" again becomes important. If one conceives the achievement of movements in terms of the institutionalization of rights (as we have defined them), the disappearance of a social movement either because of its organizational transformation or its absorption into newly created cultural identities does not mean the end of the context of the generation and constitution of social movements. The rights achieved by movements not only stabilize the boundaries between life-world, state and economy; they are also the conditions of possibility of the emergence of new associations, assemblies and movements. The classical rights achieved by the democratic revolution and the workers' movement have already functioned in this way vis-à-vis later civil rights and other movements. To be sure, practice and theory have yet to formulate the new rights appropriate to the current challenge to both the state and economy by contemporary movements. The historical inventory of rights gives little guidance here, precisely because, in the past, movement challenges were restricted to either state or economy.

The achievement of rights and the transformation of political culture do indicate how "thresholds of limitation" can be established to block the colonization of the life-world. They do not help, however, with the establishment of "sensors" capable of indirectly influencing the operation of the steering media.[30] The third antinomy appears the most intractable. Self-limiting radicalism is often interpreted to mean the abandonment of all projects of democratization of the state or the economy. In our view, this is the mistaken path taken by otherwise very insightful post-Marxists such as André Gorz. This path is mistaken because without the further democratization of state and economy the autonomous institutions of civil society, no matter how internally democratic, would be extremely vulnerable to the far more powerful organizations of the two subsystems. Consequently, fundamentalist programs of de-differentiation would be permanently on the agenda of movements. Habermas himself, because of his distinction between system and life-world, has often been accused of delivering the economy and the state over to the powers that be, and of begging the question: How can democratic will-formation in civil society attain even indirect influence over functional subsystems which are "self-referentially closed" and, hence, "immune to direct intervention"?

Such formulations, and Habermas's own tendency to self-misinterpretation notwithstanding, critics of the system/life-world duality conflate the level of analysis of coordinating mechanisms, the institutional level, and both of these with the analysis of various types of action (strategic, instrumental, communicative, normative, etc.).[31] We propose, in reply, a set of distinctions that goes beyond Habermas's analysis of the system/life-world duality, which we nevertheless continue to accept on the abstract-analytical level. We are thus able to show that there is no theoretical reason for ruling out the influence of communicative and democratic impulses from civil society on the state or the economy.

Let us explain. The abstract categories of system and life-world indicate only where the *weight of coordination* lies in a given institutional framework. Cultural, social, and personality-reproducing institutions have their centre of gravity in communicative/normative forms of action-coordination. Normatively speaking, this allows us (and Habermas) to speak of decolonization on the basis of the immanent possibilities within such institutions. *But we go further, by insisting on the possibility of democratizing political and economic institutions.* Here, to be sure, the centre of gravity of the coordinating mechanisms (in a modern society) is and must be on the level of steering performance through the media of money and power, i.e. system rationality. But that does not preclude the possibility of introducing communicative action into state or economic institutions. All types of action can and do occur in societal institutions—not even the market economy can be understood exclusively in terms of instrumental or strategic calculations. Moreover, the theory of civil society traditionally contained a "vertical" dimension, usually in the form of parliaments, that mediates between state and society. The normatively desirable project of introducing economic democracy (on the workshop level) or further democratizing these "vertical" institutions (including neo-corporatist arrangements) must be tempered, certainly, by the necessity of keeping intact the self-regulation of steering systems. But the mere existence (however inadequate) of parliaments, of forms of co-determination and collective bargaining indicate that publics can be constructed even *within* the institutions which are primarily system-steered. Institutions which must be coordinated communicatively come under the heading of civil society", whereas those which must be *steered* by money and/or power come under the institutional level of system. Neither dimension ought to be conceived of as "self-referentially closed" for both are open to democratization (albeit to different extents). Moreover, both can be "colonized" by the functional imperatives of the steering mechanisms, and thus distorted by the logic of reification and domination. The contemporary capitalist control of the sphere of production, and the elitist model of democracy operative today are examples of colonization of economic and political *institutions* by the functional requirement of the two steering mechanisms and the interests of domination and exploitation. Finally, the locus of a particular institution in civil society or in the media-steered subsystems depends on its organization and purpose. For example, if a university were to be totally functionalized to serve the economic needs of vocational training, it would migrate from civil society to the level coordinated primarily by the media, even if internally, a good deal of democratic communicative interaction were to obtain in decision making among peer (faculty, student groups etc.).

This rather rough sketch shows that the political issue is how to introduce public spaces into state and economic institutions (without abolishing mechanisms of steering or strategic/instrumental action) by establishing a continuity with a network of societal communication consisting of public spheres, associations, and movements. Here one could debate, for example, the determination of preferences among economic and political choices, keeping in mind the needs articulated in societal publics. However, self-limitation would mean that the debate over how much and which forms of democratization are desirable in economic and state institutions must grant in each case the necessities of system maintenance. Such is the meaning of democratization that complements Habermas's idea of decolonization. Correspondingly, the elimination or pure instrumentalization of political and economic participation constitutes the form of unfreedom that is the counterpart to the colonization of any institution.

The contemporary crises of the welfare state bring some urgency to these questions. Historically, the creation of democratic and rule-of-law states involved not only the creation of rights defending society against the state and guarantees of political participation for societal actors. It also strengthened the institutional forms of the capitalist market economy that were and still are pervaded by domination. The establishment of welfare states, on the other hand, involved not only the securing of worker, consumer and other rights, but also the strengthening of the modern administrative state, which was never a neutral agency for the use of societal subjects. Indeed, the unprecedented role of the state in welfare capitalist systems, and the fact that it shares steering functions with the capitalist market economy, account for the self-conception of the new movements as "society-strengthening" with respect to both subsystems. As a result of important historical learning experiences, victory is no longer seen as the inclusion in state power (reform) or in smashing the state (revolution) but, among the most reflective segments of the movements, as the rebuilding of civil society and the controlling of the market economy and the bureaucratic state.

Our reconstruction of the concept of civil society aims to defend these projects. Along with Habermas, we find both the neo-conservative return to the programme of property rights (along with retraditionalization of civil society minus democracy) and the welfare state loyalists' defense of the *existing* form of social rights (and their paternalist, clientelist underside) historically one-sided and normatively ambiguous. With Habermas, we stress instead the "reflexive continuation of the programme of the welfare state". This involves, first, the construction of a new type of civil society delimited by a partially new set of rights with communication rather than property rights as their core. As such, the autonomy of civil society from state and economy could be reestablished and the further modernization of civil society pursued. Secondly, "reflexive continuation" would involve the creation of forms of social control over state and economy (through the expansion of sets of representative institutions within and between them) that are compatible with a modernized life-world. The two steps presuppose each other: only an adequately defended, differentiated and organized civil society is capable of monitoring and influencing the outcomes of steering processes, but only a civil society capable of influencing the state and economy can help to maintain the structure of rights that are the *sine qua non* of its own existence. These two steps were always implicitly true, of course. But what is new is that civil society can no longer be made autonomous by blindly strengthening one steering mechanism in the fight against the other. The reflexive continuation for the welfare state needs to be seen not only as the continuation of the project of the working class movement by other subjects, but also as the resumption of the project of the democratic revolutions which created modern civil society. Such is the meaning of an equally distanced and reflective relation to both modern economy and state.

The norms of the classical notion of civil society imply the project of democratization. Habermas's theory, without this concept, would help to thematize ultimately *only* necessary self-limitation (along with the democratization of political culture). The reconstruction of civil society in terms of the system/life-world duality *or* the translation of this duality into the categories of civil society can do both. Today, we know of no better theoretical interpretation of the self-limiting, radical democratic politics of Polish Solidarity and of key dimensions of the new social movements of the West.

Notes

1. A. Arato and J. Cohen, *Civil Society and Democratic Theory* (Boston, MIT Press, 1992), Chapter I. Also see A. Arato, "Civil Society against the State: Poland 1980–1981", *Telos* 47 (Spring 1981); A. Arato, "Empire vs. Civil Society: Poland 1981–1982", *Telos* 50 (Winter 1981/82), Jean L. Cohen, "Strategy or Identity: New Theoretical Paradigms and Contemporary Social Movements", *Social Research* 52 (Winter 1985), pp. 663–716; A. Arato and Jean L. Cohen, "Social Movements, Civil Society and the Problem of Sovereignty", *Praxis International* 4, 5 (October 1985), pp. 266–283. For Southern European and Latin American comparisons see the four volumes (especially the last one) edited by O'Donnell, Schmitter and Whitehead, *Transitions from Authoritarian Rule* (Baltimore, Johns Hopkins University Press, 1986). The classical articles on the concept of civil society and its history are: Manfred Riedel, "Gesellschaft, bürgerliche" in *Geschichtliche Grundbegriffe* (Stuttgart, 1975); Jenö Szücs, "The Three Historical Regions of Europe" in J. Keane (ed.), *Civil Society and the State* (London, Verso Press, 1988); Niklas Luhmann, "Gesellschaft" in *Soziologische Aufklärung I* (Opladen, 1970); Norberto Bobbio, "Gramsci and the Concept of Civil Society" in Keane, *op. cit.*

2. The practical justification of precisely this theoretical ensemble could be provided on the basis of an interpretation on the discourse ethics of Apel, Habermas, and Wellmer. We attempt this in A. Arato and Jean L. Cohen, "Discourse Ethics and Civil Society" in our *Civil Society and Democratic Theory*.

3. See our contribution to the forthcoming Habermas Festschrift edited by Honneth, McCarthy, Offe, and Wellmer (Suhrkamp, Verlag, 1989).

4. Habermas, of course, reintroduced the concept of civil society in his study of one of its central categories: the public sphere. But in this study he also appropriated a version of Schmitt's argument involving state-society fusion by tracing out the decline of civil society. Later attempts to reconstruct key notions of the classical doctrine of politics like *praxis* and *techne* stresses the metatheoretical elvel. But as long as Habermas engaged in a reconstruction of historical materialism, he could not free himself from Marxian prejudices against civil society. It is our thesis that a fundamental break occurs in the two-volume work, *Theory of Communicative Action*. See Jürgen Habermas, *Die Strukturwandel der Öffentlichkeit* (6th ed., Berlin, Neuwied, 1974) and *Theorie des Kommunikativen Handelns* (Frankfurt-am-Main, Suhrkamp, 1981). See also, Jean L. Cohen, "Why More Political Theory?", *Telos* 40 (Summer 1979), pp. 70–94.

5. *Theory of Communicative Action: Theorie des Kommunikativen Handelns, op. cit.* Habermas's development nevertheless provides the means of defending our theory

of civil society. We can document this development in terms of the transformation of the theory of discourse ethics, which was initially a utopian model defining the ideal speech situation as the basis of a new, homogeneous form of life that tended to correspond to the institutions of a mono-organizational version of radical democracy (council communism). In part, under the influence of A. Wellmer, in the late seventies and early eighties, Habermas has transformed this conception in a pluralistic direction, making the (now only regulative) idea of discourse compatible with a plurality of forms of life, even a plurality of forms of democracy that is possible, we maintain, only on the ground of civil society. In the process, Habermas reduced the gulf between rational and empirical consensus and replaced the stress on post-modernity in his notion of emancipation by that of the completion of modernity. See "Discourse Ethics and Civil Society", Chapter One of *Civil Society and Democratic Theory, op. cit.*

6. Ever since Aristotle, the normative thrust of the concept of civil society (*koinonia politike*) entailed a vision of an autonomous-domination-free association of peers who communicatively establish their goals and norms and regulate their interaction according to standards of justice. The early modern version of civil society added to this (now, to be sure depoliticized conception) the principles of individual autonomy, social and moral plurality, and, of course, universality.

7. See Habermas's chart, *Theorie* II, pp. 182–228.

8. We discuss these issues in greater depth in *Civil Society and Democratic Theory, op. cit.* By "the traditional version of civil society", we mean one that assumes that the differentiated institutions and various pluralities of civil society are normatively integrated through an overarching collective definition of the good and the just (*Sittlichkeit*—Hegel, Parsons) and/or through an overarching corporate organization of the whole society (Parsons' "societal community").

9. This is the step beyond Parsons, whose concept of "societal community" allows only for the normative coordination of action and a conventional relation to standards.

10. Luhmann, like many contemporary neo-communitarians, believes that the social integration of interaction through norms is possible only on the basis of a unified world-view or *Sittlichkeit.* Unlike contemporary neo-communitarians, however, he is convinced that modern differentiated societies preclude such forms of social integration and can only be integrated functionally.

11. Indeed, Habermas presents us with an historical typology that shows how the processes of differentiation of system and life-world yielded a modernity burdened by its negativity. The analysis partially parallels works such as Karl Polanyi's *The Great Transformation* and Robert Nisbet's *In Search of Community* but avoids the naive expectations of the former vis-a-vis the state and the innocence of the latter vis-a-vis the capitalist market economy. The historical changes of juridification are presented explicitly in terms of the concept of civil society. See *Theorie* II, pp. 524–531.

12. Habermas's definition of cultural modernity as the decline of substantive and centred reason and the differentiation of the value sphere of art, science, and morality

follows Weber. Weber attributes to this and to secularization the phenomena of the loss of meaning and the loss of freedom. Horkheimer and Adorno reproduce this assessment. See *Theory of Communicative Action* I, pp. 346–352.

13. *Ibid*, pp. 221–223, 233.
14. *Theorie* II, pp. 229–93.
15. This involves changes in all the institutions of civil society responsible for cultural reproduction, social integration and personality development; see Habermas's discussion in *Theorie* II, pp. 229–294.
16. *Ibid*, p. 471.
17. *Ibid*, p. 488.
18. Cf. N. Fraser, "What's Critical about Critical Theory? The Case of Habermas and Gender", *New German Critique, op. cit.*, p. 112. Fraser's article suffers from misinterpretations common to many interpreters of Habermas's text. She mixes up the issue of analysis of action types with the different analytical level of the distinction between social and system coordination, between life-world and system. She also confuses the distinction between the modes of action-coordination (via communication or via media of money and power) with the differentiation between the symbolic and material reproduction of the life-world. The first error has no basis in Habermas—all forms of action can be found in institutions of the life-world and in those that are media steered: what distinguishes life-world and system is not the action types found there but the mode of action coordination. The second confusion is due to Habermas's own unnecessary tendency to link the system/life-world distinction with the symbolic/material reproduction distinction. Fraser wants to throw away the baby with the bath water by claiming there is nothing to the distinction between system and life-world. We fully disagree with this claim and with her corresponding critique of Habermas on the gender issue.
19. Of course, there are strategic action and power relations in both domains.
20. *Theorie* II, pp. 530–531.
21. Jean L. Cohen, "Strategy or Identity: New Theoretical Paradigms and Contemporary Social Movements", pp. 663–715.
22. *Theorie* II, pp. 536–537.
23. This could include decentralization, new forms of representation such as functional representation, the democratization of neo-corporatist arrangements, and more public spaces in politically relevant arenas such as corporations.
24. The absence of the concept of association, both within the institutional analysis of civil society and with respect to social movements, leads Habermas to revive the classical breakdown thesis, which understands movements as mere reactions to normative disintegration or other dislocations accompanying modernization. See Jean L. Cohen, "Strategy or Identity", *op. cit.* This also leads to an almost exclusive focus on issues of democratic legitimacy at the expense of a concern with solidarity.
25. *Theorie* II, p. 485. Of course, in this context *l'homme* means humanity, not men.
26. *Ibid*, p. 471.

27. Habermas, "Die Neue Unübersichtlichkeit" in *Die Neue Unübersichtlichkeit* (Frankfurt-am-Main, Suhrkamp, 1985), where this dimension is expressed in the more aggressive terms of the development of a new "cultural hegemony" (p. 153). On the development of the politics of Habermas's earlier theory, see Jean L. Cohen, "Why More Political Theory?", *op. cit.*; Jean L. Cohen, "Crisis Management and Social Movements", *Telos* 52 (Summer, 1982), pp. 21–40.

28. Habermas, "Die Neue Unübersichtlichkeit", *op. cit.*, p. 156.

29. Andrew Arato and Jean L. Cohen, "Social Movements, Civil Society and the Problem of Sovereignity", *op. cit.*, and Jean L. Cohen, "Strategy or Identity", *op. cit.*

30. Habermas, *Der Philosophische Diskurs der Moderne* (Frankfurt-am-Main, Suhrkamp, 1985), pp. 422–423.

31. See McCarthy, Fraser and Misgeld in *New German Critique* (Spring–Summer, 1985), a special issue on Habermas.

ARE WE LIVING IN A WORLD OF EMOTIONAL IMPOVERISHMENT?

Agnes Heller

I

Women and men normally associate emotions with feelings. In my book *A Theory of Feelings*, I make distinctions between "emotion" and "sentiment" as subgroups of "feelings".[1] To be in an emotional state such as anger, joy, anxiety, is tantamount to *feeling* something. Behaviourists, as well as those in certain branches of cognitive psychology, do not accept this everyday experience at its face value. The latter insist that emotions are, in fact, cognitive-evaluative processes, and for that reason cannot be accepted as "feelings".

However, one can accept the premise without subscribing to the conclusion. From Plato's *Philebus* to Aristotle's *Rhetoric*, philosophy has established the tradition of understanding emotions as "cognitive and situated feelings". This means, on the one hand, that emotions affect judgement. On the other hand it means—and this is the crucial issue—that the kind and intensity of a particular emotion is dependent on our understanding of a situation.

Aristotle remarks that "the frame of mind is that in which any pain is being felt".[2] This is also true of all kinds of pleasure. The juxtaposition of reason and emotion is a heuristic device forged by rationalist philosophies, but if something has gone wrong with this device, it will not be rectified by placing emotions in the territory of "the cognitive" while leaving feelings and the body stranded on the other side of the great dividing line.

Let us then accept as a starting point that emotions as well as sentiments are feelings. Let us further accept that to the same extent as sentiments, emotions are also cognitive and judgmental processes. Once this is granted, we can see that the link between the feeling-aspects and the judgmental-aspects of a particular emotion can be theorized as follows: there are two (or more) "unspecific" feelings, such as the feelings of pain and pleasure, which occur *in*

Thesis Eleven 22
©1988 *Thesis Eleven*

conjunction with our evaluation of situations or persons. The feeling-aspects remain unchanged, for it is the *evaluation* which defines them and makes them perceived as a particular emotion. For example, the feeling of displeasure (discomfort) is *defined* or *perceived* at one time as grief, at another time as envy, at yet another time as anxiety or expectation or bad news. Certain experiences lend credence to this view. For instance, sometimes we feel displeasure without being able to give the feeling a name, simply because we are not aware of its causes. Yet once we find "reasons for feeling displeasure", we identify the feeling as "expectation of bad news", "pangs of conscience", "being angry"— we *identify* it as a distinct emotion.

However, sometimes we are unable to identify the feeling regardless of the emotional terms applied to its description. In such situations we often feel—and this too is a feeling—that no emotional terms can describe (express) properly its quality, because the quality is too particular and unique. We then try to delineate the quality of the feeling through a combination of several emotional terms.

This second and elementary experience suggests that our feelings are unique and qualitatively distinct. It further suggests that the relationship of an emotion to its cognitive aspects is not merely external, but that the cognitive-evaluative-situational aspect is *inherent in the very feeling itself.*

The fact that emotional terms do not do justice to the complexity of feelings lends further support to the thesis of inherence. The emotional term "to be afraid", for example, is an umbrella term for several qualitatively different feelings. An obvious objection to this would be that the cognitive aspect does not reside in the emotional term alone, but also in the concrete situation in which it is being used, as well as in the valuation of the situation; "being afraid of being found out", "being afraid of death", and the like.

In my view, both kinds of experience tell us something about emotions. If the cognitive-evaluative aspect of emotions *inheres in the feeling itself,* we then have a variety of shades of feelings which are qualitatively distinct, and we will also have the (secondary) feeling that standardized emotional terms and expressions do not do them justice. But if the connection between the feeling and the cognitive-evaluative-situational aspect of the emotion remains merely *eternal*, we will have no problem identifying our pleasure or displeasure with the emotional expressions adequate to them (e.g. comfort-discomfort, pleasure-pain, to list the distinction in terms of their intensity). Furthermore, certain situations or persons will always elicit the same particular feelings; for example, "beauty therefore appeal", "competition therefore envy", "enemy of my community therefore hatred".

Something similar can be asserted about sentiments. They are emotional dispositions. "Having a sentiment" or "being in a sentiment" such as friendship or love of any kind, does not indicate the constant and continuous presence of the same feeling or emotion. Rather, it indicates the presence of a disposition to develop certain feelings and emotions every time the object of our sentiment—or our relation to the object of our sentiment—is affected. Whenever the cognitive-evaluative aspect of the emotion *inheres in the sentiment itself*, one's love or friendship for different people, ideas or things—that is, for different beings—will be qualitatively distinct. In such a situation, one's world of feeling will be like a palette with a rainbow of colours. Contrariwise, whenever the cognitive-evaluation aspect of the sentiment is *externally* related to the simple feeling of pleasure-displeasure—with all their degrees of intensity—the same "condition" will evoke the same emotional response, and the problem of identifying sentiments will not arise.

II

Emotions as well a sentiments can be good or bad, strong or weak, deep or superficial. However, it is difficult to translate an individual's whole emotional universe into such categories. One can say tentatively, for example, that a woman's emotions and sentiments are weak even if a few of her emotions make themselves felt "strongly". Or a man can be described as "emotionally deep" despite several rather superficial sentiments. If the moral yardstick of "good or bad" serves as the criterion of categorization, neither frequency of occurrence nor numerical superiority of one feeling over another will be decisive. In our final judgement, one evil passion will render a person's entire emotional universe evil.

However, despite the difficulties in evaluating a particular case, the criteria of evaluation are eminently clear. Traditional character types such as melancholic, choleric, etc. were constructed on the basis of everyday observation. They undoubtedly rested on combinations of deep superficial and strong-weak emotional "units". The *moral* assessment is different in kind, therefore it does not yield clusters of temperamental character; although both "good" and "bad" can show a strong affinity with intensity—that is, the "proper" feeling response should not be too weak nor should it be too strong.[3]

The binary category of "rich-poor" has a distinct feature in comparison to all others. One cannot be characterized as either rich or poor on the basis of single emotions. An instance of fear or anger can be strong or weak, deep or superficial, good or bad, but it cannot be either rich or poor. However, a sentiment can be rich or poor, because a an emotional disposition it may give rise to quite different kinds and shades of emotion, as well as other feelings which cannot be discussed within this framework. In a similar way, an individual's emotional universe can be termed rich or poor. Yet it is not accidental that the distinction between "rich" and "poor" emotional worlds cannot be translated back into the old categories of human temperament. Obviously emotional poverty or wealth has nothing to do with temperament; or for that matter, with terms created by inhabitants of the ancient world, who devised the clusters of the types of temperament out of their own particular conditions.

We may even wonder if the designation of a person's whole emotional universe as "poor" or "rich" can be taken for granted. We are accustomed to such judgments, and we believe we understand how to appraise the "poverty" or "wealth" of a person's emotional universe. But was the inner world of Odysseus or Don Quixote "rich" or "poor"? Without artificial intellectual efforts and devices, the question cannot be properly answered. The question itself seems somehow to be misplaced— although the same question would be properly posed if asked about the heroes and heroines of 18th or 19th century novels. Titles like *Sense and Sensibility* needed no interpretation in their own time.

Hegel praised the ancient world for its plasticity. The modern world, however, lacks plasticity. Modern, "romantic" art excels in painting, poetry and music; they are the genres *par excellence* of subjectivity. The distinction between a rich and poor emotional life makes perfect sense in a world where subjectivity develops in full and is ever being cultivated; but only in a world like this.

I am not here equating "subjectivity" with the subject-object distinction, as Horkheimer, Adorno and Heidegger sometimes did. Nor would I restate the Lukácsian position that the heroes of Homer were no subjects at all. I am convinced that subjectivity comes about through the self-reflexivity of the subject. The emotional life of men and women can be rich or poor under the condition of "subjectivity" alone. Subjectivity establishes a personal, individual and unique relation of the subject to intersubjectivity (and not to the object). In this context, the subject is no longer a distinct but exhaustive incarnation of intersubjectivity, the sense in which Lukács denied the "subject character" of the Homeric heroes. Rather, it separates itself in order to unite itself with such aspects of intersubjectivity that have been re-confirmed, re-affirmed and condoned by the subject himself or herself. The circumstance that the subjects themselves are intersubjectively constituted is irrelevant for the hermeneutics of subjectivity.

What I term the self-reflectivity of the subject is an interplay of reflection/self-reflection. On the one hand, a person makes use of the cultural language of intersubjectivity for self-understanding, on the other, s/he makes use of his/her own self-understanding to accept or reject single practice, norms and rules put forward by the prevalent language of culture.

The moral implications of the interplay of reflection and self-reflection are manifold. I will mention only the most important. The dangers of empty subjectivism and relativism can be avoided under the condition of a kind of reflection which I have termed "double-quality reflection".[4] Reflection becomes "double-quality reflection" when a subject distinguishes between concrete and abstract norms, and when s/he keeps the second as a moral authority for the subject even if s/he rejects the first as null and void. This issue would be of prime importance if we examined the distinction between "good" and "bad" emotions. However, at least on the theoretical plane, the juxtaposition of emotional wealth and poverty is a completely different matter. The devil is certainly an emotionally poor person. Evil normally appears in the shape of a person with strong but undifferentiated impulses, or a cold person who is incapable of bringing manipulative-calculative logic to perfection. Yet an emotionally rich person can remain morally infantile or irresponsible if she does not cultivate her moral sensibility.

Subjectivity as self-reflectivity opens up a treasure trove of potentials for emotional differentiation. The person becomes the hermeneut of his or her own emotions. Of course hermeneutics is neither a subcategory of observation, nor an area of self-knowledge alone. In interpreting her emotions, in putting them under hermeneutical scrutiny, a person creates an "emotional palette" of different shades of one particular emotion. This is not creation but, as mentioned, interpretative differentiation. Given that the interpretation is inherent in the quality of feeling itself, one or another shade of the palette will be *felt* in subsequent contact with other people, children, books, flowers, or anything else. The tension between the (relative) poverty of emotional language and the richness of feelings themselves will assert itself.

Solutions of this tension can be sought in two ways. One can try to adapt the language to the self-differentiation of feelings. Or, one can try to erase the self-differentiation of emotions and make attempts to regain emotions which are—once again from the perspective of subjectivity—strong, fundamental and undifferentiated. Once the split between emotional terms and personal-emotional differentiation widens into an abyss, the differentiated self of emotional sensitivity becomes incommunicado.

Emotional differentiation (wealth) should not become prohibitive of communicability. If that happens, the real subjectivity of the person disappears. We have been repeatedly told that our age has brought about the end of the subject. If this is indeed so, the question of emotional wealth and poverty is outdated, and the interest of this paper is only historical.

III

Let us suppose that in a group of people, each individual cultivates his or her own emotions, sensibilities and sentiments. This group of people can establish *collectively* a kind of culture which institutionalizes, so to speak, emotional cultivation. Emotional density can be cultivated collectively. The shared language of this sort of emotional culture can be the language of art, particularly the language of painting, poetry and music. In addition, new gestures and ceremonies, that is, a completely new, esoteric world of signs, can be inserted into the common language of signs, forming a network of interpretation of differentiated significations. Someone who is a member of a group like this will perceive the absence of the same or similar emotional culture in others as the manifestation of utter emotional impoverishment—and not without reason.

This scenario is far from hypothetical. It is real. It is exactly what happened in the 18th and 19th centuries, when certain groups of the bourgeoisie, the bourgeoisified aristocracy and gentry, developed an esoteric culture of emotional refinement and self-cultivation; certain groups, that is, not the bourgeoisie or the gentry *in toto*. An esoteric culture is by definition one of separation in which the act of separation implies a claim to superiority, although not necessarily social superiority or privilege. Rather, cultural superiority is a tool to *compensate* for social inferiority. Cultural differentiation with the claim of cultural superiority requires the cultivation of ways of life which do not, or do not entirely, correspond to the lifestyle of the framework of the class from which they emerge.

The subjectivity of a modern individual can surface in various areas of life, and can open up diverse fields of possibility for itself; the venture of emotional differentiation is only one among many. The cultivation of sensitivity is esotericism with a flavour of cultural opposition. The emotionally rich person despises possessive individualism, has nothing but contempt for the business-man, the petit bourgeois, the politician. The oppositional drive is perhaps the main driving force behind the cultivation of sensitivity, for it requires intro-spection, and introspection in turn requires leisure, freedom from the ordinary business of life. Ceremonies develop that both segregate and cultivate specific emotions and sensibilities.

At the same time, the central category of emotional self-cultivation is wealth. The millionaire and the bohemian artist are equally "wealthy", the only difference being that their wealth consists of different coins. The wealth of money is external, that of sensitivity is internal. A person and his money are different, and this wealth can be lost. A person and his sensitivity are identical, the person *is* the bundle of emotions and they cannot be taken from him. Furthermore, the millionaire's wealth has not been created by him but by others (in terms of a 19th century socialism, by the proletariat). However, an esoteric person's (emotional) wealth has been created by the person, and cannot be taken way. Money is alienated and alienable, so is political power or fame. But the wealth of emotional density is inalienable. In terms of this vision, there is a dirty, alienated and inferior kind of wealth, and there is one which is shining, non-alienated—the real one.

The 19th century spoke the language of wealth and poverty, and Marx was no exception. Communism ensures the appropriation of the wealth of the species by every individual. The ideal is the person rich in needs as well as, needless to say, rich in emotional culture. For the 19th century, scarcity was a heavily negative term, the shame or "dark side" of human existence. The cultivators of sensitivity failed to notice that the spectre of scarcity made its appearance among them as well.

The dialectics of cultivation of sensitivity became progressively perceived. I will exemplify this development in an abstract model rather than in an analysis of historical processes. As is well-known, the subject faces the dilemma of communicability after having differentiated her emotional world. It is precisely this dilemma that seems to be solved by creating a special, esoteric culture for the cultivation of sensibility, including of course artistic sensibility. The creation of such a network of esoteric cultural signs sublates the contradiction, but only under one condition: that the original normative framework of behavioural patterns, duties and rights remain intact, and the esoteric cultivation of sentiments be practiced within this broader framework, creating an esoteric niche within a broader, established way of life.

However, once the binding character of the socio-political intersubjective norms and rules disappears, leaving only the esoteric sign-world of the ceremonies of sensibility, the person—carrier of this sensibility—is cut off from the network of the active participant members of his/her society. The private world of esoterics is further sheltered from the broader world; those submerged exclusively in the cultivation of sensibilities rarely earn their daily bread. It is in this respect that Thomas Mann mentions *machtgeschützte Innerlichkeit* (inwardness shielded by power). Submerged in their hypercultivated sensitivities, these overrefined plants of the European soil fail to notice, or choose not to notice, the glass roof protecting them from an early frost. Moreover, to an ever-increasing extent, they despise the frosty outer world of insensitive, "dull" masses.

Subjects relate subjectively to the world of political-social norms, institutions, rights and obligations, insofar as they re-cast and re-activate them within their frameworks at the same time as they reject those which cannot be condoned by conscience. As long as they re-cast and re-activate these norms, as long as they go on about their everyday and non-everyday business in company with their fellow creatures, they have to make choice. In an active life, there are major commitments and minor commitments. There are lifelong as well as merely temporary preferences. *Therefore there is a hierarchy, and not merely a difference.*

This hierarchy is not social in nature, nor is it the internalization of social hierarchy (though it may be). Yet it is a value hierarchy in a double sense of the word. We may ask ourselves, which value is preferred over another? We may also ask ourselves, which thing, person, activity or profession of value is more valuable for me, my personality, for me as a subject? In a scenario like this, the "old" distinctions between particular emotions maintain their relevance. Deep emotions are steady, constant, essential to the subject. They are not just one among several emotional shades. They stand out, they steer and sometimes even compel. Superficial sentiments, in contrast, are vested in insignificant instances. They can wither, and we will not miss them if they vanish from the palette. Certain other emotions are strong if the situation so requires, and weak if it does not. Certain sentiments are strong while others are weak. Not all of our sensibilities are of equal relevance; one can cultivate some and neglect others.

This is not a scenario of less subjectivity, but one of less subjectivism. It is one I like to call the "emotional household". Like every household, it too copes with scarcity. It is a scenario of subjectivity because it is precisely the *person* who has to learn to cope with the limitations of his/her own emotional resources and use them properly, in good measure, in accordance with his/her obligations and desires. It is a scenario of less subjectivism because one manages a household (including an emotional household) for others as well as for oneself related to others. Cultivation of sensibility is a constituent of a household like this, but one which must be held in correct proportion.

Subjectivity is the condition of the differentiation of emotions and the cultivation of emotional sensibility. This cult of sensibility had its finest hour *ante rem*, in Clarissa, Werther, Marianne. *Ex post facto*, that is, after the Napoleonic wars, the same cult began to display its more problematic face. From Flaubert's *Sentimental Education* to Proust's "lost time", the infinite wealth of shades of feeling began to destroy the personality itself. The cult of sensibility finally comes to an end in *Man Without Qualities*. If one endlessly continues to differentiate one's own emotional life, refinement at last becomes so subtle, so manifold, elastic, vacillating and ephemeral that nothing steady is retained, no personal quality persists. But the person of an esoteric culture remains a part of that particular culture. The ceremonies of sensitivity remain intact, while subjectivity vanishes from sight behind them. What lingers is the discourse itself: the discourse of esotericism.

It is precisely this constellation which has been projected onto so-called "mass culture" and "mass societies" by the spokesmen for an esoteric cultural milieu. When they contend that the subject and subjectivity have disappeared, and that it is no longer the person but the language itself which speaks, they give voice to their own predicament.

Naturally I am not saying that philosophers who describe our world as one without subject, are not subjects themselves. Rather, I contend that they have had a primal experience of esoteric discourse totally void of subjectivity, and that they project this primal experience onto the modern world as a whole. To describe a theoretical proposition as a projection is an act of "exposure" or reversal, and as such it cannot have truth claims concerning the issue which has been projected. So the question of whether or not the subject has disappeared from the (post)modern world, or whether or not we live in a world of total emotional impoverishment, is not posed here let alone solved, because the proposition itself has been unmasked as a gesture of projection.

IV

In *The Charterhouse of Parma*, when after Waterloo Stendhal's hero Fabrizio del Dongo toys with the idea of trying his luck in America, his aunt the Princess Sanseverina mockingly asks the youth if he could imagine himself living in "the democracy of merchants". The answer is obviously negative. "The democracy of merchants" is repulsive not because it is a democracy; Sanseverina would have no trouble relocating her refined nephew into the age of Pericles. But for this kind of subjectivity, merchants are rude, materialistic, uncultivated, prosaic. They have neither taste nor good manners.

The great-grandchildren of similar "merchants" in Western, Southern and Central Europe followed the tradition of Stendhal's heroes. They held everything popular in contempt, the sole exception being *le peuple*, the mythological People, or the proletariat writ large. They were the heirs-designate of a fading culture. Lukács, for instance, did not need to indulge in projecting the disappearance of the esoteric-bourgeois subject onto the emerging mass of society. He could afford to negate the over-refinement of the esoteric-aesthetic culture in direct speech. The price he paid was his enthusiastic appeal to the new barbarians, who would supposedly reintroduce to society grandeur, individuality and subjectivity, along with strong emotions and a thriving new culture, while tearing to pieces the ceremonial ties of an already subjectless world. So far only the first part of this prediction has come to pass. The cultural threads of an over-refined world have been torn to pieces, but no individuality, heroism or authentic personality have emerged; only naked barbarism. Yet this unhappy historical development cannot be taken as proof of the "disappearance of the subject", or of the emotional impoverishment of modern, or "herd" man.

"Impoverishment" is a relative term. It means "poorer than before". An impoverished man of material wealth can still be fairly well off. But the term "emotional impoverishment" carried strong negative connotation. Yet, if one compares the postmodern individual with the high priests of the cult of emotional refinement, the "emotional impoverishment" detected in the former does not necessarily indicate simply a loss of value. One can imagine men and women making up for the loss of certain emotional shades through greater emotional depth and a sensible emotional household. In what follows, I will use the term "emotional impoverishment" only when the absence of emotional differentiation is accompanied by emotional superficiality. "Emotional impoverishment" occurs when the dominating emotional language turns banal, and when the alternative "imaginary institutions of signification" which might induce emotional refinements or sensibilities are not apparent.

When it comes to a criticism of "one-dimensionality", mass culture, mass media and mass technology are usually the prime targets. The assumption is that responsibility for cultural decay and impoverishment of emotional life rests with the industrial mass production of records, record players and television sets. I have tried to prove that such and similar accusations should be viewed with scepticism. Those accusing, in fact, are the great-grandchildren of Fabrizio del Dongo, people highly suspicious of "masses" and "merchants", those who project their own experience of the loss of over-refined subject, onto a world which is alien to them.

In this atmosphere, emotional terms and expressions become suspect. They lose ground in "high" culture at a time when they still capture the imagination of "low" culture. Musil pointed out this development in the theoretical chapters of *Man Without Qualities*. Emotional refinement empties out the emotional expressions themselves. If shades of emotions can no longer be communicated in direct speech, it stands to reason that traditional emotional terms—those vehicles of direct communication—turn banal. And since a refined person cannot be "banal", s/he must shy away from using traditional emotional terms. "Shy away from" is not a metaphor. Over-refined persons are actually deeply ashamed of using "common" emotional expressions. Since their subjectivity does not become manifest in action, moral resoluteness, or behaviour, but rests in their sensibility alone, they are afraid of losing this subjectivity by using "common" emotional terms. An over-refined person is less afraid of denouncing his neighbour than of talking banalities. "Common" emotional terms are banned as "banal", thus the language of the cult of refinement will be emptied of such expressions. To turn to someone and simply say "I love you", becomes ridiculous-banal, and therefore emotionally prohibited.

At the same time, mass media continued to produce its one-line emotionalism, "I love you"—"I love you too"; and occasionally it still produces such texts. Emotional expressions flooded the lyrics and music of popular culture. But it could not resist for long the trends which filtered down from high culture. Popular culture soon began to contribute to the anti-sentimentalist drive. At last everyone grew ashamed of using straightforward emotional language, everyone began to feel that such language was "banal".

However, without an emotional language, including the language of sentiments, even the ingredients of an emotional household will be in short supply. Although emotional terms are merely forms and frameworks, it is within such forms and frameworks that sensibility develops and blossoms. If the form, the framework, is absent, the result is emotional impoverishment in the strictest sense of the word. Emotional impoverishment does not mean the absence of emotions but the absence of emotional refinement and the absence of sentiments. It is tantamount to the absence of emotional culture, sensibility. Although people in "real" life still use emotional expressions, sometimes lavishly, the anti-sentimentalist drive, which has temporarily conquered the world of contemporary imagination, does not provide much support to a sensibility-oriented emotional household.

One can, of course, tell a different story by insisting that men and women in modern life no longer need emotional refinement in their daily lives. Men and women perform functions in a variety of institutions, and they develop simple functional relationships to their fellows. Functional relationships of this kind do not call for emotional differentiation.

Sentiments are not only superfluous, they are also dangerous. It was, after all, the sentiment of love which enslaved women to men in an epoch when, objectively, they might have been free. As far as the enjoyment of artworks is concerned, we enjoy them with eyes and ears, not with sentiments. To develop a special sensibility called "taste" is superfluous. At any rate, tastes are subjective, or alternatively, they are manipulated. If this is the viewpoint of appraisal, the disappearance of emotional expressions and patterns from "high" as well as "low" culture can be accounted for by the reflection theory, or the theory of "homology"; that is, high and low culture only reflect what is going on in "life", or in another rendering, the disappearance of emotional language from most of our media is homologous with the disappearance of emotions from "life", or with the modern trend of putting a premium on the disappearance. This explanation might account for the phenomenon that emotional terms and expressions are felt banally, and in fact are banal. For what is felt banally, is banal. We have no other criterion for assessing banality.

Since emotional differentiation is one of the hallmarks of subjectivity, a story like this lends credence to the thesis of "the end of the subject" even if it does not corroborate it, for subjectivity has other constituents as well. It is certainly possible to speak a cultural language which is not conducive to the subjectivization of the human individual, but which is nevertheless capable of guiding men and women in their daily lives. An example is the language of "health versus sickness". One can discuss calories, headaches, heartbeats and exercises to the same extent that others discuss love, friendship, the colour of the sky, the modulation of a voice; with the difference that no health-talk will differentiate one's subjectivity (although it will sharpen one's sense of observation of one's own body). A personal household of health is just as possible as an emotional household. Scarcity is characteristic of both. Yet whereas in the second case a well-conducted household results in "personality quality", in the first case it results in "bodily quality" . Obviously "the discourse on the body" so widespread in recent years is only partly a liberating act against the soul/body dualism. It also serves as an arrow pointing at the "heart"—a well-known metaphor for emotions. However, this arrow can also turn into a boomerang.

V

If different people discuss the end of the individual, the end of the sub-ject, the end of the mono-centred personality, they mean completely different things. Given the popularity of terms predicting "the end" of something, as well as the unpopularity of the term "subjectivity", all such meanings are fused. Let me make a distinction among several meanings. The subject does not exist, for the person is no longer subjected to hierarchical norms and entities. The subject has ceased to exist, for the person no longer understands itself as "the human essence" who sub-jects nature. The subject has disappeared for the subject-object relationship has disappeared. The subject has disappeared because all that remains is the discourse by which the person is progressively devoured.

From the aspect of the differentiation of emotions, the subjection of nature is irrelevant unless we believe that emotions and sentiments belong to "nature". However, our own sub-jection to something else, to something which is "higher" and "normative", is definitely not irrelevant. Blind, one-way subjection is detrimental to both emotional depth and refinement, yet reflective/self-reflective subjection is the precondition of the latter. Mono-centred individuality is neither the result nor the condition of emotional wealth, yet an individual without (polyvalent) personality centres must be impoverished. Cogito-centred world visions have nothing to do with emotional density. Neither individualism nor rationalism prevents our emotional world from differentiation; but neither do they further it. However, if the person is completely absorbed by an anonymous discourse, inwardness is completely destroyed.

Put briefly, some understandings of the thesis of "the end of the subject" (or the end of the individual) are compatible with the presence of emotional subjectivity, while others are incompatible. My concept of the subject eschews linguistic (not language) games, and it places the emphasis on relation, not on sub-jection. Even if we make a case for the disappearance of the subject (both as being sub-jected and as sub-jecting), we can still maintain that subjectivity itself has changed into a "relationship to", and that it can no longer be understood and explained in terms of its original meaning. If subject is a relation to intersubjectivity and/or nature, then subjectivity is not necessarily on the wane in the world we have learned to call "postmodern". It can remain with us, or it can disappear. Similarly, emotional "wealth" can remain with us; or rather, it may reappear. But one need not be clairvoyant to stake one's bet on the reappearance of emotional culture, or on a *particular* emotional culture.

Postmodernity belongs to modernity. It is nothing but modernity slowed down, modernity which has become self-secure, which no longer considers itself an intermundium between past and future. Postmodernity is a new attitude, more self-reflective, more ironical, more pluralistic, than the old modernist attitude. It is the retrospective glance and the emphasis on pluralism as difference and variety, that brings about the constant recycling of ideas and practices so characteristic of our age. Recycling does not mean putting on an old-fashioned suit of clothes. Rather, it means that cultural patterns will become different yet similar, modified by new experiences, new ways of feeling. Emotional culture—the cult of emotional wealth—this major offspring of the modern age—is also very likely to be recycled. If this happens, emotional culture will not be the privilege of a few. In the postmodern condition, different groups consisting of people of different backgrounds with a great variety of cultural traditions can create parallel and distinct emotional cultures. In all probability the subjects of "low" culture termed "mass" by adamant culture critics, men and women from all walks and avenues of life, will grow bored with the cult and games of "body". Bodies are not differentiated enough, they are not even sufficiently erotic if they lack the appeal that can only be conferred on them by emotional differentiation. What is it that can be new and at the same time different? Only emotional refinement, which once again can become new, and which is by definition different.

Notes

1. cf. *A Theory of Feelings* (Assen, Van Gorcum, 1979).
2. Aristotle, Rhetoric, 1379(a) 10, *The Complete Works of Aristotle Vol. II*, ed. By J. Barnes (Revised Oxford Edition, Princeton University Press, 1984), p. 2196.
3. Aristotle's theory of the proper mean explores exactly this situation.
4. cf. *General Ethics* (Oxford, Blackwell, 1988).

INDIVIDUAL, SOCIETY, RATIONALITY, HISTORY

Cornelius Castoriadis

As an old admirer of Max Weber,[1] I want to take the opportunity here to reexamine a series of questions which, as far as I am concerned, have been settled for a long time but which the "spirit of the times" has raised again in a fashion I find to be regressive, and whose decisive elucidation a critical confrontation with Weber, it seems to me, would allow.[2]

THE QUESTION OF INDIVIDUALISM

We all know that Max Weber taught what he called an individualist method. The ultimate goal of sociological and historical inquiry—for Weber, and rightly so, there is at bottom no distinction between these two objects of inquiry—would be to refer all phenomena investigated back to the effects of the acts and behaviour (*Verhalten*) of "one, few or many" determinate—that is to say, separate and definite—individuals. As he himself says in *Economy and Society*,[3] it is only in this way that "something more" becomes accessible, something "never attained in the natural sciences": "the understanding of the behavior of the singular individuals that participate in these social structures". This is certainly a very important point: all physical processes are describable, and they are often explainable, that is to say, they lead us back to "laws" which govern them. But they are not understandable, and in truth there is nothing there to be understood. On the other hand, various instances of human behaviour are—at least partially, at least virtually—understandable. Squabbles between children, a fit of jealousy, most often these sorts of behaviour can be understood as such and as they unfold, even in extraordinary and improbable ways (whereas it would be, strictly speaking, impossible to provide an "explanation" in the sense of the exact sciences). This task of the understanding is conditioned by the possibility that we can have what Weber calls *sympathisches Nacherleben*, a sympathetic (or empathic) reliving or recapturing of the behaviours and motivations of another.[4] But this "empathic reliving" is not, as we shall see, the basic characteristic of "understanding".

What Max Weber calls the individualist method seems to be opposed to a substantialist or ontological individualism. The sociology Weber wants to promote proceeds by constructing (or restituting) a subjectively understandable meaning of the behaviour (*Verhalten*) of single (*einzelnen*, "one or more"[5] individuals. It accedes to this meaning all the better, or rather it can attain it, to the extent that this meaning is "rational". This attainment of meaning is accomplished via the construction of ideal types (of individuals, or of instances of behaviour). I will return to these as well as to the enormous question of whether "the *signification* of social phenomena is constructed by the social scientist starting from a particular standpoint"[6] and of whether or not presuppositions are made during this construction relative to its object.

Fully anticipating the possible perversions of this view, Weber characterized in advance as a "monstrous misunderstanding" (*ungeheuer Missverständnis*) the attempt to draw from this "individualist *method*" an "individualist system of values" in any sense, as well as every attempt to draw from "the unavoidable tendency of sociological *concepts* to assume a rationalist character" any conclusions concerning the "predominance of rational motives" in human action or even a "positive valuation of rationalism" (*E&S* 18, no. 9.[7] Those who are familiar with his violent and obsessively repeated criticisms of Rudolph Stammler can easily imagine the harsh sarcasm he would have heaped upon the "individualism" and "rationalism" found in the social sciences today—not to speak of the pseudopolitical conclusions that have been drawn therefrom, using arguments that resemble nothing so much as the syllogism that "unicorns exist, therefore the universe is made of quince preserves". Upon such arguments Friedrich von Hayek has made his reputation.

From this perspective, what can be said of "social collectivities" or "social formations"? Weber's expressions are, in these cases, so categorical that it can immediately be seen that if the individualist method does not involve taking an "evaluative", and still less a political position, it is nevertheless tantamount to an ontological decision concerning the Being of the social-historical: "For the interpretive understanding of behavior . . . these social collectivities must be treated as solely (*lediglich*) the resultants and modes of organization of the particular acts of individual persons since, for us, these alone can be treated as comprehensible agents of meaning-oriented action" (or "bearers of meaningful behavior": *sinnhaft orientiertem Handeln*.[8]

This powerfully-worded statement is accompanied by three remarks concerning the relation between "the subjective interpretation of action" and "these collective concepts":

(a) It is often necessary to use expressions such as "State", "family", etc.— but one must avoid confusing them with the corresponding juridical concepts by imputing to them a "collective personality".

(b) The process of understanding must take into account that these "collective formations" are also "*representations* in the minds of real men", and that they thus can "have a powerful, often a decisive (dominant, *beherrschende*) causal influence on the course of action of real individuals". But clearly, in this context such "representations" can be thought of only as the *result* of the action of other "real individuals".

(c) There is an "organic" school of sociology that tries to explain social behaviour on the basis of "functional" considerations, the "parts" accomplishing the functions necessary for the existence of the "whole". These kinds of considerations may have value, says Weber, as a "practical illustration", for they may establish a "provisional orientation" for one's investigations (but beware of the risk of "reifying concepts"!) or they can be heuristically useful (allowing one, for example, to detect the most important actions within a given context). But all this is just a prelude to the work of sociology proper, which alone accomplishes the true task: the understanding of the behaviour of individual participants.[9]

These remarks clearly have no import on the level of basic principles. Weber's individualist method does not prevent him from ultimately deciding the ontological question in the most categorical of terms: "The real empirical sociological investigation begins with the questions: What motives *have determined* and *do determine* the singular (*einzelnen*) members and participants in this 'collectivity' to behave in such a way that this community came into being (was formed, created: *entstand*) in the first place and that it *continues to exist?*"[10]

Only individual acts, therefore, would be "understandable" or "interpretable". But in what does this comprehensibility of theirs consist? Weber's "initial" formulations are broad and exhibit his prudence in this matter: "The basis for certainty in understanding can be either rational ... or it can consist of an emotionally or artistically appreciative empathic reliving (*einfühlend Nacherleben*)"; at the same time, he speaks of how difficult it is for us to understand "many ultimate 'ends' or 'values' toward which experience shows that human action may be oriented" if, when we "relive them in the empathic imagination" (*einfühlende Phantasie*), they depart too radically "from our own ultimate values".[11] He thus seems to maintain a balance between the two opposing poles, and their difference arises only from the relative difficulties involved in understanding each one. Let us note in passing, however, the underlying imprecision of this opposition: we understand more easily an action oriented toward ends or values which are near to our own and (or which unfold according to a rationality of means relating to ends; we have more trouble understanding, and sometimes we do not understand at all, actions which occur in conformity with ends that are not our own) or whose application appreciably departs from the rationality of means relating to ends. (In line with what is becoming more and more the current usage, I will call the later "instrumental rationality". Weber's term, *Zweckrationalität*, which in this one case is rather unfortunate, really means *Mittelrationalität*, rationality of means used, which obviously can be adjudged only in relation to an end that an actor has set forth and intended, whereas the literal translations, "end-related rationality" or "rationality according to ends" create an intolerable ambiguity.)

But in reality, if one attentively rereads the section of *Economy and Society* entitled "Methodological Foundations" while keeping this problematic in mind, there is little possible doubt about the double movement being made there. On the one hand, the "understanding" is reduced more and more to the understanding of instrumentally-rational action. On this point, let me quote at length from this section, for the passage[12] sheds light on almost all aspects of the entire matter at hand:

> These laws (which interpretive sociology tries to establish) are both comprehensible and univocal to the highest degree insofar as at the foundation of the typically observed course of action lies pure instrumentally-rational motivations,... and insofar as the relations of means and end are, according to the rules laid down by experience, also univocal ... In such cases one may assert that *insofar as* the action was rigorously rational in an instrumental way, it *would have had to* (*musste*, in the sense of necessity and not obligation) occur *in this way and no other...*

The examples cited (arithmetical calculation, insertion of such and such a proposition in such and such a place in a proof, rational decision of a person acting according to the determinate interests involved in undertaking an action corresponding to the results s/he would expect) are clear-cut. On the other hand, Weber amasses a series of examples of behaviour which are not instrumentally rational: *all* traditional activity, many aspects of charismatic actions[13]—and of course, reactions—then[14] the quasi-totality of "real action" which "goes on in the great majority of cases in a state of apathetic (vague, numb: *dumpf*) semi-consciousness or unconsciousness of the 'meaning one intends' ". "In most cases the individual's action is governed by impulse or habit ... Really effective meaningful behaviour (*sinnhaftes Handeln*), where the meaning is fully conscious and explicit (whether it be 'rational or irrational') is a marginal case". Whence the conclusion, already formulated: "All these facts do not discharge interpretive sociology from the obligation, in full awareness of the narrow limits to which it is confined, to accomplish what it alone *can* do".[15]

So that no one hastens to object that within traditional, habitual, semi-conscious or unconscious behaviour can be found a sort of "rationality", let us note that there are two unsatisfactory options: either we know nothing about it or, in order to establish its existence, we would have to have recourse to ideas of "objective rationality" which Weber had dismissed in advance—and rightly so, given the horizon of his philosophical views—for, as Weber says, "we shall speak of 'action' insofar as the acting individual attaches a subjective *meaning* to his behavior". Such meaning "may refer first to the actual or effective (*tatsächlich*) existing meaning in the given concrete case of a particular actor, or to the average or approximate meaning attributable to a given plurality of actors; or second, to the meaning subjectively *intended* by the actor or actors *thought of* as types within a conceptually constructed pure type".[16] And in any case, a mystery would remain: Why and how do the great majority of individuals in the great majority of their acts act simply because they have become habituated to act in that way, what does it signify in relation to the *very being* of human individuals, and what can we say of the *instauration* (each time pristine) of these "habits" or of "tradition"? What can we say, too, of the prospects and chances for interpretive sociology if the latter, when faced with 95 percent of human history, must confine itself to saying: that is not understandable, but it is traditional?

We will have to criticize the philosophical foundations of Weber's position. But before doing that, we must understand the logic (and, arising from its foundations, the necessity) of his attitude.

Sociology must understand, and not (or not simply) explain. (I will return below to the mistaken idea that one can *separate absolutely* these two moments.) What can one understand? Meaning. And, according to Weber, there is no meaning except "in", "through" and "for" actual individuals (even if as simply for the social scientist who "constructs" this meaning)—in any case, it is an *intended* meaning (*gemeinter*; the German word strongly suggests the "subjective" side, and it is quite close to the Greek *doxazō*. But what sociology is to understand is not simply an "isolated" meaning, supposing that such a thing could exist. It has to understand the concatenation of people's acts—the socially oriented behaviour of individuals—and not "explain" them, as physics does, by mere acknowledgment of incomprehensible irregularities. And as far as possible, sociology has to understand these concatenations as *necessary*. It is thus, and thus alone, according to Weber, that it can be a science. Its task[17] is to furnish "a *correct* causal *interpretation*," and this requires that "the process which is claimed to be typical must appear adequately grasped on the level of meaning and at the same time that its interpretation must to some degree be shown to be causally adequate". For Weber, causality is essential. Now, what must really be called, in the last analysis, Weber's rationalistic (methodological, but also ontological) individualism depends entirely upon this connection between causality (necessity) and understanding, which is inevitably represented (we shall soon see why) by rational intelligibility. Indeed, in opposition to the "stupid regularities" of physical nature, a rationally connected concatenation of acts is bound to appear to us as both intelligible and necessary—intelligible in each of its moments and in their connection, and likewise necessary. (To Weber's chosen examples, cited earlier, one can add that of the general who, under given circumstances and with given means at his disposal, would have made those decisions that were instrumentally rational in view of the end he had set for himself; here we would be able to "*explain* in causal terms" the distance, the margin of deviation of his actual acts, by the intervention of "misinformation, strategical errors, logical fallacies, personal temperament or considerations outside the realm of strategy".[18]

Now, causality signifies neither "irreversibility" nor any kind of temporal ordering and still less, quite clearly, a mere, empirically established, regular succession from one phenomenon to another. Causality signifies the regularity of a succession whose *necessity is expressed by a universal law*. In the case of the physical sciences, the universality of the law, *formaliter spectata*, is a prerequisite for scientific thought and, *materialiter spectata*, it is represented by the, in principle indefinite, reproducibility of the particular succession under investigation. (I am leaving aside here such distinctions as experimentation, observation, indirect inference, and so on, which are of only secondary importance in relation to my theme.) But in the case of social-historical phenomena (I repeat that for Weber there is in this regard, and rightly so, no essential distinction between society and history) both reproducibility and even non-trivial repetition properly speaking are beyond our grasp, for a thousand reasons that have been stated many times and which still could be enlarged upon. Now, it is precisely this absence of reproducibility which, from his causalist perspective, gives substance to Weber's remarks on "rationality" and intelligibility. The intrinsic intelligibility of a concatenation of motivations and acts is precisely what effectively substitutes for the kind of reproducibility found in the experimental sciences (as it increases, moreover, our "understanding"). Experimental reproducibility is replaced, in effect, by a *statement of potentially indefinite reproducibility* of the sort: "Every other rational individual in X's place would have decided, when faced with the same circumstances, to employ the same means, Y". Or, if you prefer: *qua* rational individuals, we are all substitutable for one another and each of us "would have to reproduce" the same sorts of behaviour when confronted with the same conditions. (Let us note that under these conditions the very singularity of historical events is dissolved, except in the form of a numerical singularity, or of irrational deviation: "What would you have done under these conditions?" "Exactly what he did". "And why didn't you do it?" "I drank too much champagne".)

If such potential reproducibility, itself issuing from considerations of "rationality", is, however, lacking, what Weber calls the *Fehlen an Sinnadäquanz*—a lack or shortage of adequation of meaning—comes into play, thus reducing the observed regularity to an "incomprehensible" or "statistical" regularity[19]—that is to say, it makes us retreat to the side of the observational physical sciences. And this is true even for "psychic elements": "the more precisely they are formulated from the point of view of natural science, the less does one understand them. This is never the road to interpretation in terms of an intended *meaning*".[20] Certainly, as Weber adds, incomprehensible processes and regularities are not for all that any less "valuable"; but for sociology their role is the same as that of all factual situations established by other scientific disciplines (from physics to physiology). They belong to the conditions, obstacles, requirements, incitements and so on that the non-social world presents to people in their capacity as social actors.

Is there not then beneath all of this any philosophy (other than a "theory of knowledge of the social sciences")? Oh, indeed there is! It is not even worthwhile entering into discussion over the untenable idea of the existence of some "method" (or "theory of knowledge") that would involve *no* ontology. Without the two interconnected assertions—viz. that *there is* something comprehensible in society and history and that what is understandable *is* (*par excellence*, if one wants to insist on the point) the "rational" dimension of *individual* action—Weber's method would no longer possess an object of investigation (and one would no longer understand why he has chosen to apply this method to society and history rather than to the expansion of galaxies). There is no point in adding such phrases as "we do as if . . ." (why not use this same "as if" in molecular biology?) or "we are speaking of the parts covered by our method without making any judgements about the totality" (therefore *there very well are* parts which your method takes in, and this fact cannot depend upon your method alone since the other parts resist its application). The origin of the idea that the comprehensible is the product of individual action can be traced back to Vico and his celebrated statement, *verum et factum convertuntur*—truth and (human) deeds/facts are interchangeable, or, more freely but still faithfully: only that which we have done is intelligible and everything that we have done is intelligible—and upstream from Vico, all the way back to Hobbes. Of course, the origin of this idea is to be found in theological philosophy: when, in the *Timaeus*, Plato wants to "explain" the world, he makes its constitution *understandable* "as much as possible" by putting himself in the place, so to speak, of a "rational" demiurge (indeed, one placed at the summit of "rationality": a mathematician and geometer) who works on the basis of a model that is itself "rational". (If the world is not completely "rational", it is that Plato, who in spite of everything remains Greek, has contrived for his demiurge to work upon matter that is itself irrational and independent. This option is not open for the Christian theology of an omnipotent God.) Clearly, the same scheme predominates in German idealism (the intelligible is correlative to the action of a subject—finite in Kant, infinite according to Hegel). In all events, Weber's Kantian and neo-Kantian roots are well known and quite evident, especially in this regard.

To air out the discussion a bit and to expose more clearly the stakes involved, let us take our distance in the most brutal terms possible. Without prejudicing the moment of partial truth it contains, Vico's statement as well as the whole constellation of ideas denoted by it is false. We would not live in the world we live in, but in another, if everything we did was intelligible and if what we did was alone intelligible to us (—as individuals or as a collection of individuals designatable by name). It is hardly worth recalling that not all of what we do or of what others do or have done is intelligible (or, oftentimes, even understandable, however broadly we expand the meaning of this term). And many things—the most decisive—are intelligible to us without us having done them or without us being able to "redo" them, to reproduce them. I have not made up the idea of a norm or law (in the effective, sociological sense, not in the "transcendental" one); I might invent a particular law but not the *idea* of a social law (the idea of institution). In vain will it be said that concretely designatable persons have taught me language; to teach me language, they already had to have possessed it. Will one go so far as to maintain that "rational individuals", driven by their "interests" or their "ideas", have *consciously* made up language (language in general, or some particular language)? ("Will one go even further and maintain that it is only to the extent that language has been done *consciously* that it is intelligible?") Let us stop laughing, and simply ask: *Without language*, is a "rational" and "conscious" individual conceivable as an effective individual (*and even* as a "transcendental subject")?

We know how Dilthey, starting from a perspective of "individualistic" (and, at the beginning, "psychological") understanding and borrowing from Hegel while rejecting Hegelian metaphysics, was led to take into account the manifestations of what he calls, following Hegel but with a meaning much larger than is found in the latter's philosophy, the "objective spirit" (which practically overlaps completely with what I call the institution): language, custom, forms of life, family, society, State, law, etc. Though as early as 1883 he had characterized the individual as an abstraction, one may also rightly note the persistence in Dilthey of the principle of *verum factum*: "The field (of the sciences of the mind) is identical to that of the understanding and consequently the object of understanding is the objectivization of life. Thus the field of the sciences of the mind is determined by the objectivation of life in the outer world. *The mind can understand only what it has created*".[21] Dilthey's philosophical position here is clearly confused. Something is objectivized which is not Hegelian Reason or the World Spirit; it is called, incidentally, "life" or "mind"—and that in which it objectivizes "itself" is de jure understandable to us (across differences in times and places). Also, the conditions for this understanding remain obscure: it could be said that we participate in this "life" and in this "mind"—but is that a sufficient condition, especially once it is no longer a matter of understanding "rational" activities alone but also the totality of human experience *and above all* its "objectivized" forms?

This was not a problem for Max Weber—since, as we have seen, collective entities "appear anew as simple givens which the understanding must seek to reduce to the activity of individuals".[22] But at what cost! One must endorse an ontology (that of critical philosophy) which affirms: *If there is* meaning, it is because there is a subject (an ego) that posits it (intends it, constitutes it, constructs it, etc.). And *if there is* a subject, it is because it is either the source and unique origin of meaning or meaning's necessary correlate.   That this subject is named, in philosophy, "ego" or "consciousness" in general and, in sociology, the "individual" undoubtedly creates serious questions (notably the problem of how to pass from the transcendental subject of critical philosophy to the individual effectively acting in society, who, according to the principles of Kantian and neo-Kantian philosophy, can only be the "psychological", "empirical", "phenomenal" subject), but it basically changes nothing. In both cases, the postulates and intentions of thought are clearly *egological.* Whatever one then does, there is one thing one cannot avoid doing: viz. presenting the social-historical as the "product" of the cooperation (or of the conflict) between "individuals" (or claiming, in an attenuation of this individualist methodology, that we can think about it only to the extent that it is individual).

What are these "individuals"? Two paths open up, and both lead to untenable conclusions:

(a) Either it will be said that the essential aspect of individual behaviour is "rational" (or progress toward "rationality")—and if I can understand the individual, it is because I participate in the same "rationality". We immediately proceed, full steam ahead, toward a (Hegelian) absolute idealism as concerns history, even if this is labelled "reconstruction of historical materialism", as it is in Habermas. That one might happen, within this "rationality", to distinguish between a "logic of interests" and a "logic of ideas" (or "representations") changes nothing: it is still a matter of logic; and if there be conflict, it would be a conflict between two logics. Everything that does not come under this heading, everything that cannot be rationally reconstructed in a philosophy seminar—not much, really, just the totality of human history—is scoria, a gap to be filled in progressively, a learning stage, a passing failure in the "problem solving" exercises assigned to humanity (by whom and for what purpose?) or—why not?—"primitive nonsense", as old Engels said.

(b) Or, following Terence (*humani nihil alienum puto*) and the great classical philosophers, I take the "individual" in its fullness, with its capacity for "rationality" but also with its passions, affects, desires, etc. I then find myself faced with a "human nature" that is more or less determined but assuredly identical across space and time—and whose latest avatar is a pseudopsycho-analytical marionette which, it must be said, Freud himself had a substantial hand in fabricating. Even supposing that, following the path that leads from *The Republic, The Leviathan, Totem and Taboo*, etc., I might be able to under-stand why and, above all, how this being could produce a society, I remain with the following enigma: why and how has it produced so many different societies, and why has it produced a history (and indeed many of them)?

Two things fill me with an ever-renewed sense of wonderment: the starry sky above me and the ineradicable hold these schemata have on my contempo-rary fellow authors. Learning, we are told once again today, is the basic motor of human history. Considering the ease with which people "forget" psycho-analysis, ethnology, prehistory, history—or, more concretely, two world wars, gas chambers, the Gulag, Pol Pot, Khomeini, and so on and so forth—we must concede that learning is not a motive force, not even a secondary one, for contemporary reflection in this domain.

THE SOCIAL-HISTORICAL AND THE PSYCHICAL

We do not "understand" all individual acts of behaviour, not even our own—far from it—and we can understand "objects" that are irreducible to in-dividual acts of behaviour when they belong to the field of the social-historical. The social-historical world is the world of meaning—of significations—and of the *effective* or *actual (effectif)* meaning. This world cannot be thought of as a mere "intended ideality", it must be borne by *instituted forms*, and it pene-trates into the very depths of the human psychism, decisively fashioning it in almost all of its discernible /*repérables*/ *manifestations.* "Effective meaning" does not necessarily mean (and, moreover: never exhaustively means) mean-ing for an individual. The dividing line between "nature" as the object of the "experimental" sciences and the social- historical does not have to do with the existence or non-existence of individual behaviour. Whether it is a matter of acts of individuals, collective phenomena, artifacts or institutions, I am always dealing with something that is constituted as such by the *immanent actuality of a meaning*—or of a *signification*—and this is sufficient for me to place the object within a horizon of social-historical apprehension. That there may be limit-cases (Is this pebble "natural", or has it been worked upon?) does not weaken our assertion any more than does the fact that we might have trouble deciding whether someone is trembling with rage or shaking because s/he is suffering from a neurological condition. The understanding is our mode of access to this world—and it does not necessarily, nor by its essence, require recourse to the individual. If, in reading the *Parmenides* or the *Lex duodecim tabularum*, I understand these writings, it is not because I am sympathetically reliving someone's behaviour. Faced with a social-historical phenomenon I have the (in the immense majority of cases, enigmatic) *possibility* of "sympathetically reliving" or "reconstituting" a meaning *for* an individual; but I am *always* gripped by the presence, the "incarnation" of meaning. That I might try to make understandable as well the "intentions" of an author, the possible "reactions" of his/her potential readership, changes nothing. The social/historical object is co-constituted by the activities of individuals, which incarnate or concretely realize the society in which they live. And in extreme cases I can take account of these activities only "nominally". A dead language studied as a no longer evolving corpus, Roman law as a system, these are *institutions* that are accessible as such; they do not refer back to individual actors except "at the margin" or in a wholly abstract manner. And, far from considering language as the "product" of cooperation between individual thoughts, it is language that tells me, first of all, what was thinkable for individuals and how it was so.

In opposition to a substantialist or ontological individualism, a methodological individualism would be an approach that refuses (as Weber does explicitly) to ask questions of the kind: "Is it the individual or society that comes 'first'?"; "Is it society that produces individuals or individuals that produce society?" while asserting that we are not obliged to answer such "ontological" questions, the only thing that we might (come to) understand is the behaviour of the (actual or ideal-typical) individual—this behaviour itself being all the more comprehensible when it is "rational" (or at least "instrumentally rational"). But what is the actual (*effectif*) individual—and what is *effective* rationality?

The individual is not, to begin with and in the main, anything other than society. The individual/society opposition, when its terms are taken rigorously, is a total fallacy. The opposition, the irreducible and unbreakable polarity, is that between *psyche* and society. Now, the psyche is not the individual; the psyche *becomes* individual solely to the extent that it undergoes a process of socialization (without which, moreover, neither it nor the body it animates would be able to survive an instant). We need not pretend we do not know when we do. Surely, Heraclitus has not been "surpassed": as he says, we will not reach the limits of the psyche, even after having traversed its entire path (or all its paths). But we know that human beings are born with a given biological constitution (which is extremely complex, rigid in certain respects and endowed with an incredible plasticity in others) and that its makeup includes a psyche so long as it is functioning. Though we are far from knowing everything about the latter, we nevertheless know quite a lot. The more we explore it, the more we discover that it is essentially alogical, that in this regard the terms "ambivalent" and "contradictory" give us an idea of its mode of being only to an immensely slight degree. But we also know when exploring the psyche that we encounter on all its strata the effects of a process of socialization that it undergoes as soon as it comes into the world—and this is so not only because the patient of psychoanalysis must put his dreams into words or because the psychoanalyst must think on the basis of certain categories.

This process itself is certainly a social activity. And as such, it is always necessarily mediated by identifiable individuals, the mother for example—but it is *not only* them. Not only are these individuals always already themselves socialized, but what they "transmit" goes far beyond them: let us say, roughly speaking and so as to point out merely one feature, that they provide the means and the modes of access to virtually the whole of the social world as it is instituted in each instance, this whole being a totality which they in no way need to possess in actuality (*effectivement*) (and which, moreover, they could not in fact "possess" in actuality). And there are not only individuals: language as such is an "instrument" of socialization (though it certainly is not only that!) whose effects go immeasurably beyond everything the mother who teaches it to her child could "intend". And as Plato already knew, children (and youths and adults) are socialized by the very walls of their city well beyond any explicit "intention" of those who constructed them.

I will not repeat here what I have set forth at length elsewhere upon many occasions (*Institution*, Ch. 6; *Subject*, passim).[23] I will simply summarize my views by saying that the socialization of individuals—itself a socially instituted process, and in each case a different one—opens up these individuals, giving them access to a *world* of social imaginary significations whose instauration as well as incredible coherence (the differentiated and articulated homology of its parts as well as their synergy) goes unimaginably beyond everything that "one or many individuals" could ever produce.[24] These significations owe their actual (social-historical) existence to the fact that they are *instituted*. They are not reducible to the transubstantiation of psychical drives: sublimation is the psychical side of the process whose social side is the fabrication of the individual. And they are obviously not reducible to "rationality", whatever breadth one grants to the meaning of this term. To state that they are is to oblige oneself to produce, here and now, a "rational dialectic" of history and even of histories in the plural; one would have to explain, for instance, in what way and how during the 14th and 15th centuries, the civilizations of the Aztecs, Incas, Chinese, Japanese, Mongols, Hindus, Persians, Arabs, Byzantines and West-Europeans, plus everything that could be enumerated from other cultures on the African, Australian, Asian, and American continents, represent simply different "figures of rationality" and, above all, how a "synthesis" of them could be made—here's the state of the World Spirit in 1453, for example, and here's why, in and through this diversity on the phenomenal level, the underlying unity of Reason, whether human or not, manifests itself—or, lacking this, here's how these civilizations could be *ordered* rationally (for, a Reason that could not, even "dialectically", give order to and establish a hierarchy for its manifestations should be put out to pasture). The thick-headedness displayed in the various versions of contemporary rationalism when confronted with these questions—which questions themselves could be multiplied indefinitely and which are as basic as they are incapable of being circumvented—clearly shows that it represents much less a stage in the history of thought than a regression of an *ideological* nature (the motivations behind this ideology cannot detain us here). The philosophy of history does not begin with a reading of Kant but with a study of human sacrifices among the Aztecs, the massive conversions of Christian peoples to Islam in half of the Eastern Empire, or Nazism and Stalinism, to take a few examples.

On the other hand, if we grant the existence of a level of Being unknown to inherited ontology, which is the social-historical *qua* anonymous collective, and its mode of being *qua* radical imaginary in its capacity as *instituting* and *creative of significations*, we will be able to keep in mind the weighty evidences social-historical phenomena themselves present to us—viz. the irreducibility of the institution and of social significations to "individual activity"; society's coherence, beyond the functional level, in matters relating to *meaning*; the mutual irreducibility of different social-historical formations and of all of them to some sort of "progress of Reason". The existence of this level is shocking only because people do not wish to depart from settled habits of thought; in itself, there is nothing more (or less) astonishing about it than that other level of being whose existence everyone stupidly accepts, if I dare say so, because they believe they have always seen it: viz. life itself. The existence of the social-historical is revealed (and even "proven") by its irreducible effects; if we do not grant its existence then we must, in no uncertain terms, make of language, and of languages in the plural (and this is only *one* example), a biological phenomenon (as Habermas practically does). These same effects reveal its creative character: where else does one see a *form of Being* like the institution? It is a creation that manifests itself, *inter alia*, by the enormous diversity of social forms as well as in their historical succession. And this creation is *ex nihilo*: when humanity creates the institution and signification, it does not "combine" some "elements" that it would have found scattered about before it. It creates the *form* institution, and in and through this form it creates *itself* as *humanity* (which is something other than an assembly of bipeds). "Creation *ex nihilo*", "creation of form" does not mean "creation *cum nihilo*", that is to say, without "means", unconditionally, on a *tabula rasa*. Apart from one (or perhaps several) point(s) of origin which is (are) inaccessible and unfathomable and which itself (themselves) *lean(s) on* properties of the first natural stratum, of the human being as biological being, *and* of the psyche, all historical creation takes place upon, in, and through the already instituted (not to mention whatever surrounding "concrete" conditions there may be). This conditions it and limits it—but does not *determine* it; and quite clearly, still less does it do so in a "rational" manner since in major instances what occurs is a passage from one magma of social imaginary significations to another.[25] Thus it is a mere rhetorical objection to state that if there is a creation in history then Homer could have been located somewhere between Shakespeare and Goethe. None of these "phenomena" (authors) can be detached from its own social-historical world—and it just so happens that, in *this* case, these worlds succeed one another by "being conscious", more or less, of those that preceded them in *this* segment of human history. The existence of conditions during a succession of such phases does not suffice to make such a succession "rationally causal". My reading of Hegel enters into the conditions for my thinking at this moment; if, against all odds, I succeeded in thinking something *new*, Hegel will not have been the "cause" of such an occurrence. The world built upon the ruins of the Roman Empire from the 5th century onwards is inconceivable without Greece, Rome, the New Testament, and the Germanic barbarians. This in no way signifies that it springs from an "addition", "combination" or "synthesis" of elements from these four sources (and others one could think of). It is a creation of new social-historical forms (which are, moreover, radically other in the Eastern Empire and in the Western barbarian kingdoms); they confer an essentially new meaning upon the very elements which pre-existed them, and which they "utilize".[26] To speak of a "synthesis" in such instances is pure mental laziness and a dreary repetition of old clichés; they blind one, for example, to the fact that the "utilization" of Greek philosophy by Christian theology would have been impossible without a huge distortion of this philosophy (whose effects, moreover, are still making themselves felt) or that the institutionalization (and already the spread) of Christianity has required the abandonment of essential elements of the New-Testament faith, such as its acosmic outlook and the purported imminence of Parousia (the Second Coming). Far from being able to "explain" or "understand" the Byzantine world on the basis of these elements, I must, quite to the contrary, understand the Byzantine world as a form for itself and a new magma of instituted significations in order to "explain" and "understand" what its pre-existing elements have become through the new meaning they have acquired. In the actual practice of such an investigation, there is certainly always a give-and-take between the two approaches, but this in no way alters the main point on the level of principle.[27]

Of this, at least, Weber was thoroughly convinced *as well*, even if his terminology differs from ours. The true referent for the "incomparability" or "incommensurability" of "values" and ultimate "ends" of "people's social acts" and for the "war of the gods" is the otherness or *alterity* of different social-historical worlds and of the imaginary significations that animate these worlds. They express his acute perception of the problem created by the irreducible multiplicity of the forms through which the social-historical deploys itself as well as his profound awareness of the impossibility of giving these forms, when considered in themselves, any hierarchical ordering. But this allows an ineradicable antinomy to remain in his thought. As clear as is his refusal to consider modern "rationality" and "rationalization" as *de jure* "superior" to other forms of social existence—and I will add, for my own part, that from other points of view, notably philosophical and political, this refusal is highly criticizable and ultimately unacceptable—his "violent rejection (*refus*) of historical irrationalism"[28] *obliges him*, due to the irreducibility of "ultimate values" (i.e. of other imaginary significations), to set up a rationalist individualism (which, as we have seen, cannot simply be "methodological" in character) and to establish instrumental rationality as the horizon of intelligibility for the social-historical. We should now be capable of seeing how the two terms of the antinomy feed upon each other: the more people's acts are motivated "in the last analysis" by adherence to mutually irreducible "ultimate values" (and, of course, to "Reason"), the more "scientific" analysis has to fall back on instrumental rationality as the only solid field of investigation; and the more "rationality" is postulated as the ultimate horizon of the understanding, the more the "ultimate values" of different cultures become *de facto* inaccessible and the understanding of the social-historical world finds itself reduced to the reconstitution of a few fragments, or instrumentally-rational dimensions, of human action.

But what is this "instrumental rationality" itself? The "instrumental rationality" of human individuals is, each time, socially instituted and imposed. (That this imposition encounters in the psyche what, through a difficult and painful process, makes it possible, is another question.[29] It is, for example, impossible without language. Now, every language conveys the totality of the social world to which it belongs. There are, of course, some "elements" of this rationality which, in the abstract, are transhistorical: $2 + 2 = 4$ is undoubtedly valid in every society. These are the elements which belong at the intersection (the Common part) of the ensidic (the ensemblistic-identitary) understanding which every society must, at minimum, institute and which also correspond, sufficiently as to need, (as Aristotle would say), to the ensidic component of the first natural stratum upon which every society lives.[30] *However*, these elements are *always* co-determined to a great extent by the magma of social imaginary significations in which they are immersed, and which each time they instrument. With out such instrumentation, these significations could not even be *voiced*. But without these significations, the "rational" (ensidic) elements would have *no meaning*. A book in mathematics written entirely in formalized terms and containing *no* explanation of its symbols, its axioms and its rules of deduction, is totally incomprehensible. Thus, if one cannot avoid taking these transhistorical elements into consideration (a condition which does not take us very far, however), it is impossible to have a *correct* access to these same elements as they are actually given in a certain society unless one first has viewed the imaginary institution of this society. I must know something of the Christian religion to avoid seeing in the statement "$1 = 3$", as propounded by a believer in or a theologian of the Holy Trinity, a pure and simple instance of absurdity. It is therefore impossible for me, in trying to carry out the Weberian "methodological" program, to consider individual behaviour as composed of a central "rational" (ensidic) component that is supposed (be it (only) "method-ologically") *everywhere and always the same* and of *individual* deviations from this "rationality". The understanding is instituted social-historically, and it is im-mersed in the overall imaginary institution of society. To speak in crude but clear terms: what is different in another society and another epoch is its very "rationality", for it is "caught" each time in another imaginary world. This does not mean that it is inaccessible to us; but this access must pass by way of an attempt (certainly always problematical; but how could it be otherwise?) to reinstitute the imaginary significations of the society in question.

In the second place—and this is another aspect of the same thing—the dif-ference, the alterity, the deviation through which the object of social-historical inquiry is presented—and which constituted the principal difficulty for this inquiry—is of an entirely other order than the deviation of an instrumentally-rational form of behaviour from the actual behaviour observed. Marc Antony gave up the battle of Actium when he saw Cleopatra's vessel depart—though, "rationally speaking", he still had a chance of winning; this interference of pas-sion in the application of instrumental rationality offers us no great enigma to resolve. What really astonishes us, and what constitutes the difficulty involved in the attainment of social-historical knowledge, is the enormous and massive alterity separating the representations, affects, motivations and intentions of the subjects of another society from our own. How can we begin to understand the behaviour of Arab warriors during Islam's great period of expansion, Christian soldiers during the Crusades, participants in the religious wars that tore apart Europe from 1530 until the Treaty of Westphalia, if the only instrument we have at our disposal is the ridiculous comparison between the instrumentally-rational component involved in each of these cases and that which deviates from this component? I will have understood nothing if I have not tried to penetrate an entirely other *world* of significations, motivations and affects; these certainly contain an ensidic component of *legein* and *teukhein*, but they are irreducible to it. And nearer to us, or rather closer to home: What good would it do me if I tried to understand the behaviour of Hitler, the SS and members of the Nazi party or Stalin and members of Stalinist parties as instances of instrumentally-rational behaviour which, on certain precise points, have deviated from this rationality (the two parts of this statement being, moreover, quite true)? What would I have understood then of totalitarianism? And how can one avoid see-ing that in this case the very implementation of such a demented "instrumental rationality", sometimes applied down to its tiniest details, has been dependent to a massive degree upon the imaginary of totalitarianism as well as decisively codetermined by it? Once again, one cannot avoid thinking that the return in force of such a "rationalist" individualism, and even of a certain rationalism, is actually motivated today as well by the desire to put an end (in words and philosophically) to the horrors of the 20th century, even while these horrors continue to happen and diversify before our very eyes.

The situation is reversed, but the question is rendered no more solvable, in the opposite case: alterity tends toward a minimum—and ideally toward zero—when the object of investigation is the researcher's own society. In this case, the risk is that the researcher will consider the "rationality" of his/her society (and his/her very own rationality) as going without saying, as unquestionable, and that, for this very reason, s/he will fail to recognize the imaginary that lies at the basis of his/her society and founds it in its singularity. Need we recall to what extent this risk has trapped some of the greatest thinkers—from Hegel and Marx to Freud and Max Weber himself, not to mention those among our contemporaries who are legion? It is in this way that the Prussian monarchy, capitalist technique and the capitalist organization of production, the patriarchal family and the modern bureaucracy have, each in their turn, appeared as the incarnations of an unquestionable ("instrumental" or substantive) rationality.

IDEAL TYPES

As conceived by Weber, the intended purpose of the ("scientific") construction of ideal types is to establish "typical" concatenations of individual motivations and acts (which ought, in the "perfect" case, to be both "adequate as to meaning" and "causally adequate") and thereby also to establish ideal types *of individuals*, at least with regard to an aspect of their activity ("king", "official", "entrepreneur", "magician", to take examples Weber cites.[31] Now, one of the paradoxes of his work is that several of the ideal types he has constructed (or elucidated)—and among these, some of the most important are terms which were formerly imprecise or vague and to which he has given a much more rigorous content—do not refer to individual behaviour or to individuals but to great collective artifacts; that is to say, they refer in fact to institutions and types of institutions: the city, the market, varieties of authority, bureaucracy, the patrimonial or legal State, etc. Of course, what Weber was seeking to do was to see to what extent in each case a specific instance of a class of phenomena, taken as belonging to the same term, approaches or diverges from its ideal type,[32] which is not of interest to us here, and on the other hand, to reduce these artifacts each time, ideally, to "individual behaviours"—an objective which is in truth rarely, not to say never, attained, given that it is intrinsically unattainable. To reduce, for example, the "market" to the maximizing behaviour of "rational individuals" is both to make individuals of that type fall down into place from the sky and to neglect the social-historical conditions by which the "market" as institution has been genuinely *imposed* upon people (Polanyi has already said a good deal of what there is to say about this). What is constructed in each case is the ideal type of an *institution* which certainly has to accommodate "individuals"—no institution can survive if it does not—but which concerns another level of being than "purely individual" existence and which, more importantly, is the general and specific *presupposition* for our being able to speak about the "rational behaviour" of individuals. It is because *there is, already there,* a bureaucratic universe that my behaviour *qua* bureaucrat would or would not be "rational"; even in modern bureaucracy, to be a bureaucrat with instrumentally-rational behaviour signifies behaving according to "rational" (and just as often, "absurd") rules instaurated by the bureaucracy in general and by the particular bureaucratic corps to which I belong.

But there is much more. The social-historical world is a world of effective and immanent meaning. And it is a world that has not waited around for the theoretician in order to come into existence as a world *of meaning,* nor in order to be, to a fantastic degree, *coherent,* for without coherence it would not exist. ("Coherent" means neither "systematic" nor "transparent".) This sets requirements on the construction of ideal types; to an extent, these requirements were tacitly admitted by Weber; to another extent, he ignored them.

Ideal types have a *referent* which is the effective social meaning of the "phenomena" (behaviours) observed. That this actual meaning is never "given immediately", that there is always necessarily an (in principle interminable) circulation back and forth between the theoretical construct and its confrontation with the (significant) "facts" changes nothing on the level of principle. Contrary to what Popper believes, one can say idiotic things about ancient Greece (I am not speaking here in terms of geography or demography) or about any other society—and one can show, with the aid, for example, of an ancient Greek text, that they are indeed idiotic. There are an infinity of absurd "interpretations" and few prima facie plausible ones relating to the historical "material" at hand. The validity of an ideal type can only be judged by its capacity to "make sense *(sens)*" of the historical phenomena, which are already *in themselves and for themselves* bearers of meaning *(sens)*.

Now, such meaning is never "isolated". It always participates in the overall institution of society as institution of imaginary significations, and it is of a piece *(solidaire)* with it. This is also why—and independently of all "empirical" and "vulgar" refutations—I cannot insert the ideal type "shaman", for example, in a capitalist society or the ideal type "financial speculator" among the Arunta. *It just won't stick.* More generally speaking, the ideal types that I construct for a given society under study have to be *coherent, complementary,* and (ideally) *complete* or *exhaustive.* If I construct an ideal type of "Roman patrician", for example, it must be able to *hold together* with the ideal type "Roman plebian", the two with that of "Roman slave", Roman *"pater familias"* and *"mater familias"*, etc.; but none of these ideal types can be constructed without reference to Roman law, Roman religion, the Roman army, the possibilities of the Latin language, etc. It is not that, *at the end* of this work, I will have reconstructed Roman society in its entirety; rather, it is that I cannot undertake *the first step* in this task unless I have this society *as such* in view. "Social facts" and "individual behaviours" are *effectively* possible (as "facts" *and* as meaning) only because there is, each time, a society which "functions", as is said in English, "as a going concern". (This has nothing to do with any sort of "functionalism": I simply mean that society exists, that it reproduces itself, changes, etc.). It is not because the ideal types constructed in order to grasp a given society have been constructed with an eye toward its coherence that they "produce" a coherent society—it is because society *is* coherent (even during civil war and in concentration camps) that the theoretician can try to construct ideal types which hold together somehow or other. I do not "freely" construct the Athenians' relation to their *polis*; it is because this relation has actually (*effectivement*) existed, in its historical singularity, in its coherence, and in its relative permanence, that I have before me the *polis* and the Athenian as objects of knowledge. As a coherent totality, society exists first of all in and for itself; it is not a "regulative Idea". "Total understanding" of it is, of course, an inaccessible ideal—but that is something else entirely.

RATIONALITY AND POLITICS

In order to appreciate the *constraint* that Weber's idea of "rationalization" as a *historically active factor* (and therefore one which is *immanent* to history and not "constructed" by the theoretician in order to better understand it) imposes, we should have discussed in precise detail Weber's immense work on the question of religion.[33] It is impossible to do so here: given the intrinsic importance of the subject and its revival in contemporary discourse, I hope to be able to return to this topic very shortly. Nevertheless, in the meantime I want to note that I consider completely false Weber's idea, which has been revived and expanded by Habermas, that "all religions have to resolve the problem of theodicy" and that there is an "*internal logic of religious representations*" which drive them toward a *movement* of "rationalization", whatever qualifications one will add to fix up this thesis.

I will conclude with a few remarks concerning Weber's political views and their relation to his philosophy and social theory, especially with regard to what must be called Weber's "decisionism" in matters political, or the idea of a "politics of the will".[34]

Ultimately, Weber's "decisionism" boils down to saying that just as in the social-historical world the ultimate "values" orienting human activity are mutually irreducible and incommensurable, so the action of the politician (and of each of us, inasmuch as we are political subjects rests on ultimate values which no amount of "rational" argumentation can impose upon those who do not share these same values. Let us note, first of all, that if Weber did not free himself, as we have seen, from Kantian rationalism in the domain of knowledge, he breaks with it in the domain of action; second, that this position (the "politics of the will") is in reality hardly weakened at all by Weber's marked preference for an "ethics of responsibility" (which takes the results of action into account) as against an "ethics of conviction" (which enjoins one to act according to certain principles or "for the greatness of the cause", whatever the real consequences of one's actions might be). The distinction is itself untenable, if not on the (descriptive) sociological plane, then in any case on the logical and normative, the only one of interest to us here. All "responsibility" is responsibility with regard to certain *ends*. If my "ethic of responsibility" prevents me from undertaking some political action—because, for example, it might entail the sacrifice of human lives—it is quite obviously because I posit human life as the supreme value, or at least superior to all others, this being a "conviction". And if I want to promote the "greatness of a cause" by any means possible, come what may, I greatly run the risk of destroying this cause. (One can think in terms of an absolute "ethic of conviction" without contradicting oneself only if this ethic is oriented in a completely acosmic fashion.) Third, quite obviously the choice to take on "responsibility" itself follows from a "conviction". Finally, as Philippe Raynaud notes, "the ethic of responsibility itself presupposes the limits of its own validity *and can thus grant the irreducibility of conviction*".[35]

The irreducibility of conviction to anything else is another way of saying that nothing allows one to provide a "foundation" for ultimate choices and to escape the "combat of the gods". Nothing can save us from our *ultimate responsibility*: to choose and to will in view of the consequences. Not even Reason, that latest historical figure of a Grace that would shower upon those who entreat her with sufficient ardour.

There are two ways to attempt to go beyond—or, I would rather say, avoid—this situation, and both appear to me untenable.

Raymond Aron thought he could "escape from the circle in which he (Weber) enclosed himself" by invoking "universal rationality" as exemplified by "scientific truth". But "scientific truth" (and even the fact that "it addresses itself to all men") is a value and criterion only for those who have *already accepted* the value of "universal rationality" *and* who (this additional condition is absolutely essential) have passed from the latter to a practical and political/ethical universality. The first condition makes this statement into a tautology, the second reveals the fallacy that lies within. I see no incompatibility between the acceptance of "$2 \times 2 = 4$" (Aron's example) or quantum theory, and a call to kill the infidels, to convert them by force, or to exterminate the Jews. Quite the contrary, the *compatibility* of these two classes of assertions is the massive fact of human history. And it is particularly striking to witness the fact that it is smack in the 20th century—the century that, more than any other, has monstrously demonstrated, and continues to demonstrate, that it is possible to dissociate the techno-scientifically "rational" from the politically reasonable—and *after* the experience of Stalinism and Nazism, that people have begun again to whistle in the dark the tune of universal rationality as a way of building up their courage.

We must again, we must always, make distinctions. An ensidic "rationality" exists, it is universal up to a certain point, and it can take us very far (up to the point of manufacturing H-bombs). It was there before Greco-Western science and philosophy, it does not commit anybody to anything, and it could continue, for an indefinite period of time, upon an inertial course even if philosophy and science in the strong sense were to suffer a temporary or definitive eclipse. And Khomeini can, without any contradiction, consider Western science null and void—since all truth is in the Book—and buy from Satan such effective products as Stinger missiles so as to put them in the service of the One True God. And even if this were a contradiction it would change nothing. Contradicting oneself never prevented anyone from existing. But scientific *truth*—which is of the same nature as philosophical *truth*: namely, it perpetually puts to the test the closure in which thought is every time caught—contains the possibility of a *historically effective* universality only by effecting a *rupture* with the world of traditional or authoritarian instituted representations. (It is actual historical universality with which we are concerned when we confront the political question, not "transcendental universality"). Now, to "give oneself" this rupture as something already effectuated—which is what Aron does when he speaks of a "community of minds across boundaries and centuries"—is to assume that the problem is already resolved. In this effective sense, scientific or philosophical universality presupposes subjects who have *actually* put into question their belonging to some particular social-historical world. In a sense, it is, even, just that. It is therefore tied to the exigency of a universal ethics and politics only *at its root*: both of them express and try to realize the project of autonomy. This project therefore has to be posited *before* one can draw out any argument whatsoever in favour of scientific universality—and the latter will be valid only for those whom this project is valid. *Downstream* from this project, everything becomes effectively an object of reasonable debate from which gains can be expected in all domains. But these gains, this debate, this project itself, what value have they then for a genius like Pascal, who renounces, so to speak, the invention of infinitesimal calculus because everything that *distracts* the soul from its relation to God is pure diversion or *distraction*? ("Martha, Martha, thou art careful and troubled about many things; But one thing is needful", *Luke* 10, 41–42.) And upon what basis other than personal faith ("conviction"!) or a parochial cosmo-historical prejudice will one judge Pascal's and Kierkegaard's God worthy of respect while saying that of Khomeini is not?

Certainly, the term (or idea) of "authenticity" is not useful for this debate, and the idea that an "autonomous" individual is one that, in its actions, "obeys values" is untenable. In what way is a religious fanatic who drives an explosives-filled truck against an embassy's gates "inauthentic", and how could it be said that s/he does not obey "values"? Either "values" are arbitrary and mutually equivalent or else not all values are the same, and to say this already means that one has already accepted the reasonable discussability of values as one's supreme value and criterion. It is impossible to circumvent the necessity of affirming the project of autonomy as the primary position, one which can be elucidated but which cannot "be founded", since the very intention of founding it presupposes it.

I cannot take up here again the discussion of the idea of autonomy.[36] But we must reiterate that the question will remain intractable so long as autonomy is understood in the Kantian sense, viz. as a fictively autarchic subject's conformity to a "Law of Reason", in complete misrecognition of the social-historical conditions for, and the social-historical dimension of, the project of autonomy.

Let us now take up the normative standpoint (the political/ethical one, the two being at bottom indissociable). There is a goal which a few of us have set for ourselves: the autonomy of human beings, which is inconceivable except as the autonomy of *society* as well as the autonomy of *individuals*—the two being inseparably linked, and this link being in fact an analytic judgment (a tautology) when we understand what the individual is. We set autonomy in this sense as the goal for each among us, both with respect to each one of us and with respect to all the others (without the autonomy of others there is no collective autonomy—and outside such a collectivity I cannot be *effectively* autonomous). Since 1964[37] I have called the activity that aims at autonomy praxis: this activity aims at others as (potentially) autonomous subjects and tries to contribute to their efforts to attain full autonomy. (The term "*praxis*" therefore has here only a homonymic relation to the meaning Aristotle assigns to it.) This activity may take on an intersubjective form the precise sense of unfolding in a concrete relation to determinate beings *intended as such*. Its most obvious cases are then pedagogy (also and especially "informal" pedagogy, which occurs everywhere and always) and psychoanalysis. But it also has to, under penalty of lapsing into total incoherence, take a form that goes far beyond all "intersubjectivity": *politics (la politique)*, namely, the activity that aims at the transformation of society's institutions in order to make them conform to the norm of the autonomy of the collectivity (that is to say, in such a way as to permit the *explicit*, reflective and deliberate self-institution and self-governance of this collectivity).

It is by starting with this position that we can understand why, contrary to what some may think, Habermas's efforts to found a theory of action on the ideas of "communicative action", "interpretive understanding" and "ideal speech situations" do not really go beyond "the mere critique of Max Weber's subjective convictions" and cannot "culminate in a fruitful attempt to redefine the tasks of social theory" (contrary to PhR, 190).[38] There certainly is a "communicative" dimension (more simply put: there is communication) almost everywhere in social action (just as there is, everywhere, "instrumental i.e. ensidic activity", a *legein* and a *teukhein*). Communication, however, is hardly ever an "end in itself", and it is totally inadequate as a way of bringing out criteria for action.

Let us consider the simplest cases, those apparently most favourable to Habermas's thesis. Both in pedagogy and in psychoanalysis, "communicative action" and "interpretive understanding" are certainly important *moments* of these activities. But in no way do they define either their *meaning* or their *end*. The *end* of psychoanalysis is not "interpretive understanding" between the analyst and the patient (which in no way is intended *as such*, and which is highly asymmetrical, as also is the case in pedagogy)—but rather a contribution to the patient's access to *his/her own* autonomy (his/her capacity to challenge him/herself and lucidly to transform him/herself).

And again, these are (the most important) instances of "intersubjective" action. Now, activities that aim at autonomy have to (under penalty of succumbing to an annihilating incoherence) take on a *social*—that is to say, a political—form. And here we must dispel a radical misunderstanding and expose an ideologically-based terminology that has reigned in philosophy at least since Husserl. The philosophers do not know (or rather, what is worse, do not *want* to know) what *the social* (*le social*) is. The term "intersubjective" systematically serves to evacuate the genuine (theoretical as well as practical) question of society and to mask their inability to think it. The term "intersubjectivity" expresses their continued enslavement to a metaphysics of the "substantive individual" (of the "subject") and the desperate attempt (already found in Husserl) to escape from the solipsistic cage to which egological philosophy leads—an attempt which, moreover, fails, the "other" always remaining in this perspective an incomprehensible prodigy.

But the social is something entirely other than "many, many, many" "subjects"—and something completely else than "many, many, many" "intersubjectivities". It is only in and through the social that a "subject" and an "intersubjectivity" may become possible (even "transcendentally"!). The social is the always already instituted anonymous collective in and through which "subjects" can appear, it goes indefinitely beyond them (they are always replaceable and being replaced), and it contains in itself a creative potential that is irreducible to "cooperation" among subjects or to the effects of "intersubjectivity".

It is the *institution* of this social (sphere) (*le social*) that is the aim of politics, which therefore has nothing to do with "intersubjectivity" or even with "interpretive understanding". Politics intends the institution as such, or the grand options affecting society as a whole. It "addresses itself" to the anonymous collective, both present and to come. Certainly, it always acts through a determinate public, but it does not *aim for* interpretive understanding between the political actor and this public; rather, it aims at the fate of the collectivity for a period of time that is, in principle, indeterminate. The fact that the orator has to express him/herself in a comprehensible way, or even that we want, and consider of capital importance, that the decision result from the most reasonable discussion possible, is not even worth mentioning here. The intended end, and the actual result, are something else entirely, these being the adoption of a new law, or engagement in some important common endeavour. In important cases, all these decisions *modify* not only the individuals presently involved but also those to come. All this goes far beyond "communicative action" and "interpretive understanding". These latter are, so to speak, only the atmosphere indispensable to *political* life and creativity—and their very existence depends upon instituting acts. The *end* or *goal* of these acts goes far beyond the establishment of an ideal communication situation, which is only part of that end, and really just a mere *means*.

Now, if one adopts not a normative standpoint (we want autonomy, what it presupposes and what it entails) but rather a descriptive-analytic one concerning society and history in their actuality—as is, in reality, the case with Habermas—Habermas's attempt to elicit from the *very fact* that "communicative action" occurs everywhere and always some sort of *exigency* can be seen only as an enormous logical blunder. As a "reproducing product" of society, "interpretive understanding" is everywhere: among 5th century BC Athenians, New Yorkers and French people today, the Communards of 1871—as well as among the oligarchic Spartans, the Waffen-SS or Khomeini's pajdarans. What distinguishes for us the second group from the first does not relate in any way to some kind of deficiency in the capacity for intersubjective communication (which is, perhaps, at a maximum within a homogeneous group of fanatics of any sort) but to the fact that such communication is *always already structured* exhaustively by the given institution of society in such a way that it is *effectively impossible*, from the social-historical point of view, for the participants to put into question this institution (which they are doomed to reproduce indefinitely) and, *by this very fact*, to open themselves to the reason of others. It is the institution as it is given each time that always assures communication and traces the limits of the humanity with which one can, in principle, "communicate". It is therefore this *institution* as such that has to be aimed at if the field of such communication is to be enlarged. And if we will to enlarge it, it is not because we will communication for itself, rather we will it in order that all humanity be put in a position where it would be able to work in common toward the creation of institutions that will advance its freedom of thought and creative making/doing (*faire*).

Habermas's attempt "rationally" to educe, once again, right from fact—the idea of a "good" society from the *reality* of the conditions of social life—appears to me just as untenable as the other attempts of the same kind that have been made in the past, and which he repeats. It lends him, in a totally characteristic way, to seek a mythical *biological* foundation for the questions of social theory and political action. The following passage, one among many others, bears witness to this: "The utopian perspective of reconciliation and freedom is ingrained in the conditions for the communicative sociation of individuals; it is built into the linguistic mechanism of the reproduction of the species".[39] Since when has biology (the "linguistic mechanism of the reproduction of the species") ever "built into" it a "utopian perspective"? Why would such a "mechanism" not be compatible with the preservation of closed societies—which it has, on the contrary, safeguarded almost everywhere, almost always, throughout history? And why would freedom be "utopian"? Freedom is neither a "utopia" nor a fatality. It is a social-historical project without whose already occurring, yet still partial, realization neither would Habermas be in a position to write what he writes nor would I too object to it. (Here, as in all contemporary parlance, "Utopia" clearly is a replacement for the Kantian "regulative Idea"; it removes the disagreeable "idealist" connotations as it confers upon it, now that Marxism has gone bankrupt, an agreeable "pre-Marxist revolutionary" scent.) To found the project of freedom philosophically in reason is already a bad usage of reason, for the very decision to philosophize is but a manifestation of freedom; to philosophize is to try to be free in the domain of thought. To want to "found" it on "the linguistic conditions for the reproduction of the species" is to revert to a biological positivism that leads to an incoherent paradox: it makes of freedom both a fatality inscribed in our genes and a "utopia".

From the moment we have left the closure of the sacred institution, from the time when the Greeks posed the questions: "What ought we think?" "What ought we do?" in a world they had built in such a way that the gods had nothing to say about these questions, there is no longer any possible evasion of responsibility, choice and decision. We have decided that we want to be free—and this decision is already the first realization of this freedom.

Tinos, August 1987—Paris, January 1988

Notes

*   Originally published as "Individu, société, rationalité, histoire," in *Esprit*, February 1988, pp. 89–113. Translation by David Ames Curtis. For reasons of space and interest to English-speaking readers, several references to Philippe Raynaud and his *Max Weber et les dilemmes de la raison moderne* (Paris: PUF, 1987) which occasioned this essay, have been eliminated. This essay appears in my volume *Philosophy, Politics, Autonomy* (Oxford University Press).

1. My first published writings in Greece (1944), which Ypsilon has just republished in Athens (1988), included among other things a translation with extensive commentary of Weber's "Methodological Foundations" from *Economy and Society* and an "Introduction to Theory in the Social Sciences", the composition of which was heavily influenced by Weber.

2. I will cite Philippe Raynaud's book by the abbreviation PhR; *Economy and Society*, Guenther Roth and Claus Wittich (eds) (Berkeley, University of California Press,

1978) will be indicated by *E&S* followed by a page number, and by a section number in those cases where the "Methodological Foundations" section is cited. (Translator's note: I have in many instances altered this translation of Weber's posthumous work in order to make the English conform more closely to Castoriadis's original French translation from the German.) As I have treated this question at length elsewhere, the reader may, if interested, consult my 1964–65 essay, "Marxism and Revolutionary Theory", which now appears as the first part of my 1975 book, *The Imaginary Institution of Society*, trans. Kathleen Blamey (Cambridge, Mass., MIT and Oxford, Polity, 1987), and is cited here as *MRT*; the second half of *The Imaginary Institution...*, cited here as *Institution*; also, *Domaines de l'homme* (Paris, Seuil, 1986), cited here as *Domaines*; and finally my 1986 essay, "The State of the Subject Today", trans. David Ames Curtis, *Thesis Eleven* 24 (1989), cited here as Subject. All italicized words and passages are in the original, unless stated to the contrary.

3. Weber, *E+S*, p. 15, section No. 9.
4. Let us note in passing that not so long ago this possibility of a sympathetic or empathetic reliving of experience provoked bursts of laughter from progressive Parisian psychoanalysts. Quite clearly, without this possibility social life itself would simply be impossible.
5. *E+S*, p. 13, No. 9.
6. Raynaud, PhR, p. 51.
7. *E+S* p. 18, No. 9, emphasis added; cf. also *E+S*, pp. 6–7, No. 3.
8. ibid., p. 13, No. 9.
9. ibid., pp. 13–14, No. 9; cf. also the remarks on Othmar Spann's "universalistic method" or "holism", ibid., pp. 17–18.
10. ibid., p. 18, No. 9; emphasis added.
11. ibid, p. 5, No. 3.
12. ibid., pp. 18–19, No. 10; emphasis added.
13. ibid., p. 17, No. 9.
14. ibid., pp. 21–22, No. 11.
15. ibid., p. 17, No. 9; emphases added.
16. ibid., p. 4, No. 1; emphases added.
17. ibid., p. 12, No. 7; emphases added.
18. ibid., p. 21, No. 11.
19. ibid., p. 12, No. 7.
20. ibid., p. 13, No. 9; emphases added.
21. From Dilthey's *Der Aufbau der Geschichtlichen Weltin der Geisteswissenschaften*, in *Gessamelte Schriften*, 1915, Vol. 7; emphasis added; cited by PhR, p. 86.
22. ibid., p. 121.
23. *Institution*, Ch. 6; *Subject*, passim.
24. *MRT*, pp. 135–156.
25. *Institutions*, Ch. 7; *Domaines*, pp. 385–418.
26. *Domaines*, pp. 231–333.
27. For a sketch of the problems involved in, and the means available to the under-

standing, see "The Greek *Polis* and the Creation of Democracy", *Graduate Faculty Philosophy Journal*, New School for Social Research, Vol. 9, No. 2, Fall 1983, pp. 81–93; also in my *Philosophy, Politics, Autonomy*, Oxford University Press.

28. *PbR.*
29. cf. *Subject.*
30. *Institution*, Ch. 5.
31. *E+S*, p. 18, No. 9.
32. cf. what he says about "the market", ibid., pp. 82–85.
33. The three volumes of the *Gesammelte Aufsatze zur Regionssozilogie*, as well as Ch. 5, ibid., pp. 399–634, in particular the paragraphs on "theodicy" pp. 518–526.
34. *PbR*, p. 183.
35. ibid., p. 184; emphasis added.
36. cf. *MRT*, pp. 101–114; *Domaines*, pp. 241–260 "The Greek *Polis*"; "The Nature and Value of Equality", trans. David Ames urtis, *Philosophy and Social Criticism*, Vol. 11, No. 4, Fall 1986, pp. 373–390; forthcoming in *Philosophy, Politics, Autonomy*; and *Subject.*
37. *MRT*, pp. 71, 79.
38. Contrary to *PbR*, p. 190.
39. *The Theory of Communicative Action*, trans. Thomas McCarthy, Boston, Beacon Press, 1984, p. 398.